Whistling in the Dark

Whistling in the Dark
Of the Theology of Craig Keen

EDITED BY
JANICE McRANDAL
STEPHEN JOHN WRIGHT

CASCADE Books • Eugene, Oregon

WHISTLING IN THE DARK
Of the Theology of Craig Keen

Copyright © 2024 Wipf and Stock. All rights reserved. Except for brief quotations in critical publications or reviews, no part of this book may be reproduced in any manner without prior written permission from the publisher. Write: Permissions, Wipf and Stock Publishers, 199 W. 8th Ave., Suite 3, Eugene, OR 97401.

Cascade Books
An Imprint of Wipf and Stock Publishers
199 W. 8th Ave., Suite 3
Eugene, OR 97401

www.wipfandstock.com

PAPERBACK ISBN: 978-1-4982-7876-8
HARDCOVER ISBN: 978-1-4982-7878-2
EBOOK ISBN: 978-1-4982-7877-5

Cataloguing-in-Publication data:

Names: McRandal, Janice, editor. | Wright, Stephen John, editor.

Title: Whistling in the dark : of the theology of Craig Keen / edited by Janice McRandal and Stephen John Wright.

Description: Eugene, OR : Cascade Books, 2024 | Includes bibliographical references.

Identifiers: ISBN 978-1-4982-7876-8 (paperback) | ISBN 978-1-4982-7878-2 (hardcover) | ISBN 978-1-4982-7877-5 (ebook)

Subjects: LCSH: Keen, Craig. | Philosophical theology. | Theology, Doctrinal.

Classification: BT40 .K446 2024 (paperback) | BT40 .K446 (ebook)

03/27/24

for Craig and Elesha

Contents

Introduction: Risky Words, Dissenting Bodies | ix
Janice McRandal

PART I | THEOLOGY

1// Writing and Reading: Why Language Matters Theologically | 3
Stanley Hauerwas

2// The Place of the Bible in Our Civic and Political Life | 13
William J. Abraham

3// Apophasis and Abasement: Writing Jesus with Søren Kierkegaard and Craig Keen | 24
Peter Kline

4// What Does Theology Promise? The Folly of the Cross and the Theology of Glory | 34
John Caputo

PART II | BODIES

5// Corpus Christi | 61
Christina M. Smerick

6// Knowing an Unseen God: Thoughts from Neuropsychology | 70
Warren S. Brown

7// Precarity and Disruption | 81
David Reinhart

PART III | HOLINESS

8// Before Eucharist: The Politics of Food in Plato and Paul | 99
  Theodore Jennings

9// "Sometimes Nothin' Can Be a Real Cool Hand" | 107
  Bryan Stone

10// On Loving Spiders | 123
  Stephen John Wright

11// The Hallowing of the Flesh in Biblical and Patristic Christology | 137
  Thomas A. Noble

AFTERWORD

12// Tending to Dogma a Long, Long, Long Way from Home | 153
  Craig Keen

Bibliography | 173

Introduction

Risky Words, Dissenting Bodies

JANICE MCRANDAL

Particularity and the hallowing of crucified flesh. This is how Craig Keen speaks theologically of bodies, which is to say, how he speaks theologically. To introduce his theology is to draw attention to how he speaks of God by speaking of the particular, crucified body of Jesus bathed in God's glory. "Glory," for Keen, names the outgoing embrace of God in which flesh rendered unclean and vile, flesh lacking integrity, flesh to be expelled from the community, is made to be the site where God's holiness and eschatological gathering of creation is enacted. This strange holiness does not require or enact the repair of the body. Holiness opens space for the hospitable embrace and welcome of the body in its disrepair. That the body in its disrepair is made to shine with the glory of God, and that the body in its disrepair can be set to work to welcome other disintegrous bodies into the glory of God—this is for Keen the sum of the good news, the gospel. It is why his theology turns especially to the poor and hopes for and imagines the working of God's glory among those crushed and forgotten by the "glory" of the world.

What form does such a theology take? Keen speaks of and to particular bodies. Words about bodies, especially bodies enacting resistance to the norms on purity and integrity, are risky words. It is not that Christianity has ignored the body. As Eugene Rogers has insisted, "Christians have always been debating some practical issue about the body . . . [but rarely have Christians connected] doctrines like incarnation, election, and resurrection, with race, gender, and orientation"[1]—that is, with enfleshed differ-

---

1. Rogers, *Sexuality and the Body*, 17–18.

ence and the norms that regulate it. What difference does bodily difference make? How is theological work done differently now that abnormed bodies are being spoken of, now that such bodies are speaking themselves? On one level we might claim great progress has been made in theologizing the body beyond the norm or beyond integrity. But what is theology actually doing with those bodies? Could contemporary theology be read as giving rise to another way of ignoring the body, appropriating bodies, commodifying bodies, for the sake of its own rhetoric? In such performances, the body is reduced to a hermeneutical key allowing the theologian to inject credence into the debates surrounding the differentiated and embodied postmodern subject. Clearly the practice of theology finds itself in a delicate space. Craig Keen is a theologian who has sought to wrestle with many of these questions, not as a way out of the entanglement of words and embodiment, but a way back in. Keen is especially attentive to this dialectic: bodies in words; words embodied. His theology is done is such a way "that we take our body experiences seriously as occasions of revelation."[2] *After Crucifixion* is, according to Keen, a work of theology written for:

> past and present and future students, among whom are undergraduate students, graduate students in professional programs, graduate students in more strictly academic programs, pastors, laborers, university and seminary professors, social workers, artists, drug traffickers, corporate professionals, military professionals, NGO professionals, psychologists, writers, community organizers, musicians, small business owners and employees, pre- and elementary and middle and junior high and senior high school teachers, chaplains, blue-collar workers, medical doctors and nurses and technicians, politicians, farmers, corporation executives, as well as, of course, those unmarked by formal titles; gentle, violent, kind, cruel, forgiving, exacting, faithful, and treacherous people; victims and perpetrators of child abuse, victims and perpetrators of spousal abuse; people with plans, property, and prestige; people adrift, jobless, homeless.[3]

It is for all these bodies, somebodies, nobodies, that Craig Keen has offered his theological words. And Keen takes these bodies up in his work. He remembers them, speaks of them, and tells their stories. In short, he prays for them. If there is a danger in such a work, and in the words that form such a work, it is in the very act of taking up and speaking for. As I have suggested, such theological moves may be and often are, nothing more

---

2. Nelson, *Body Theology*, 9.
3. Keen, *After Crucifixion*, xi.

than a sleight of hand, a way in which the theologian buries bodies in the production of theological capital. At his best, Craig Keen works to provide a path into embodied words in such a way that we theologians may learn how to listen and allow bodies to speak, to move out of the way, even, as bodies generate their own words.

This kind of work is done by Keen as he refuses universals. Keen is always thinking after the particular—particular bodies with particular narratives, doing a particular work. It is not that he does not understand the philosopher's impulse, who in considering the gathered people "wrap their minds around their ideas, finding about them nothing seriously anomalous, [or] that, in gathering, these people might have a particularity, a particularity like and secondary to the particularity to which they prayer-fully defer, a particularity that would elude all apprehension and exhibition, we are tempted to say, is unthinkable."[4] Rather, it is that Keen understands the way in which the universal seeks to grasp and tame the particular, to enact the kind of ownership such works performs.[5] As Keen notes: "They have told me that it is all about absolutes and universals and all I seem ever to see and hear are contextualized particulars, the life-stories of people with *particular* faces and voices, of a God with *particularly elusive* faces and voices."[6] These are risky words for the theologian. They are words that want to take up particularity precisely in order to let it go. To give bodies over to their own particularity, or rather, to deny the universal and therefore acknowledge a multiplicity of particularities beyond the grasp of our words (our work), is to accept, quite simply, that there are other-bodies. And this is no mean feat, not for the theologian, the would-be queen of all sciences. Of course, for Keen, all particularity is given over to the particular body of Jesus, a body the theologian also takes up in order to let go of. Certainly, this is how Keen reads the gospel of Mark. All embodied particularity is to stand up to this, in time and in facing the future. "This is to be read as the future to which all of the world opens, it is also precisely what comes to pass to one very particular first-century Galilean peasant. That is, the localization of the coming of God's reign in Jesus does not shrink the eschatological field. His crises are particularly but not exclusively his."[7] As such, the particularity of each body, each word, each name, does not denote boundaries in Keen's work, but opens the future, a particular future framed in the mystery of the coming of God. It is why Keen observes Peter's claims upon the Messiah as

4. Keen, *After Crucifixion*, 6.
5. Keen, *After Crucifixion*, 15.
6. Keen, *After Crucifixion*, 23.
7. Keen, *After Crucifixion*, 40, 41.

an opposition, a moment in which it "becomes manifest that he, like the demons who would put the Messiah in his place, has drawn a conceptual boundary line around Jesus, has enlisted him, has named his name."[8]

But if bodies, anybody, is open to such a future, it too is a particularized future, a future toward which the body trains for martyrdom. In this, we find a second way in which Keen gives theology away to bodies. And this too is an odd way of thinking about bodies, bodies that "slip through the fingers at the working end of the long arm of the law."[9] As Keen says, "the body will not bow out of life,"[10] but is instead called into a future "we are unable to extrapolate, a future in which the victory comes here not instead of defeat, but in defeat."[11] Bodies, then, are given to that which they already are, given to "be" a martyr, a bodily witness to the crucifixion/resurrection of Jesus Christ. The work of the martyr who testifies to Jesus is kenotic, a work of emptying. These are bodies doing away with themselves, or, coming into the coming of the slaughtered lamb:

> This is by no means "apophasis" in the rigidly propositional sense, i.e., "negative" as opposed to "positive theology." It is apophatic less properly, less acquisitively, more kenotically. It does not disregard kataphasis, i.e., what is "said," the discourse that gathers speech. Indeed, without the "said" of gathered speech this apophasis would have no move to make. And yet the "said" is regarded not with the proprietary eyes that would keep it safe, as it is, and bearing interest. Rather it is regarded with eyes that quietly welcome the sojourner—however undocumented, however alien—who might slip across heavily guarded borders into the sovereign nation-state, the sojourner "possibility." The "said" is regarded in order to give it away to the stranger.[12]

In this account—training for martyrdom—Keen fashions a wide space for both individual and social bodies. It is a means by which subjectivity is both gifted via and given over to the slaughtered lamb. It is apophatic embodiment. Again, risky words. And yet words in which bodies are neither tamed nor sublimated by the coming of God's reign. The martyr is called away from those totalizing categories that discipline bodies, that continue to abnorm the noncompliant. This body is uncapturable by categories such as authenticity, excellence, identity, and integrity. The martyr is called into

8. Keen, *After Crucifixion*, 172.
9. Keen, *After Crucifixion*, 121.
10. Keen, *After Crucifixion*, 127.
11. Keen, *After Crucifixion*, 150.
12. Keen, *After Crucifixion*, 155–56.

an embodied apophaticism, not as a simple way out of injustice, but as a way into the future. "Martyrdom is to live toward crucifixion, toward it and through it, out into the coming of a life that does not settle neatly into extant categories, a life, that is, without closure."[13]

For Keen, we are thus talking about bodies at prayer. It is to think prayer as a letting go of words and of one's body as both a kinetic and a kenotic act. Perhaps we might call this "discourse," in as much as discursive subjectivity in Foucault's account, for example, is "more than ways of thinking and producing meaning."[14] Discourse not only exercising power over the mind but also ultimately over the body in the subject produced. "Discourse runs through everything we do," Keen suggests, while pushing further. *After Crucifixion* itself is written as prayer, a prayer generative from bodies that toil the land, sleep, eat, and bleed, as much as it is generative of concepts. The inversion here is subtle, but it is an important one. For in it we learn that prayer is itself bodily dissent, a way in which the body disrupts whatever we have come to mean by discourse. "Language decenters privacy, propriety, autonomy, and individuality. It opens me, disrupts and disturbs my identity."[15] As such, Keen invites us, the reader, onto the wide well-waxed hardwood floor to dance with him.[16] He prays, more concerned with rhythm than with any attempt to make a claim, a theological treatise.

Of course, of all this is framed in Keen's work by an ecclesiology that centers upon the Eucharist, as so much recent theology does. These are prayers that can easily be reduced to bodies baptized and fed on the particular narrative of the church. And yet it is no surprise that so many bodies have fled the church for other spaces where bodies gather—dance halls, jazz clubs, protest lines, comedy clubs, and sport fields. Is there room in Keen's work for these other-bodies, bodies dissenting, bodies refusing to suffer and serve and wait with the church for the coming of God? Are these bodies simply sublimated by the body of Christ that feeds off the mutilated body of Jesus? If the Jesus who looked resolutely toward Jerusalem is anything in the work of Keen, he is a dissident. Perhaps Keen's work, then, allows for a dissident theology, for risky words that might abandon his own project, or prayer. Perhaps this, too, is what the "transgression of the integrity of God"[17] might mean.

13. Keen, *After Crucifixion*, 180.
14. Foucault, "Truth and Power," 135.
15. Keen, *After Crucifixion*, 117.
16. Keen, *After Crucifixion*, preface.
17. Keen, *Transgression*.

PART I
Theology

1//

Writing and Reading

Why Language Matters Theologically

Stanley Hauerwas

ON WRITING

"Call me Ishmael." Did Melville begin with that line or find it along the way as he wrote his great novel? I would like to think he found it along the way and that is one of the reasons it is so unforgettable. I would like to believe he found the sentence along the way because such sentences are so important that one suspects they could only be discovered with great difficulty. Sentences like "Call me Ishmael" seem so organic, as if they just "happen"; but once they are found they can never be replaced. Their very existence as a sentence creates a kind of necessity. Once a sentence like "Call me Ishmael" exists we know it cannot not exist.

A first sentence must be written to seduce the reader into reading the next sentence, and the next, and the next, until all the sentences have been read. That is true, for example, of the sentence I have just written. I wonder if the sentences with which I began meant whoever is now reading this could not resist reading this far? I should hope that to be the case as I hope to seduce any reader of these sentences to read further.

Yet why am I writing about writing when I am trying to convince you to read? The reason that I can only write about reading by writing about writing is, as Verlyn Klinkenborg writes in his marvelous book, *Several Short Sentences About Writing*, "You can only become a better writer by becoming a better reader."[1] It may even be true for some that you can only become a better reader by becoming a better writer.

That reading and writing are inseparable crafts is a widely shared presumption by writers and readers. Writers, however, are more likely than readers to argue that you only become a writer by reading what other writers have written. Some writers even report that they learned to write by copying sentence after sentence from another writer's novel or essay. Some readers who have become writers tell us that in the process of copying one sentence after another sentence, before they knew it they had copied a whole novel.

Most readers of this essay, I suspect, are willing to grant that there is an important relation between reading and writing, but they might wonder why reading and writing matters theologically. I want to explore that question by attending to two writers, Rowan Williams and Craig Keen, who have written on the theological significance of writing, or, more accurately, on why language matters theologically. I will also take a side glance at Alasdair MacIntyre's account of language because MacIntyre develops an illuminating account of language by exploring how other species besides humans may develop innovative modes of communication. MacIntyre helps us see how at once we share many characteristics with other animals as well as the difference language makes.

Williams and Keen, however, are crucial for the case I want to make about the significance of how we write as theologians. Williams and Keen are crucial for the case I want to make because they are eloquent writers of theology who share in common a sense of how difficult it is to say what we mean. Crucial for both is Williams's contention that "the labor involved in scrutinizing and using language about God with integrity is bound up with the scrutiny of language itself."[2]

I focus on Williams and Keen because they write beautifully about the importance of writing beautifully about God. That is a great achievement because it is generally acknowledged that many theologians do not even write clearly much less with beauty. The reasons theologians do not write well are no doubt complex, but at least one of the reasons is the relegation of theology to the university with the result that theologians now write mainly for other theologians. That theology has become primarily an academic specialty

---

1. Klinkenborg, *Several Short Sentences*, 17.
2. Williams, *Edge of Words*, 17.

means theology—like many academic subjects—has confused incomprehensibility with profundity. Williams and Keen do not make that mistake.

It may be objected that Williams and Keen write primarily not about writing but about language. That is not surprising if you take notice of the fact that without language there would be no writing or reading. There is no correlate between those who write well and reflection on the nature of language itself, yet we should not be surprised that writers cannot resist trying to understand the words they use. Williams and Keen are theologians who not only develop accounts about the theological significance of language but they write beautifully about why language is so important. I begin with Williams because his account of the incomplete character of language illumines Keen's work.

ROWAN WILLIAMS ON LANGUAGE

It is not surprising that Rowan Williams chose to concentrate on language in his Gifford Lectures delivered at the University of Edinburgh. It is not surprising because anyone who has followed Williams's work over the years finds familiar themes in the published version of his lectures entitled, *The Edge of Words: God and the Habits of Language*. Deeply influenced by Wittgenstein, at the heart of Williams's theological project has been what Charles Taylor has identified as the constitutive understanding of language. Taylor contrasts the constitutive view of language with what he calls the "enframing" account of communication. The enframing account of language assumes that life, behavior, purpose, and mental functioning can be described without reference to language.[3] In contrast to the constitutive view of language, a view Taylor attributes to Herder, there is no "outside" to language because any attempt to get at "reality" without language flounders on the reality that "reality" is linguistically constituted.[4]

The constitutive understanding of language, an understanding possible only by having at our disposal linguistic resources, is the condition of the possibility of our being able to think at all. Yet because we are possessed by language we are able to have ever-changing emotions, goals, and relationships. Language, therefore, by its very nature, cannot avoid nor should language users try to escape the necessity of new meanings being introduced into the world. Meaning is created because through language new

---

3. Taylor, *Language Animal*, 3.
4. Taylor, *Language Animal*, 4.

properties, for example, new objects of admiration and/or indignation, are introduced into the world.[5]

I have begun with Taylor's account of language to introduce Williams's very sophisticated account of what it means for us to be language constituted beings. Though he does not use the term "constitutive" Williams's view of how we become language users is very similar to Taylor's. Thus Williams remarks that "the fact of language is a good deal more puzzling than we usually recognize."[6] It is so even though we normally think our language represents to us, makes present to us, the patterns and rhythms of our world, but representation is not a passive process.

Williams challenges the assumption that the primary task of language is to describe the world by distinguishing two ways of thinking about how we speak about our linguistic encounters with the world. Description is the name he gives to our presumption that the task of language is to produce a map that makes possible a structural parallel between what we say and what we perceive. Such a view of language, however, fails to account for what Williams calls the representational work of language, which seeks "to embody, translate, make present or reform what is perceived."[7]

Williams's intent in *The Edge of Words* is to illumine the representational process that he takes to be more significant than our mistaken presumption that description is more basic. The representational character of language presumes as well as expresses our ability to be an agent. To be sure, on Williams's reading, we are complex agents but nonetheless because of speech we are capable of acting in the world. We cannot, however, describe the world any way we want. "We cannot in human discourse simply say what we please."[8] Yet we cannot know the limits of what we can say in principle because we cannot know the full range of possible schemata.[9]

That means we cannot place a limit on possible conceptual possibilities. The diversity of representational possibilities points toward an understanding of our language as fundamentally unfinished. But the unfinished character of language establishes us as speakers who must constantly seek to respond to changes in our place in the world. Metaphysically, this means that claims to represent our environment presupposes, as Herbert McCabe suggested, that the universe not only looks like but is a network of communication.[10]

5. Taylor, *Language Animal*, 47.
6. Williams, *Edge of Words*, ix.
7. Williams, *Edge of Words*, 22–23.
8. Williams, *Edge of Words*, 26.
9. Williams, *Edge of Words*, 26.
10. Williams, *Edge of Words*, xi.

We are at once determined and freed by our ability to speak. The freedom that characterizes language, a freedom that makes it possible to be truthful by what we say, comes through the struggle to say the right words in appropriate contexts. To test our language requires intelligent discernment because our language "creates a world, and so entails a constant losing and rediscovering of what is encountered. In other words the human speaker takes the world as itself a 'project': the environment is there not as a fixed object for describing and managing but as a tantalizing set of invitations, material offered for reworking and enlarging."[11]

This incomplete character of language makes it necessary to reach for the perspective of another. When we speak we are engaged not only with other speakers in our immediate context, but with those represented by time-constituted rituals and fictional narratives. That language is inherently filled with time is an indication of our finitude. Constituted by time, our thoughts and words presuppose as well as indicate the necessity of community for our ability to speak truthfully to one another and to avoid deceiving ourselves.[12]

We are always saying more than we know but that is simply a reminder that language is, as we are, finite and historical. While language can be used to distort the truth as well as lie, the very ability to lie depends on our ability as language users to use language to represent that which is not itself. In short, without language we would be incapable of being truthful. According to Williams, however, the truth is often to be found in the silences that surround what we say. Silences are testimony to the unfinished character of language manifest by the very fact that we are often aware of what has not been said that needs to be said even though we are unsure how to say what needs to be said.[13]

The incomplete character of our language is an indication that what Williams describes as "the sacred" is present in our lives. The sacred names the fact that just to the extent we are able to speak we cannot escape the reality that we are related to something that is other than ourselves. Yet that "something" is closer to us than we are to ourselves because in a certain sense it speaks us. The indeterminate, incomplete, embodied character of our language expressed in metaphor and formal structure is "interwoven with a silence that opens up further possibilities of speech."[14]

"Opening the possibilities of future speech" Williams takes to be a description of how theological language must work. Knowing God is not

11. Williams, *Edge of Words*, 59–60.
12. Williams, *Edge of Words*, 86–87.
13. Williams, *Edge of Words*, 167–68.
14. Williams, *Edge of Words*, 170.

to be found in the experience of religious ecstasy or when we feel alone in the universe. Rather to know God is to develop an understanding of how our thinking and feeling become decentered if not disposed through the very ability we have to speak. Any claims to represent God are thereby to be tested by whether such a representation entails a dispossession and deepened capacity to be still. Williams sums up his view by quoting Maggie Ross: "Every true sacred sign effaces itself."[15]

Williams disavows any suggestions that his appeal to silence is a way to "prove" the existence of God. Rather he thinks the complexity of language that he has tried to describe is what we should expect if Christ is in fact the Word of God. In short, what we find revealed in Jesus Christ, and why what is revealed must be revealed, illumines what we find true of our ability to speak a language that we discover at the edges of language is silent about itself. Christian doctrine, therefore, points to the irony that unconditioned reality communicates itself in the conditioned reality of the death of a Jewish man.[16]

Williams concludes his investigation of the character of language by observing that in our day it is worth remembering that it is not simply God's existence that is at issue, but the existence and continuation of what it means to be human. Thus, Williams chose to focus on language because our humanity is to be gained through the distinctively human ability to speak. By developing an account of our continuity as well as difference from animals, Alasdair MacIntyre provides an account of language that I think supplements what we have learned from Williams.

A MACINTYRIAN INTERLUDE

MacIntyre develops his account of language, an account that reflects his indebtedness to philosophers in the Wittgensteinian tradition, in his book, *Dependent Rational Animals: Why Human Beings Need the Virtues*.[17] I call particular attention to his account in this book because as he helps us better understand how communication is possible between animals who do not have a language.

Drawing on studies of dolphins by Louis Herman, MacIntyre observes that no one who has studied dolphins doubts that dolphins have a sophisticated system of communication. They not only communicate to one another but they also have a remarkable capacity for innovative and creative forms of communication that are responses, for example, to the challenge of

---

15. Williams, *Edge of Words*, 175.
16. Williams, *Edge of Words*, 180.
17. MacIntyre, *Dependent Rational Animals*, 26–27.

capturing schools of fish for food. MacIntyre argues, therefore, that though animals like dolphins do not have a language they are best described as prelinguistic, which means they have the capacity to communicate with us.

MacIntyre directs our attention to the ability of dolphins to communicate to suggest that though we are linguistic animals like dolphins our linguistic ability draws on prelinguistic capacities. Yet that we are animals that can talk means, however, our ability to speak to each must have at our disposal a stock of expressions with syntactical rules that make possible the matching of names to the bearers of those names. Our sentences must be embedded in forms of social practice, practices often rooted in the body, that make possible our ability to know what kind of speech act has been or is being made, e.g., whether I am asking a question or making a request.[18]

MacIntyre develops these reflections about language to suggest that adult human behavior and activity develops out of, and in many ways is dependent on, modes of activity that we share with other intelligent animals. Accordingly, the behavior of those species of animals such as dolphins must be understood as kin to language users such as ourselves. As language users we rely in large areas of our lives on the kind of recognitions, discriminations, and perceptual attention that shape our linguistic powers.[19]

MacIntyre's suggestion about the life shared by language users at once supports and extends Williams's account of the significance of language. In particular, MacIntyre's emphasis on the dependence of language on a tradition with a stock vocabulary that makes possible innovative interventions is important if we are to understand how Christians talk. In MacIntyre's terms, Christian speech depends on the practices of a people called Christian, but that does not mean the language of the faith is esoteric. It does, however, require innovative interventions because what it means to be Christian is a matter of an ongoing discovery.

Another way to put the matter, a way that I have called attention in earlier work, is that the necessary innovative character of theology demands we see and make connections.[20] I have long wanted to entitle a book *Connections* because if I have any talent it is for seeing connections. It is not just seeing connections, for example, between words and sentences, though that is very important, but to see connections between social and political

---

18. MacIntyre, *Dependent Rational Animals*, 29–30.

19. MacIntyre, *Dependent Rational Animals*, 40–41.

20. Hauerwas, *Sanctify Them in the Truth*, 1–3. I begin the "Preface" to *In Good Company* with the sentence, "Christianity is connections," xiii. At that time I was thinking of connections between people across time and space. Such connections make possible the innovative character of Christian speech.

realities and what and how we say what we say. That is Craig Keen's great gift, to help us see that our very humanity is at stake in how we speak.

CRAIG KEEN ON WRITING THEOLOGY

In the "Preface" to his book, *After Crucifixion: The Promise of Theology*, Keen begins with this surprising sentence: "Not only a writer's pride or her humility may lead her to settle on the conviction that the book she has written is extraordinary."[21] That sentence is not in the league of "call me Ishmael," but it does the work Keen meant for it to do. Namely, the sentence sets the context for his confession that though he is both proud and humbled he nonetheless believes he has written an important book. He is quick to observe that "an extraordinary book is not necessarily a good book,"[22] but it remains clear he is not trying to win the reader's agreement by practicing false humility. He observes that "pride and humility are complicated phenomena that not uncommonly rub off on the work in which they are complicit."[23] A beautifully written sentence in which Keen rightly should take pride while being reminded that humility cannot be left behind.

It is not surprising, therefore, in the sentence that follows his claim to have written an extraordinary book he reminds us that both pride and humility "come in handy" when we are engaged in prolonged and difficult tasks—like writing books. Keen confesses, and confesses is the right word, that he is sure he has been both proud and humble because in the writing of the book he has found himself against himself through comparison with others whose levels of energy is greater than his. Consequently, as he has written this book he has felt alternatively good and bad about a choice of word, the turn of a phrase, and the way phrases "tumble together" to make paragraphs and sections and chapters and suddenly a whole book.

After Crucifixion is a strange book that seems to have tumbled out of Keen's soul. It is a book that defies any easy description about what it is about. It does so because Keen acknowledges he introduces one subject after another with the result that one is not sure how it all fits together. For example, Keen lists the subjects he will treat: "from immigration to education, from the history of metaphysics to the Gospel of Mark, from urban planning to martyrdom, from brain physiology to ecclesiology, from wounded bodies to the forgiveness of sins, from hard work, hard death, from time to resurrection, from theological method to the doctrine of the Trinity"—and

21. Keen, *After Crucifixion*, ix.
22. Keen, *After Crucifixion*, x.
23. Keen, *After Crucifixion*, ix.

much more. Keen is unapologetic about the scattered nature of the book's subjects because he does not understand his book to be a book about anything. It is not a book about anything because he writes "what I have written is a prayer, a prayer I have prayed in the writing."[24]

The above paragraphs are meant to call attention to Keen's writing to indicate the art of his sentences that are shaped by what he takes his task to be. After the initial beginnings he tells us that his book is meant to be an introduction to theology. But he knows it is a *weird* introduction to theology because the "position" taken in the book "will not stay still long enough to stake a claim."[25] Yet he persists in calling the book an introduction because, "*After Crucifixion* is an invitation to you, and invitation to dance, to think, to pray, to hear an extraordinary, weird, uncanny beat and move to it—with me."[26]

Keen's writing has the character of poetry. Indeed he tells us that he has spent an enormous amount of time agonizing over word choices. He explains such attention to words is required when you are writing as he is for so many audiences. He uses puns and etymologies of words to signal the extent to which words often speak with more than one voice. Accordingly, he lets the awkwardness of certain phrases gesture in the direction of "the text's multiple concurrent personalities."[27] If you have had any doubt that Keen has a poetic sensibility, "concurrent personalities" should be sufficient to still such worries.

Having directed attention to the care he has used in his choice of words, Keen then makes explicit why he takes this to be so important for theological writing. For Keen, the task of theological writing is "to write words off themselves."[28] That words must do such work in and for theology is because words about God are "entangled in an overtly or covertly memorial past and a wonderfully or fearfully anticipated future."[29] That our words are so entangled is but the expression of the fact that "to follow Christ is with him perpetually to be emptied."[30]

The way Keen writes as a theologian turns out to be an expression of his theological convictions. As followers of Christ we are led to care for the poor, but such care is a very particular kind of care found in the life, death,

---

24. Keen, *After Crucifixion*, x.
25. Keen, *After Crucifixion*, x.
26. Keen, *After Crucifixion*, xi.
27. Keen, *After Crucifixion*, xiii.
28. Keen, *After Crucifixion*, xiii.
29. Keen, *After Crucifixion*, xiii.
30. Keen, *After Crucifixion*, 29.

and resurrection of that man, the Jewish peasant, Jesus, the son of God. Keen thus acknowledges that he is to hope and remember the poor with his words. The words must be words disciplined by Jesus who called the poor to be as he was—poor. Keen, therefore, writes in a way to make the words he uses empty themselves in a manner that exemplifies the silence that Williams suggest surrounds all speech but particularly speech about God.[31]

CONNECTIONS

I suggested above that the unfinished character of our language forces us to discover modes of expression that can surprise us. I observed that such discoveries are often made by seeing connections that had not been seen prior to their discovery. Reading Keen is an ongoing training in seeing connections. Connections like his argument that there is an intrinsic relation between ecclesiology and martyrdom. Which forces the further question of what it might mean, or perhaps more accurately, what will the church look like when she no longer lives as if she must insure her own existence?

That Keen describes his book as a prayer is the kind of discovery I suspect Williams presumes theology requires if it is to be truthful speech about God. Of course if theology is prayer that means theology cannot be "about" God but must be an address to God. That, I take it, is Keen's great gift, that is, his studied refusal to write as if theology is but another form of information. As a result, he has written theology in a manner that makes unnecessary any apology. That he has been able to do so is testimony to a soul that has no need to prove itself. We are in his debt.

---

31. What it means for words to "empty themselves" is echoed in Stephen Mulhall's recent Stanton Lectures, which are now published in his book, *Great Riddle*, 57. Mulhall uses the language "kenotic or self-emptying" to describe how words mean. He understands such self-emptying to be a christological expression.

2//

The Place of the Bible in Our Civic and Political Life

WILLIAM J. ABRAHAM

IT IS A GREAT pleasure to contribute to a volume celebrating the work of Professor Craig Keen. While I do not know all his work intimately, I have always been provoked by his interventions. For the most part I have seen them as a lively and unique appropriation of the Barthian tradition expressed with a Wesleyan accent. However one traces the genealogy, the crucial insight is that the Christian tradition has its own contribution to make to the crucial issues not just of theology but of our existence as a whole. On the one hand, there is no square inch of our life that may not be radically effected by our theology as Christians once we cross the threshold of divine revelation. We cannot lay claim to some sort of autonomy or private space where God can be excluded. We have to wait and see how things fall out. On the other hand, the faith cannot be swallowed up in alien categories; nor can it be marginalized to make room for more privileged resources. Put differently, the Bible has its own voice in any serious conversation about our manifold and mysterious existence. Buried in this claim, of course, is a conviction that the Bible genuinely mediates special revelation. For this reason alone I find myself wanting to listen very carefully to what Professor Keen has to offer us as a provocative and penetrating theologian.

In this tribute I want to pursue the place of the Bible in our civic and political existence. I take this theme as illustrating one way in which the Christian tradition has a distinctive place to play in our thinking about life in the public arena. At the very least it is an initial challenge to the view that our social and political life should be governed solely and exclusively by secular categories and modes of thinking. As I proceed I shall draw on my experience in Ireland and the United States.

Let's begin by noting that many insist that the Bible cannot have a role, much less be pivotal in our civic and public life. Here are three objections that come to mind immediately when any move to bring the Bible and its attendant moral and theological teachings into the public square becomes a live option.

First, this will involve intolerance and potential violence. Any and all claims to divine revelation will do this. Radical Islam, it will be said, shows this clearly. At the very least, religious believers will seek to impose their views on others, as the standard polemic of the New Atheism proclaims.

Second, this move will poison our political discourse by introducing data and warrant that necessarily can only appeal to one section of the community. Initially we can think of Catholic versus Protestant, and then Christians against all the rest. Public discourse must of necessity be generic, universal, and restricted to public canons of rationality. This is the only way to secure peace.

Third, this move will undercut a critical distinction if not separation between the church and the state that is essential to democracy. Democracy means diversity and pluralism across comprehensive doctrines over against a confessional uniformity or privileged majority ranked against a marginalized minority.

Space permits me only the option of quick nuclear strikes against all of these objections. All of these objections are really surface objections.

Against the first, this objection overlooks the radical differences between different claims to divine revelation. It is built upon inexcusable ignorance and willful stupidity. Every serious Christian vision of the content of divine revelation undermines the generalization deployed.

Against the second, the appeal to some kind of universal reason is severely limited when it comes to our civic and political life. We need more than general moral and rational platitudes to build a comprehensive life together as citizens. More importantly, the move to a post-Christian world dominated by secularism has given us no agreement on moral and political goods agreed by all rational agents. Secular reason is riddled with deep divisions that show up in intense disagreements between democrats, republicans, socialists, communists, fascists, and their many hybrids. Secularism in some instances has led to more killings than the many centuries put together before the fall of Christianity in Europe.[1] The promises of both minimal and maximal visions of the Enlightenment opened up most famously by Immanuel Kant have not been fulfilled. Postmodernists have pounced on this and they are readily taking us from the frying pan into the fire of identity politics, verbal bullying, hasty slogans, and a nasty descent in some cases into hard-core sensuality in the public arena. Work through a good biography of Michel Foucault[2] or ponder Susan Nieman's fine study on evil in modern philosophy[3] and you will find yourself rocked to your foundations when you witness the collapse of the modern appeal to reason and experience. David Hume, that canny lapsed Presbyterian, captured this when he noted that reason has and always should be the slave of the passions. To quote him in full: "Reason is, and ought only to be, the slave of the passions, and can never pretend to any other office than to serve and obey them."[4]

Against the third, any democracy worth its name has to include all people within its boundaries and that includes robust Christian believers, as well as other believers or those who would see themselves somehow as nonbelievers. Secularism simply creates its own atheological confessional states and readily imposes its own privileged commitments in law, education, medicine, and the ethos of public life as a whole. Secularists will readily use the organs of state to shut down any alternatives that threaten their hegemony. The resort to legal measures is the more visible kind of coercion and the overriding of conscience. A more insidious form of taking control is to limit what kind of argument can be brought into the public square or allowed in legal briefs. Equally insidious is the insistence that the language that shows up in public records and documents be sanitized and rendered in the most generic and deflationary way possible. So we will speak, say, of parent one and parent two rather than mother and father.

Let me turn the corner and go a tad deeper. As we do so, we can see that claims about divine revelation, say, through Scripture, or the wisdom it imparts, cannot be neatly partitioned off as irrelevant and not worthy of public relevance or articulation. Let me sketch one way into this thicket. Consider three theses, two very briefly and the third at greater length.

---

1. For a compelling study of the situation in the Soviet Union, see Yakovlev, *Century of Violence*.
2. See, for example, Miller, *Passion of Michel Foucault*.
3. Nieman, *Evil in Modern Thought*.
4. Hume, *Treatise on Human Nature*, 2.3.3.

Thesis one: the nature of our civic and political life is expressed in our laws and legal arrangements. These cannot be reduced to law, but legislation is a crucial if not core phenomena.

Thesis two: our legal arrangements are inescapably moral in character and content. Even the decision to live by authorized law is a moral one as it rejects, say, the choice of anarchy where we all do what is right in our own eyes. The very form of our laws are morally loaded for they are prescriptive; they are endorsed as good; they include practices for distinguishing between the innocent and the guilty; and they delineate various forms of penalty and punishment. Materially, our laws presuppose all sorts of moral judgments. Thus, they capture what we might call moral platitudes, for instance, that rape is intrinsically wrong. Likewise with theft, slander, cruelty to animals, the degradation of the environment, the trafficking of underage girls for sexual services, and acts of terrorism. Move up the line of contestation and consider unfair discrimination in the workplace, unfair dismissal, and the rules of engagement in war. Further along the line, consider how the state makes provision for education, care of the elderly, protection for minors, delivery of road infrastructure, the presence or absence of capital punishment, regulations regarding family law (say, adoption), the very conception of marriage and the conditions for divorce, and provision of basic medical care. Morality cannot be reduced to law; nor does law incorporate all our moral judgments; but moral judgments show up in our legislation; they are inescapable. We might say that they incorporate our minimal conception of what it is to be a civilized society; they reflect a consensus about what constitutes the common good.

Thesis three: moral decisions are inescapably tied to wider philosophical and theological commitments. We may all agree on a basic, baseline network of laws without which any society will fall apart. Thus, we characteristically have laws about family, the security of property, murder, theft, and the like. Consider this as akin to a core curriculum. But just as in education a core curriculum in a primary school is not enough for a well-rounded education, so in society we need what we might call further courses that are not just electives for the full formation of society. This is especially visible in two areas: in the area of property and family life. We have to choose whether we will go with private property or public ownership or some complex combination of the two as has happened in Singapore. More pertinent to recent debates we have to make decisions about family arrangements. Will we have polygyny, polygamy, polyandry, or monogamy? And when we agree on monogamy will it be exclusively heterosexual or will it include homosexual couples as well? Wider considerations about gender identity, human nature, the concept of harm, the idea of human freedom, and the concept of the common good will come into play.

Take the issue of abortion. Very often participants in the debate try to keep contested considerations off the table by going for the quick kill and trying to dissolve the debate by appeal to universal reason. So conservatives try to focus on arguments from natural law and on children's rights. Revisionists focus on generic ideas of freedom and equality and on adults' rights. These moves will not take care of business; the other side is not convinced. Hence the massive effort to resort to nonrational forms of persuasion by marches and advertising campaigns and noisy polemical debates on television that can readily become a form of perverse entertainment.

Consider why the appeal to generic forms of so-called public reason fails. The concept of reason, that is, of rational considerations that will appeal to all participants is much too thin to work. It cannot reach the deeper issues at stake. Reason so understood yields very different results. Furthermore, the debate quickly becomes one of abstract concepts and generic slogans, like equality or freedom. Worst of all, the debate requires a stripping down of our identities as full human agents who make complex synthetic judgments. Citizens are carefully house-trained before they are allowed into the discussion where the kind of evidence that will count has to be explicitly public all the way to the bottom. Appeals that go beyond the kind of evidence allowed in law courts are seen as superstition or fanaticism or sectarianism. These are the code words that are meant to shut folk down before the conversation begins. There is a complete failure even to think, for example, as to how revelation as mediated through Scripture can correct and enrich reason; it does not destroy our understanding, on the contrary, it deepens our understanding.

We need to come to terms with the complexity of the debate. Thus in debates, say, about abortion or marriage, is not a debate between secular and religious views. That perpetuates an insidious binary and disjunction. The debate is between various forms of secularism and various forms of Christianity. The conversation is whether we will have one kind of Christian faith-based state and another kind of secular faith-based state, between one kind of confessional state and another kind of confessional state. Christians are divided on what to do and secularists are divided on what to do. It is not a debate between those committed to reason and those not committed to reason, say, emotion or revelation. It is a debate between those committed to reason as healed and transformed by divine revelation and those committed to reason informed and updated by various secular worldviews.

This sounds all airy-fairy and hyper-intellectual to those who want to bully us into accepting their simplistic slogans and solutions. However, ordinary people who go to the polls do not need some kind of grand analysis; they just make the best synthetic judgments they can. Mary Kenny, in an article in the *Irish Independent* three months after a referendum on marriage, captured the point with characteristic clarity.[5] On the yes side, she noted, ordinary folk made complex judgments that drew from material all over the map. They wanted people to be happy. They wanted to be more positive and optimistic about their culture. They appealed to family considerations, like giving dignity to sons and daughters, and other person-relative family matters. They felt the church had got a lot wrong in the past and so they needed to exercise their own preferences. They just wanted to be kind. They wanted to celebrate love. On the no side, folk talked about a ying/yang complementarity that was represented by male and female. They were worried about where the culture was going as a whole. They believed marriage as traditionally understood was rooted in a Darwinian instinct to procreate that should be respected. They felt that it was not good to set aside 200,000 years where every human being born has been born of the union of man and woman and this has been codified as marriage. We see here the complexity of the many considerations that go into our human judgments. That complexity also includes different ways of incorporating the best wisdom of faith, however fitfully expressed, into the informal calculations that are made.

It helps at this point to look at the debate in the United States. There are significant differences between Ireland and the USA. There are interesting differences in the speed with which the law on marriage was changed. In the USA the process took about fifty years.[6] In Ireland we are looking at perhaps half that time. This may have been due to the fact that Ireland does not want to offend its American friends and the yes-folk were are all too ready to accept the extraordinary amount of money poured into the campaign from the USA. Nor can we discount the fact the gay rights are now a critical ingredient in the foreign policy of the USA and all that entails. Perhaps the most significant difference is that in Ireland the issue was open to the judgment of all the people in a referendum, while in the USA it was decided by a majority of one in a Supreme Court of nine judges, six of whom are Roman Catholic and none of which are Protestant.

Set all this aside. What is of interest is the way the argument of Justice Kennedy for the majority was framed and developed.[7] The crucial set

---

5. See Kenny, *Irish Independent*.

6. See Reilly, *Making Gay Okay*. We do not as yet have a study of the dramatic developments in Ireland.

7. For the details of the case consult the *Obergefell v Hodges* case on the website of the Supreme Court.

of considerations revolved around arguments about the phrase the right to life, liberty, or property taken from the Fourteenth Amendment. Here the crucial concept was that of liberty, which was then connected to equal protection under the law and to human dignity. The court decided that the state is required to identify as a fundamental right the right to decide the meaning of one's life and the practices related to their personal conception of existence. Notice that on this view the meaning of existence and its correlative practices is chosen rather than discovered. There is no prior vision of human nature that can trump this. What it is to be fully human, free, and dignified is chosen; it is not discovered. Thus, if some choose to believe that marriage can be between two people of the same gender, this choice must be allowed by the courts. More pointedly, they have a right to marry.

There is a real sleight of hand, for this vision of human nature, the vision that we are free to choose the meaning of our life, is of course itself a vision of human nature. We can readily trace its tangled origins from Rousseau through various intermediaries up to and including the great existential philosophers of the twentieth century. On this view there is no such thing as any fixed human nature or human essence as it has been classically articulated. To be human, to be free, to have dignity, to be equal, all these are located in this fundamental axiom taken up by the court. This account of the human condition is seen as self-evident and needs no defense. Yet it is denied by materialists, Marxists, and Christian theology in virtually all its forms. So the state has moved to endorse one vision of human nature (albeit in the name of endorsing no view of human nature) and this then is imposed on everyone as enacted in law.

Justice Kennedy is well aware that this view of freedom would never have been the view taken by the framers of the Fourteenth Amendment. And now we have another interesting development. The other five justices on the court who agreed with him insisted that they somehow had been given new insight into the very meaning of freedom that allowed them to reinterpret the classical language of the courts in this new way. It is small wonder that all the dissenting justices were intellectually outraged by the way this person-relative, minority report was now enshrined in the law of the land in terms of a right to same-sex marriage. My point here is not that such judgments will be absent in the making of law; it is that the court shows absolutely no awareness of what it is doing.

Take another interesting element in the decision. The obvious implication of the axiom of freedom I have explored is that this will open the door to other forms of marriage and family arrangements, most notably polygamy as endorsed by some Mormon groups. Yet Justice Kennedy blithely argues that the USA should keep intact the view that marriage is between two and only two people. This may be well and fine as far as his and his colleagues' chosen account of the meaning of life and marriage, but it makes no sense to build his conception of the meaning of life and marriage into the law given his views on freedom, autonomy, and self-realization operating elsewhere in his thinking. Equally contested is the claim that the court is simply upholding and expanding the treasures and benefits of marriage to a discriminated and excluded minority rather than actually altering the very concept of marriage itself. That this is at the very least a problem is already shown once we look at the sexual identities of the LGBTQ communities and the variety of options they will consider meaningful. Bisexuals are not likely to want to limit marriage to two people. That we have a significant change on our hands is also exposed in the effort to find alternatives to the language of husband and wife and the interrelated relatives, say, of uncles and aunts, in common discourse and in legal documents.

Again, note carefully my point here is not that substantive and moral judgments like these will not find their way into the law; it is that there is no awareness of what is going on. Alternative philosophical and moral judgments, some shaped in deep ways by the Bible and theology, are summarily ignored or dismissed. We can go further. Abraham Lincoln once noted that there cannot be a right to do what is immoral. This arose in debate with those who insisted they had a right to own slaves. By making same-sex marriage a right, rather than something permitted or tolerated, the justices doubled down on making their particular vision of human freedom, dignity, autonomy, and the like, the endorsed and mandated doctrines of the people as a whole. Hence the platform is created for making this mandatory across the board in public institutions and life. Hence the moral comparison with racism is pivotal in silencing opposition. The fears of vilification in terms of bigotry, ignorance, and the like, are simply the natural knock-on effects of the initial decisions about freedom and dignity when the issue at bottom is cast as one of a right to marry.

I hope I have said enough to provide a serious rationale for my third thesis: the moral considerations that show up in the law are intimately related to wider philosophy and even theological in character.

We now face a dilemma. With the exception of Northern Ireland, Europe and North America have decided what moral option will be enshrined in the law with respect to marriage. It involves a significant departure in my judgment from an earlier moral and theological tradition enshrined in law. The tectonic plates have shifted significantly in our moral context. We have crossed a significant threshold and I do not think there is any way back. The water has been spilt and it cannot be gathered up. To be sure, there are Christians and churches who have been deeply involved in this process. This only deepens my claim that there are very particular theological commitments now enshrined in the law; this is not a purely secular operation.

Where can we go from here? This is not a time for panic or scaremongering. As Wesley taught his Methodists, we are people who think and let think. Here are some brief suggestions.

First, Christian communities must continue to uphold their own identity and continue to make the Scriptures and related elements in their canonical heritages central in the formation of robust disciples in a world that is becoming increasingly post-Christian in Europe and to a lesser degree in the United States.[8]

Second, beyond this, churches need to work out their own distinctive position on the moral issues that are central to our culture; within this the appeal to the wisdom and revelation mediated in Scripture remains as important as it ever has been. The pressure to work from alien criteria and concepts must be resisted; we need to keep our nerve and remain faithful. Unity across our denominations will be hard to secure here. In fact, we are already in the midst of a new round of divisions; to cope with this we will need to develop a really serious theological conception of denominationalism, something that is extremely painful for many to contemplate given the quest for unity over the last hundred years.[9] My own view is that we are now in the midst of a fourth schism in the church that revolves around theological convictions about creation and marriage, a schism that may never be healed, if the experience of the first three are to be taken seriously.

Third, there is no reason why different Christian communions could not draw up a list of platitudes that would be apt for Christians in politics. Imagine a code of conduct that we could agree on and the difference this might make to the toxic dispositions and attitudes that are common in the political arena. Negatively, surely the first rule of politics would be that we will not kill one another. A second would run like this: it is fundamentally immoral to keep units of terrorists or "freedom fighters" in place just in case we do not get our way in the political arena. Perhaps we should begin with the simple rule to love God and neighbor and go from there. These are low-hanging fruit that should readily be agreed and implemented. It is astonishing to me that politicians who lay claim to the benefits of baptism and church membership seem to think that these carry no moral content when

---

8. It is far from easy to describe the situation in the USA. It is certainly false to say that we face simply a thoroughly secular culture; I am becoming more and more convinced we are dealing with a culture deeply influenced by liberal progressive forms of Christianity.

9. See the important set of essays in Collins and Ensign-George, *Denomination*.

it comes to their political life. Maybe a more generous way to put the issue would be to say that they are blind to the moral content they bring to their political life and simply assume its superiority to the alternatives available.

Fourth, Christian communions will need to figure out as best they can how they will respond to the theological and moral issues that crop up in politics and clear away the objections, polemical and otherwise, that will show up in the public arena. This cannot be confined to clergy but should involve laity who really know what it is to work in politics and related fields, like the civil service. The relevant biblical and theological content involved should be brought out into the open without apology or defensiveness. There is a work here for both individuals operating, say, as academics, leaders, writers, or journalists and for more corporate work taken up by various standing committees or task forces in our churches.

Fifth, Christians should relentlessly expose the hidden and contested assumptions that invariably lie behind their moral and legal commitments that secularists bring to the table. We can and should identify and catalogue the standard moves made to eliminate biblical and theological commitments from the public arena. This will include unpacking the use of a host of slogans, persuasive definitions, and caricatures that make the rounds. There is a real place here for hard-hitting polemical work, including the creation of slogans that will capture what is at stake and pose the issues sharply. Thus, facile distinctions between church and state should be identified and countered. On the positive side, the platitude that there cannot be a right to do what is immoral should be hammered home again and again given the overuse of this notion to morally intimidate opposition.

Sixth, in the current climate it is crucial that Christians and their churches that disagree with the reigning ideology make sure that they secure real freedom not just for their beliefs but for their practices. This means securing freedom to preach, freedom in their use of their property, freedom in making choices about employment, freedom to apply for government grants, freedom to teach according to their Scriptures, freedom to run their schools according to their faith, and freedom to evangelize in the public arena. The problem here is not some grand scheme, for example, to compel clergy to perform marriage as understood by the state. What is at issue is the use of soft power, including the power of the purse, to penalize those who dissent from the moral and philosophical assumptions that show up in legislation.

Seventh, and finally, serious and sincere Christians will disagree about a host of issues in politics. On one occasion our Lord refused to resolve a property dispute brought to him by a family member angry at a brother who would not concede his claim to the property.[10] He insisted that he had not come to resolve such disputes. C. S. Lewis made a telling commentary on this incident. Lewis drew attention to the standard temptations that go along with different ways of working out a political vision of Christianity. Those who are convinced that temporal welfare can flow only from a Christian life and who see nothing but trouble in democracy will readily look to an authoritarian state to sweep away the last vestiges of the hated liberal infection. They will tend to think that fascism is not so much an evil as a good perverted. They are therefore tempted "to accept even Fascist assistance, hoping that they [he] and their [his] friends will prove the leaven in the lump of [British] Fascists."[11] Those who stress the prophetic and the dominical denunciations of riches and are certain that the historical Jesus demands of us a Left revolution face a different challenge. They are tempted "to accept help from unbelievers who profess themselves quite openly to be enemies of God."[12] Then there are those who are acutely aware of the fall. They are convinced that no human being can be trusted with more than a minimum of power over others; they are anxious to preserve the claims of God from being infringed by Caesar; hence they readily see in democracy the only hope of Christian freedom. They too have their trial, for they are tempted "to accept aid from champions of the status quo whose commercial or imperial motives bear hardly even a veneer of theism."[13] This is a prescient observation of what has emerged for western democracies in general. We can accurately name this vice as a form of self-deception.

If this paper does nothing else I hope it alerts us to the fact that self-deception readily lurks in the wings whenever we venture into the political arena with or without our Bibles and the theologies we derive from them. However, this is not my deeper worry. My deeper worry is that as our culture moves into an aggressive post-Christian phase it is secularists (aided and abetted by "progressive" Christians and their allies) who will be more likely to succumb to this temptation. The relevant temptation is that they will conceal from themselves the radically contested convictions that they bring to our civic and public life and thus become a tyranny of the majority. We face tough days ahead. However, Christians have survived and flourished under a host of political regimes; we can surely do so in our own changing and challenging time.

10. Luke 12:14.
11. Lewis, "Meditations," 63. Lewis refers to this option as that of Philarchus.
12. Lewis, "Meditations," 64. Lewis refers to this option as that of Sparticus.
13. Lewis, "Meditations," Lewis refers to this option as that of Stativus.

3//

Apophasis and Abasement

Writing Jesus with Søren Kierkegaard and Craig Keen

Peter Kline

Let me begin with a preface of sorts. After I wrote this essay, I realized that what I'd done is basically write an essay on the preface to Craig's book *After Crucifixion*. I don't think I get beyond the preface. My interest here is not directly in theological content but in theological form. I pay attention to the rhythm and style of Craig's and Kierkegaard's writing. A preface-like standing back from the positive claims of their work, or an approach to those claims that takes them up indirectly through the question of form is, I think, a requirement for reading both of them well. Let me also say that I have chosen Kierkegaard as Craig's dance partner for this essay partly out of my own work and interests, but more importantly because Craig has been dancing with Kierkegaard for many years. The dance moves he's learned from Kierkegaard are on every page of his work. My aim here is to move along with just a few of them.

To the essay.

In 1841 Søren Kierkegaard broke off his engagement with his fiancé Regine Olsen. He found himself unable to enter into the long conversation that is marriage. He got out a few syllables, a few words perhaps, but then found himself unable to get out any more marital speech. There was another sort of conversation to which Kierkegaard felt compelled to devote his life. His authorship, his pseudonyms, his journals and papers, this immense outpouring of speech and writing, they trace this other conversation. Who is the partner of that other conversation that occupied him his whole life? Himself? God? Himself before God? However we might think of it, it is clear that, for Kierkegaard, this "religious" conversation caused other sorts of conversations to tremble, break, and lose their ultimacy—in short, one might say, to stutter.

Kierkegaard's authorship bears traces everywhere of this stuttering. The form of his thinking and writing is a stuttering form. For example, on my count, *Fear and Trembling* begins itself nine different times before it actually gets underway. Johannes de Silentio can't seem to get his speech up and going, and then once it does it derails into bewilderment and silence as it confronts the paradox of Abraham's faith. Or take the book of prefaces that Nicolaus Notebene put together. A book of nothing but prefaces that collectively stutter by repeating over and over the beginnings of books that never get written. Or take the concept that Kierkegaard bequeathed to twentieth-century philosophy that, as he predicted, has played a central role—repetition. It is a stuttering concept that refuses to be a proper concept. The book in which it is introduced, *Repetition*, published on the same day as *Fear and Trembling* as a kind of stuttering gesture, is a stuttering book, written by a pseudonym with a stuttering name, Constantine Constantius. It is a book about failure, the failure to repeat a magical first trip to Berlin, the failure of a relationship to get past its first syllable, the failure of a concept to make present what it is trying to name.

All of this performs what might be called the apophatic quality of Kierkegaard's thinking and writing. What language is finally good for, for him, is not direct or finalized articulations of truth but rather its own failure before what it cannot represent or pin down or enforce. The glory of language, or its poverty, depending on your point of view, is that it sets itself up for fantastic failures. It is in and through these failures that the earnestness of thought and existence is evoked as a relation to what cannot be said. Kierkegaard's authorship stages a dizzying array and variety of such failures in order to witness to unspeakable truths. His intention is to draw his reader toward the passions, possibilities, deceptions, and difficulties of life and faith that inevitably resist and escape direct and final representation, or any representation at all.

In 2013, Craig Keen published a book titled *After Crucifixion: The Promise of Theology*. In the first weeks of its debut, it received a series of very strange reviews on Amazon.com—mostly over-the-top admiration and fantastic misreading. They were written by Craig's friends and were intended as friendly satire. They are all a bit ridiculous and are certainly failures of the book review genre. In the preface to *After Crucifixion*, Craig calls his book a dance, and he imagines himself crossing a wide, well-waxed hardwood floor and with downcast eyes asking his reader to dance. Well, what he got was a bunch of drunken hooligans doing the chicken dance with him. It is a bit of ridiculous nonsense that should probably be quickly forgotten, but indulge me here, and let me play with the nonsense a bit.

What if we read this display as an instance of that elusive sensibility that Susan Sontag identified as "camp"? Camp occurs in various ways as strange mixtures of earnestness and irony, sincerity and satire, or excessive passion for unlikely objects that transgresses and fails at good taste. Drag performance is a site that excels at the tropes and gestures of camping. Or passionate enthusiasm for certain unclassy movies. Or some of Andy Warhol's pieces. To camp is to desire passionately—but in a way that refuses any easy or straightforward relationship to its object. It is to desire by holding one's object away from direct recognizability and identification and therefore away from manipulation and conscription into normative circuits of knowledge. It therefore risks becoming ridiculous or abased before normative identities and acceptable attachments.

So why camp Craig Keen's book? Why surround it with speech that dislodges it from the normative circuits of academic commentary? Craig calls his own book "extraordinary," and by that he doesn't mean that it will launch a new epoch of academic theological discourse. I take it that by "extraordinary," Craig is telling us that he has situated his book outside of, or as a surd within, the normative circuits of academic discourse and desire. This is why he also calls his book "weird," the way an unpopular junior high boy is weird, and says he is unconcerned with whether what he has written "measures up." So his book calls for weird responses and extraordinary desires, readers who don't measure up. Satire and irony are probably not the sort of weird responses Craig is ultimately hoping for, but better this—camp sensibility would say—than being reduced to a suffocating academic definition, or worse, "contribution." As Johannes Climacus says, referring to his own book that aroused no sensation among the academic commentary crowd, "better well hanged by a hapless marriage than to be brought into systematic in-law relationship with the whole world."[1]

Further, I'd venture to say that *After Crucifixion* itself does a bit of camping. If the heart of camping is over-the-top passion for objects or persons that are not easily recognizable in terms of the good, the true, and the

---

1. Kierkegaard [Johannes Climacus], *Concluding Unscientific Postscript*, 5.

beautiful, then Craig can be read as a writer of a kind of camp theology. His passion for the abased, earthly Jesus, for unclassy little local churches in their awkwardness and unimpressiveness, for puns, for etymologies, for using lines from pop music as epigraphs, for the undoing of integrity and wholeness and refinement—all of this rubs shoulders with camp. The fifth interlude of *After Crucifixion* especially walks this line. It meditates on the Trinity by way of a recollected encounter with a discarded and disintegrating pear core sitting on the edge of an anonymous student's window within the Christ's Church College in Oxford. Craig here flirts with irony, and does it earnestly. That ambiguity is the space of camp, of weird desire.

Kierkegaard, under various of his pseudonyms, might also be read as a writer of a kind of theological and philosophical camp.[2] *Fear and Trembling* is a camp-like staging of Johannes de Silentio's over-the-top passion for the Abraham and Isaac story, and so it destabilizes and defamiliarizes the reader's relation to that story. Johannes Climacus is a kind of philosopher in drag who stages philosophy through exaggeration and self-subverting irony. *Practice in Christianity* is not an ironic or satirical text, but it too might be read as a kind of camping, since it aims to awaken in its reader an infinite passion for a despised and ridiculed object—the abased Jesus. Anti-Climacus writes of Jesus' divine compassion that makes itself "one with the most wretched," that it is "something that [people] can shed a few emotional tears over during a quiet Sunday hour and involuntarily burst out laughing over when they see it *in actuality*."[3]

Theological camp is therefore a contribution to negative or apophatic theology. It aims to introduce productive failures into normative discourses by abiding with what refuses to be assimilated into such discourses. It aims to stutter before the good, the true, and the beautiful in order to disrupt their eloquence, in order to make room for what even highly refined classificatory schemas never quite lay hold of.

This is why, like Kierkegaard, Craig's writing takes on a stuttering, apophatic form. Craig's writing aims not to capture but to stop and interrupt itself so as not to capture—to release and make room. Consider the chapter structure of *After Crucifixion*. Between each chapter is an interlude that I take to be a kind of stuttering. Not the kind of stuttering that repeats syllables but the kind that pauses just a bit too long between words, causing the expected rhythm of language to tumble offbeat.[4] These interludes open

---

2. I owe this way of reading Kierkegaard to Mark Jordan in his essay "Modernity of Christian Theology."

3. Kierkegaard [Anti-Climacus], *Practice in Christianity*, 59.

4. Craig himself suggested this to me.

up fissures and gaps in what the reader might be tempted to regard as a smooth production of meaning. They are punctures that let air into what might become a suffocating linearity. They are slits in the old wineskins of thought. Each chapter is "after crucifixion," in the double sense of going toward crucifixion and proceeding from it. Each chapter is wounded and wounds. The interludes open these wounds by interrupting what might become the book's wholeness and integrity.

And so to read Craig well requires the same sort of attention it takes to read Kierkegaard well. What is required is not to take them simply at their words but for what those words stutteringly attempt to release. This is to read them for what they cannot say and yet are moving from and toward. To read them well means to let their words become traces, fragile signs of what is beyond signification, what is after crucifixion.

This is not to say that either Craig or Kierkegaard is opposed to affirmative discourse, or the focused exposition of a concept or theme, or telling a story with exquisite detail, or lively conversation. Neither is an enemy of language or thought. They are writers, after all. Yet the manner in which they inhabit and move within language is a way of holding language open, the way a lover holds itself open before a beloved. This holding open of language sometimes takes the form of interruption or explicit self-negation or silence, other times it takes the form of language becoming maddeningly indirect or poetic, still other times it takes the form of language talking itself out into exhaustion in order to open up what language has not yet and cannot ever capture—the way Luke and his chain gang in *Cool Hand Luke* open up for themselves joyful hours of nothing to do because they exhaust their assigned task by shoveling to the subversive rhythm of unregimented time.[5] I think of Craig's sometimes marathon-like sentence constructions that are often long strings of negations that clear away the clutter around the tiny, barely perceptible crack through which grace shows itself. I think of his multitude of metaphors that spin and contort the imagination, or his etymologies that trace words all the way to their strange origins. I think of the way his book ends with a flood of epigraphs spilling out as a sort of disseminating climax, the way making love climaxes not as the progression of an argument but as an unspeakable play of bodies releasing themselves into each other. I think of Kierkegaard's sentence constructions and metaphors, also often taken to exhaustion, or his patiently suffered indirection and incognito as an author, or his love for that unknown single individual that he writes for, whose edification through reading he prays will come freely as a gift, without his authority, beyond coercion and manipulation.

---

5. Keen, *After Crucifixion*, 78n10.

What spirits both writers is always before and beyond their writing in a way that pushes their writing beyond itself, beyond calculative control. Before the God whose life is freedom, language cannot congeal into stable or enforceable meanings or into a commodity to be circulated in the market economy of knowledge. Before God, language can signify or "gel" only momentarily, and so elusively, the way a wink gestures elusively and momentarily. Craig's writing, echoing the movement of Kierkegaard's writing, aims to signify in this momentary way, which is why he imagines the space-time of writing and reading as "a moment in which in some unpretentious underground venue the deep, resonant percussions of subwoofers roll as carnal waves across the chest and throat before they become the bass line in a conscious musical thought."[6] Craig here announces that his writing aims to hold itself open to, and so become an echo of, a non-graspable moment prior to writing, or perhaps in excess of it. What impacts Craig, and what he desires would impact his reader, is not captured by any conscious linguistic thought or the dried and congealed ink on the pages of a book.

So language before the Mystery of life and death that has befriended us—it fails, always fails, inevitably fails, fantastically fails, even when its possibilities are powerfully and exquisitely released and exhausted, as they surely are in Craig's and Kierkegaard's writing. Appearances to the contrary, Craig and Kierkegaard cannot say what they want to say, even at their most eloquent and articulate. What they do say is not what they want to say, because what they want to say is always slipping beyond saying, like the silent waiting and breath that remain after all the intentional words of prayer have been spoken or written. They write in order to open up this silence. Both Craig and Kierkegaard at various moments, mostly indirectly, register this inevitable failure of writing, this failure that is writing, letting it become the writing of failure. As Craig writes of himself, "I teach, which is simply to say that I 'tell'—not that I cannot keep a secret; and yet there is a secret that I cannot keep . . . or tell; mostly, I tell, as often and in as many ways as I am given the occasion, that there is a secret that I cannot by any means keep or tell."[7] This failure to keep or tell the divine secret is what incites and sustains the passion of faith. As John Caputo writes, "I cannot discern the event that concerns me ultimately, and that failure is my success, my most vital sign, my passion, the passion of my non-knowing, my prayer."[8]

The failure of language, then, its momentary and fleetingly fragile life before the mystery called God, is to be suffered, or passioned, as its liberation.

---

6. Keen, *After Crucifixion*, back cover.
7. Keen, *Transgression*, 24.
8. Caputo, *Weakness of God*, 294.

The non-ultimacy of any word or concept or construct is good news, the way the forgiveness of sins proclaims the non-ultimacy and unfinishedness of the past. Nothing as it is presently named and known is what it will be when all is finally known and named by God, when all creation is gathered into the new Jerusalem through the crucified and glorified body of Jesus. So language fails the way sin fails before the infinite mercy of God, the way death fails in the resurrection of the crucified one. Death of death. Negation of negation. Language is given to us not in order to fill the earth with objects and persons and histories named with the knowledge of good and evil. It is given so that the earth might be filled with praise and thanksgiving, filled with the self-emptying of language as it becomes a transparent and eternal Thank You.[9] On the long and difficult journey toward this eternal Thank You, language can only stutter and limp along, full of prayers and tears and laments and petitions, false starts and broken fragments, outraged cries and defiant silences, bursts of laughter and words of forgiveness—in short, full of the birth pangs of this coming Thank You. In the gift and freedom of the Holy Spirit, we may utter this eternal Thank You even now, although it is likely to sound absurd within the present evil age, perhaps like babbling tongues or some form of madness.

I am trying here to speak of grace, the way grace and gratitude spring from the same root, even etymologically. What does grace, *charis*, dare us to do, to risk? Even in our writing? In Craig's words, to get off ourselves—eucharistically. To write with grace is to write with gratitude, which is to write non-acquisitively, gathering words only to let them go, letting them become transparent to a gift that will never become a possession.

Let me turn, finally, to Jesus. For both Craig and Kierkegaard, Jesus is God's strange Word, God's Word made strange. What is to be written about this unwritable word? About this word that spoke itself onto a cross? This word of the cross, this crossed out word? Or perhaps the question I have

---

9. In his book where he reflects most directly on himself as an author and therefore as a language user, Kierkegaard concludes by writing the following about himself: "The dialectical structure he brought to completion, of which the several parts are whole works, he could not ascribe to any human being, least of all would he ascribe it to himself; if he were to ascribe it to anyone, it would be to Governance, to whom it was in fact ascribed, day after day and year after year, by the author, who historically died of a mortal disease, but poetically died of a longing for eternity, where uninterruptedly he would have nothing else to do but to thank God" (Kierkegaard, *Point of View*, 134). Craig quotes the following lines from Christian Cherge in his postlude: "I give thanks to God for this life, completely mine yet completely theirs, too, to God who wanted it for joy against, and in spite of, all odds. In this Thank You—which says everything about my life—I include you my friends, past and present, and those friends who will be here at the side of my mother and father, of my sisters and brothers—thank you a thousandfold" (Keen, *After Crucifixion*, 234).

been trying to get at here is not *what* to write, exactly, but *how*, recalling Kierkegaard's distinction between the "what" and the "how."[10] *How* does one comport oneself and one's texts to this word that would rather let itself be silenced and put to death than hemmed into a readable, speakable identity, whether political, pious, or academic? It is one of the most valuable contributions of Craig's and Kierkegaard's writing that this question, "How?," "*How* does one write Jesus?," a question that threatens to introduce a debilitatingly long pause before every blank page, is a constitutive disturbance and incitement of their writing, a thorn in the flesh, one that will not be removed, however tempting it might be to remove it and suture the wound with neat academic definitions or easy moral pronouncements.

I don't mean here to suggest some idolization of negation, any more than Craig means to suggest some idolization of crucifixion—although that is also a temptation to be aware of. It is not as if negation, or crucifixion, has the last word. The point is rather that the word is not the last in the order of what we might call revelation, nor is it the first, and this suggests something of *how* to approach the word. One could use trinitarian teaching to get at this. There is an unspeakable origin from which the Word proceeds, what is traditionally called "Father," and there is an infinite or excessive effect that the Word releases or empties itself into, what is traditionally called "Spirit."[11] The Word is always taking place between its prior, unspeakable origin and its excessive, self-emptying Spirit, always interceding here as a kind of kenotic prayer. This is the space into which Jesus is written as himself a prayer, prayed by the Father in the Spirit. It is this space into which Craig aims his theology as a kind of prayer. The "how" of writing Jesus is prayer. The space-time of writing Jesus is prayer. Self-emptying prayer—in the manner of an empty tomb.

In Kierkegaard's texts, this trinitarian space into which Jesus is written is the site of "absolute paradox." This is a space in which the eternal occurs paradoxically as a contingently singular moment. It is a space that is occupied by "the abased one," who speaks the comforting words, "Come here!" to every sufferer.[12] Yet before this abased one every would-be disciple comes to a halting, stuttering standstill before a "sign of offense," before a comforter who takes his place not in the heights of the esteem and recognition of good people, but in the depths of incognito, among the rejected and

---

10. Kierkegaard [Johannes Climacus], *Concluding Unscientific Postscript*, 203.

11. There is, we might say, a double repetition or redoubling in God that is what God is, or will be. Cf. Exod 3:22: I am who I am, or I will be who I will be.

12. Kierkegaard [Anti-Climacus], *Practice in Christianity*, 54.

mocked and scorned.¹³ Kierkegaard's pseudonym Anti-Climacus writes of Jesus as a linguistic sign, but one that is not easily readable or speakable or even meaningful. Jesus is a broken sign, an abased sign, a stuttering sign, a sign of offense, offensively unable to bring its signified into reassuring presence, instead terrifyingly unveiling a pregnant absence that calls forth not the securities of knowledge or even belief, but the precarity of faith, and therefore prayer.

In Craig's texts, this trinitarian space into which Jesus is written is populated especially by bodies, bodies thrown in with the crucified body of Jesus. It is populated, therefore, by liturgical and eucharistic bodies, bodies hard at the work of prayer. The central theme of Craig's writing is praying bodies, bodies that expend and exhaust themselves in praise and thanksgiving, in mourning, in suffering, in working, in hoping, in loving. The apophatic quality of Craig's writing is a saying that unsays itself particularly before bodies, before one body in particular, the broken body of Jesus. It is an "apophasis that bleeds."¹⁴ It is an apophasis that prays bodily, with the body, for the body, in the body, that the body might be released from its suffocating capture within capitalist, monetary economies. Craig prays the body into a different economy, a nonmonetary economy, in which the only debt is the debt of love that each body owes to every body. This is a debt so deep and bottomless so as to be incalculable and unspeakable in the language of monetary accounting. Its only language is what Kierkegaard calls "the silent and veracious eloquence of action"¹⁵ in which infinite debt becomes the source of joy because it means that the bodily work of love will never cease.

If I were to highlight an area of Craig's work that, to my mind, deserves the most constructive and critical attention, it would be this: the entanglement of bodies and prayer, the way Craig's prayers aim to release apophatic bodies, bodies unsaid before the mystery of God's mercy and righteousness and love, the mystery embodied in the abased body of Jesus. How are our embodied habits and violences productively disturbed in Craig's writing? Where might we push him further, deeper into the limitlessly complex dance of bodies that is the world God so loves? How might we prayerfully call down and write ourselves into even more disturbance? How might we face the gospel and so get off ourselves with a deeper nonheroic abandon? Those are the questions I'd like to continue to ask of his writing.

---

13. Kierkegaard [Anti-Climacus], *Practice in Christianity*, 72.
14. Keen, *After Crucifixion*, 155.
15. Kierkegaard [Anti-Climacus], *Practice in Christianity*, 13.

To conclude: prayer, like singing, whether in the form of shouts or screams or gentle melodies, enacts and activates the limit of the word, its enlivening failure. Both prayer and singing surround and saturate the word with the unspeakable breath, or spirit, upon which words float and into which they may release themselves. This is not a Kantian limit that erects tall and impenetrable walls around knowing and speaking. It is a limit more like a shoreline that allows traffic between the land and the sea and a point of entry out into the abyss. This is why all of Kierkegaard's texts, even at their most philosophical, take on an unmistakably musical, rather than scientific, tone. His texts are poetry. They are prayer. They stretch beyond themselves to the point of their own failure and abandonment in the Spirit. Kierkegaard is a religious poet of the shoreline whose authorship is not aimed inland at established circuits of discourse. He writes notes in bottles and tosses them out to sea, praying that he might make contact with just one single, unknown, struggling swimmer out there.

Craig, too, is a musical, religious poet. His preferred location is not the shoreline but rather "some unpretentious word-of-mouth underground venue" that has especially good subwoofers. There is an underground venue in Nashville, where this essay was written, called "The Basement" that I think of, and I cannot help but pun a little here: Craig's writing happens in a basement, in abasement, hearkening after the abased one, trembling from the impact of bass, from the resonant percussions of bodies moving in and around and through each other as in a friendly mosh pit, or a eucharistic feast. Craig's underground venue, like the shoreline, is a limit location, a site to which identities formed above ground in the light of day descend in order to be and do otherwise, in order to let every "is" and "am" go before an incoming, elusive future that is making all things new, a future that strangely opens up from below, from within a sealed, underground tomb. From this site of ruptured earth, following after the women at the end of Mark's gospel, we can only run away, descending into Galilee amazed, full of fear and trembling, stuttering with good news.

4//

What Does Theology Promise?

The Folly of the Cross and the Theology of Glory

JOHN CAPUTO

PRELUDE

WHAT DOES THEOLOGY PROMISE? A promising career path? A path to glory? A treasure in heaven? Does it promise something we cannot even imagine? Does theology make us a promise? Or is it rather the study *of* a promise already made, the mutual promise God and humankind make each other?

These and other questions are raised by Craig Keen in such a self-questioning and non-inquisitorial way, with such meditative and prayerful search, that even where there is a difference between us, the difference is situated within a deeper agreement. I love the way this theology goes its way, the style, the climate, the élan of this theological thinking. Praying as he writes, writing as he prays, thinking, dreaming, hoping, praying over the promise of theology, over something going on in theology that calls upon us, day and night. I sense that Craig and I are kindred souls (by souls I mean bodies), joined in the same dance, our ears cocked to the same faint and distant rumble of something sounding in the word theology.[1] What is the

---

1. Keen, *After Crucifixion*, x–xi.

event, I ask in my Derridean idiom, which Craig sometimes adopts, that takes place in and under the name of theology?

We are fellow-travelers, on the same road, a couple of intellectual vagabonds, bags on our backs, heading down a path to who knows where. That's a literary trope, of course, and it takes a lot of nerve to use it, there being only so much of the vagabond in tenured full professors, or retired ones with a comfortable pension. We are anything but real vagabonds, like homeless people, and we know it. So we beg your indulgence, Craig and I. We ask you to suspend your disbelief—especially all you young, unemployed theologians who cannot find a teaching job—and to go along with the literary conceit, his and mine, that we are a couple hobos during the Great Depression who have hit the open road on a journey to sights unseen, hoping against hope to catch a break. Tropes are not innocent; tropes can trip us up. But still, without tropes, we could not take any trip at all, hardly say anything at all, even if we must be careful not to let them run away with us.

I am just trying to say how extremely close I feel to these texts, to this voice, to this path, to this promise, to this powerful poetics, or theopoetics, to a discourse which resonates with everything I hear in the expression "kingdom of God."

PLAYING WITH WORDS

What comes after crucifixion? That is Craig's question and the title of the book, which the subtitle, the promise of theology, repeats and amplifies. Theology's promise is that something comes after crucifixion. Just as Craig Keen is playing with the slippage between the subjective and objective genitive, slippage of "of," in the subtitle, so he exploits the ambiguity of "after" in the title. *After* crucifixion in the sense of what comes after it (*post*), what follows it, which comes on the third day; after crucifixion comes resurrection. But after also has the sense of what you are going after (*ad*), like that fellow on the open road on the cover, which could also serve as a pictorial trope for following the way of the cross, or for human life itself as *homo viator*. Craig's question is quite Pauline; what sense (*logos*) does crucifixion (*tou staurou*) make (1 Cor 1:18)? Is it not pure folly (*moria*)? Or is folly the path to glory, which follows after the cross? It is not a question of choosing between *post* and *ad*, because the one is entangled with the other. Without crucifixion, there is no resurrection. Without resurrection, crucifixion would be death pure and simple.[2]

If you object to Craig playing around with words, I would say you are tone-deaf to theology. It might make more sense (*logos*) to get an MBA and

---

2. I offer my own take on the folly of the cross in Caputo, *Folly of God*.

make some money instead. No one less than Heidegger himself would rise to Craig's defense. It is not we who play with words, Heidegger would say; it is the words who play with us. *Die Sprache spricht,* which means, this is language doing its thing, this is language just being language, language up to its old tricks. It is language doing this to and with Craig, not Craig doing something to and with language. Language is playing in his ear and Craig is listening as carefully as possible and trying furiously to get it all down on paper. He is agonizing over these words, tormented half to death by its fluid, shifting, ambiguous, polyvocal play, trying to join in a bewildering dance.[3] It's a losing game. Language was already running when we arrived on the scene. This is an old story told by the poets and the mystics. Jacques Derrida became notorious for "playing" with words, which was a stumbling block to the Greek philosophers in Paris, but it did not scandalize immigrant Jews like Levinas.[4] I will get to Levinas later.

We inhabit the distance between what we can control in language and what is going on in language behind our backs—its drift, phonic and graphic, semantic and syntactic; its associative, disseminative, etymological, historical ambiguities; its irreducible recontextualizability. The idea is not to steer a clean path through the play, to achieve absolute univocity, to make three neat piles of concepts, propositions, and arguments—that's the method of logic, not the logos of the cross. The idea is to heed these ambiguities, to strain to hear the promise that is being made in them, to let ourselves be moved and instructed by them, to go out in the desert and listen. To heed is to obey, to respond to, what is calling, being called, being recalled in them. At a far remove from frivolity, the play places a very rigorous demand upon us, subjecting us, in the accusative, to an exacting, difficult, elusive, subtle imperative. It calls upon our negative capabilities, our ability to sustain an uncertainty, to make our way amidst ambiguity.

But let's stop playing around. Here's the first question this raises: does resurrection come as the *reward* for crucifixion? Does glory follow after crucifixion as its promised reward? Is that the promise of theology? If you follow the folly of the cross, you won't regret it. Go sell all that you have and "you will have treasure in heaven" (Mark 10:21). You cannot ask for a better return on your investment than that! A bit of sacrifice for three score years and ten in exchange for an eternity of bliss? Then is theology a kind of heavenly economics? Is a degree in theology an MBA after all, albeit a

---

3. Keen, *After Crucifixion,* xiii.
4. Keen, *After Crucifixion,* 163n1.

celestial business degree, specializing in deferred, (very) long-term bonds? Heavens no! Avoid economics—at all costs![5]

YESHUA THE EARTHMAN

We begin with Yeshua. Let's call him Yeshua. Speaking for myself, but I wager Craig would go along with me on this: I am sick of all the baggage, all the freight, all the power, all the intimidation, all the self-righteousness, all the sanctimonious hypocrisy, all the mythology and pathology, all the outright greed and hatred and blood-spilling, if you can believe it, with which "Jesus" is weighted. It's too much to get out from under. I can't stand it. I am like Howard Beale (Peter Finch) in *Network*, shouting out of my window, "I'm as mad as hell, and I'm not going to take this anymore!" It would take several lifetimes to shed it, and not even then. So from here on in, it's Yeshua, from Nazareth. Bracket Bethlehem and the choirs of angel, and the three wise men from the east. Just the Aramaic-speaking peasant, Yeshua. Stick to the man of flesh and bones, whose bones were broken and blood spilled. Craig and I want to get as far away as we can from Docetism, which "fails to love bodies and blood," which stands aloof from them, which turns on a "revulsion" with the body and the earth.[6] That's the second big issue here. Avoid Docetism along with economics—and they go together: don't exchange your body for a soul.

Yeshua, an erstwhile handyman, not a skilled carpenter or cabinet maker so much as a fellow who does odds and ends for people, barely eking out a living, like a Hispanic immigrant mowing lawns in the suburbs. Born and raised among the poorest of the poor, as poor as poor can be, dirt poor. Craig stresses this again and again (just check the index entry "poor"). He lives among people whose lives are completely Hobbesian—poor, nasty, brutish, and short.[7] They were lucky to make it past twenty-five years, and women are lucky to survive more than a few childbirths, and less than half the infants are lucky to survive at all. When they pray for their daily bread, don't think of a great choir singing the *Pater Noster* in Christ Church at Oxford. They meant every word of it. Day to day, bare subsistence, death's eerie grin always hovering over them. Craig drives this home, repeatedly, like the slumdogs in *Slumdog Millionaire*, he says, like Jamil Malik (Dev Patel) landing in a cesspool in order to catch sight of a Bollywood star.[8]

---

5. Keen, *After Crucifixion*, 27, 139, 185–87.
6. Keen, *After Crucifixion*, 185–87, 91.
7. Keen, *After Crucifixion*, 125.
8. Keen, *After Crucifixion*, 139. See the exchange between Craig and me in Severson, ed., *I More Than Others*.

For whatever reason—we don't know anything about Yeshua before this, this is his first public appearance—he left the dusty little village of Nazareth and took up with an exotic prophet named John. Then, after John's violent death, he struck out on his own and became a teacher, an exorcist, and a healer. That mostly meant he could look a man or woman in the eye, take their hand in his, and with the calming power of his presence drive out whatever demons were possessing that person. We have other names for that today, but even today we will sometimes put it that way. We have preserved the trope but today you better have good health insurance if you want a healer who will give you more than fifteen minutes and a pill. This was all part of his mission, to announce the "good news."

Yeshua comes announcing a promise, the coming of the "kingdom of God." The promise is described in the most material, earthy tones. Luke has Yeshua announce it with a citation of Isaiah. He has been anointed to "bring good news to the poor," to "proclaim release to the captives," to recover sight for the blind and freedom for the oppressed, to announce "the year of the Lord's favor" (Luke 4:18–19).[9] That's the Jubilee, the year the playing field is leveled, debts are forgiven, and we start all over again. (The Christian Right should try to get that in the next Republican platform.) That is how the world goes round when God rules, not Caesar. The list is extremely materialistic, extremely earthy. When Matthew, mostly out of respect for the holiness of the name of God, calls this the kingdom of "heaven," that should not result in taking our eye off the ball called earth. Matthew comes up with the same earthly list (Matt 25), feeding the hungry, slaking the thirst of the parched, releasing the prisoners. The parables, far removed from the later exercises in Neoplatonic theologizing, are about mustard seeds and leaven and treasures buried in a field. So not a heavenman, but an earthman. Yeshua the earthman.

All this eventually attracted the attention of the imperial powers that be—this was, Craig keeps reminding us, an "occupied" country—and they snuffed him out like a bug. What did he expect? After all, he was talking about a rival kingdom, not the empire's, where the rule would be wrested from the emperor and turned over to the God of the Jews. That got the attention of the Romans, fatal attention. He said this one time too many, at the wrong time and in the wrong place—at the Passover, in a crowded Jerusalem, under the very eyes of Rome worried about crowd control—and they wiped him out without so much as blinking. I think Craig would agree with that.[10]

---

9. Keen, *After Crucifixion*, 139.

10. The suggestion that a bloody Roman procurator named Pilate was actually a

So that hobo on the cover hiking down an open road—that is Craig and me and you following after Yeshua the earthman. How to move along (*meta*) this path (*odos*) is the "method," and the method is not logical but mad, the folly of following a path that stretches out before us all, its blue-black apophatic depth, *usque ad mortem*. The path is very aporetic, *a + poros*, as in dead end, literally. Does the *theologia crucis* promise a *theologia gloriae*?

HAVING FAITH IN THE PROMISE

So what happened? I am skipping ahead. So far I haven't gotten past the cover and title page and, at this rate, we would never finish reading this book. Was Yeshua right? Was the promise of the year of the Jubilee fulfilled? Not at all. The people who ran the real kingdom, the *imperium Romanum*, killed him for even bringing up the subject, especially in a crowded city during the holy days. Paul picked up the torch and rushed about Asia Minor proclaiming that the coming of the rule of God had already begun, with Yeshua, the Anointed One. So what happened to Paul? Same thing. They killed Paul, too, and the kingdom did not arrive. If anything, the opposite happened. A year of the anti-Jubilee arrived (70 CE). The Jews rose up against Rome and the Romans crushed them, destroyed their temple and scattered them to the four winds, and along with them the original Aramaic-speaking followers of Yeshua, the ones who actually knew him, headed up by James. So Yeshua and Paul were wrong, dead wrong, literally.

Now it gets interesting. Was this a false promise—the one that Yeshua is making about the coming of the kingdom, the promise that theology ponders and prays over? Two words of caution here about having faith in a promise.

1. Are we sure that the promised year of the Jubilee belongs to calendar time, that fifty was a strictly mathematical calculation, and that Yeshua was promising something that was going to happen in the measurable

---

passingly good chap who, against his personal inclinations, gave in to "the Jews" belongs to the later gospels, which for all their talk of love shows very little love for "the Jews." As if the Jew named Yeshua bar Joseph were not one of "the Jews!" That is no more to be believed than John's cynical story of Yeshua waiting for Lazarus to die so that he could put on a display of divine power by resurrecting him, a story unknown to anyone else in the New Testament. This, along with the two-worlds dualism of an eternal logos who has to come into the "world" of flesh and bones and bloody bodies, the antagonism it incites between Greek-speaking followers of "the way, the truth and the life" and "the Jews," and its soaring poetry—I read all this with great caution. The play of language is very dangerous. Theology is dangerous.

future, although we just don't know when? Might seven have symbolic significance, all the more so the year that follows seven times seven? Otherwise it is a lousy prediction. As Craig says, "After twenty centuries of waiting the eschatos has not come."[11] Eschatological time is not calendar time. A promise is risky and it not a prediction. It better not be.

2. Are we sure that what they called *pistis*, in gentile Greek, means what modern religious people call "beliefs." Beliefs are propositional assertions that pick out facts of the matter out there in the world. Beliefs come as both "secular" and what we call (in Christian Latin) "religious." The latter pick out facts accessible not by reason or by empirical investigation but only by "revelation," a special supernatural "app" you can download if you go to church. Beliefs are either correct or incorrect, properly worded or not, and if you mess up the wording, or deliberately alter it, you stand a chance of getting yourself killed. In the name of Jesus, or God, of course, or Reason, or the Nation, or the Party, or whatever alibi that is out there for killing.

Pistis, Craig and I think, is not a matter of epistemology. It means confidence, a deeper faith (*fides*) that something is being symbolized in this symbol, that something was going on (an event) in the name of God, and in Yeshua himself, God's anointed, that solicits our confidence. Events call, and we are called upon to respond. But what could that mean? Yeshua was an earthman, come to quench the thirst of people whose throats were as dry as the dusty peasant roads they traversed, to make the blind see, the deaf to hear, to release the imprisoned. Still, pretty much the opposite thing happened, and nothing ever since gives any reason to think that anything even remotely like the year of the Jubilee has ever come about. That goes for the advent of Constantine, during which time, as Stanley Hauerwas has carefully explained, Christianity converted to the empire, not the other way around.

Two thousand years and counting, and still, the same thing keeps happening. The wicked ones get rich and the just get persecuted for pursuing justice. The evil ones prosper; the good get killed. It was ever thus, before, during, and after Yeshua. How to have confidence in that? The promise of theology is more than bleak. It seems downright mad.

PAUL'S APOCALYPSIS

More than anyone else Paul appreciated the madness. "Saul" was more than a little confident that Yeshua was not the Anointed One for the simple

---

11. Keen, *After Crucifixion*, 59.

reason that he was *defeated*. He was crucified, which meant God had not anointed him, God let him get killed, ignominiously. In an honor/shame world, crucifixion meant death, and something worse than death, ignominy and shame. Then Paul had a breakthrough, an *apocalypsis*, an insight (Gal 1:12). What was that? Let's stick to his own words, please, and forget the dramatizations of Luke/Acts: no road to Damascus, no unhorsing, which was the innovation of the paintings of Tintoretto. The horse is a trope. What unhorsed Saul, what hit him, over the course of time, maybe months, maybe years, was that *God is revealed in the defeat*.[12]

This was completely mad, revolutionary, literally. It was upside down, topsy-turvy, *Alice in Wonderland* mad, looking-glass crazy, literally moronic. Gods don't get defeated. If they do, what good are they? The very idea of such a god would have reduced the raw power of the Romans to peals of laughter, scandalized the piety of the Jewish tradition who had cut a deal with Yahweh to protect them, and baffled the philosophy of the Greeks who had an idea of *sophia* as wholeness, having the whole ball of wax, the harmony of the good, the true, and the beautiful.[13] Neither power, nor piety, nor philosophy, could make any sense (*logos*) of this. It was downright foolish (*moria*), the moronic and senseless sense of the cross (*staurou*). But there it was, as big as death. God chose the weak to confound the strong, the foolish to confound the wise, the nothings and nobodies to confound the powers that be. Along with the Sermon on the Mount, there is no more confounding and explosive text in these Greek books about Yeshua than 1 Cor 1. If I were an essentialist, and thanks be to God I am not, I would say that is the essence of Christianity. Period. So instead of being an essentialist, let's just say everything depends upon it, upon a fragile and elusive and mad thought, which must be cultivated with care. Let's just say the promise of theology, of a Christian one, anyway, is lodged in there, somewhere. Craig agrees.[14]

I say "somewhere" because a promise to be crucified, to be defeated, sounds more like a threat than a promise. Surely something must be promised beyond crucifixion. Where's the glory? What comes after crucifixion? (Remember, we want to avoid economics and avoid Docetism.) Now we come to the nub of the issue in this book. There are, I think, two possibilities at this point, the way of the earthman and the way of the heavenman; the one on the cover of the book, and the other one. The first keeps its feet on the ground and continues to plod down that open road; the second wants to slip free from these mortal coils and ascend into heaven. The first is the

---

12. See the groundbreaking study by Stendahl, "Apostle Paul." Scott, *Real Paul*.
13. Keen, *After Crucifixion*, 122, 177, 231.
14. Keen, *After Crucifixion*, 99–100.

way of the flesh and remains faithful to Yeshua as a man of flesh and bones. The other is the Docetic way, which says this body, these bones, this flesh, this blood was a phantom, an appearance and the reality is a pure spirit appearing in the guise of flesh. Docetism is the poison pill, the most toxic substance one could possibly inject into Christian body. It would destroy Yeshua's good news—which is to feed the hungry, heal the sick—by making these hungry, thirsty, blind, imprisoned, paralytic, sick, and wounded bodies *unreal*. It would destroy Paul's insight (*apocalypsis*), that God is revealed in the defeat, in Yeshua the crucified, because it would make the defeat unreal, a mere appearance. The crucifixion would be nothing more than a spirit unlacing the outer garments of the flesh and leaving it behind, hanging on the cross, like a torn and soiled shirt. So the early church wisely steered a wide swath around that. It kept faith with Yeshua the earthman. Yeshua's mutilated body on the cross was not a phantom. This bloody death was real, and not Yeshua's idea. He would have been happy to have let this cup pass.[15]

GOD IS NOT DEFEATED

God is revealed in the defeat. That's the madness, the folly (*moria*), so where's the glory? To put this question in context, allow me first to go back to another Jewish defeat, one that takes us back to the originary, founding promise of the Jewish people, to the deal cut between the Jews and the Yahweh. They would be his people and he would be their God. Let us be clear. This was a completely terrestrial covenant. The Tanach is all about land and children. It "obsesses about bodies."[16] It is concerned with time and the future, with a Lord of history and a historical people, with their survival, right here on earth. The deal held up well. Until it didn't. Until catastrophe struck, when Antiochus IV (Epiphanes) attacked Jerusalem (167 BCE), defiled the temple, and suppressed the practice of the Jewish religion. Yahweh's people were mercilessly slaughtered, including the women and children. Later on, the Christians would call them the first "martyrs," the Greek word for a "witness" to one's faith, and a word central to Craig's meditations here.[17] So here was defeat, bloody slaughter, like the defeat that Jesus suffered and that Paul pondered. This was not part of the deal. This was not supposed to happen. Should the Jews begin looking around for another God who could afford them better protection?

---

15. Keen, *After Crucifixion*, 163.
16. Keen, *After Crucifixion*, 91, 126n11.
17. For a good account of the following material, see Segal, *Life after Death*, 248–81.

Enter the prophet Daniel with a novel solution (12:1-4): "Many of those who sleep in the dust of the earth shall awake, some to everlasting life and some to shame and everlasting contempt." The just—those who resisted Antiochus—will glow like stars with shiny stardust bodies and the unjust—those who collaborated with him—will rue the day they did not stand fast. This was a new deal! Daniel rewrites the contract so that the promise of Yahweh is for "everlasting" bodies that will never die, for a life insulated from death. This also sends them back to the drawing board about Yahweh. In the new revised version, Yahweh's powers are upgraded, so now he has the power not only to breathe life into preexisting elements (Genesis) but to resurrect life from death, which is getting to sound like making something from nothing. It was the first step in the Jewish Scriptures to the final upgrade God gets in the second century CE to the creator *ex nihilo*, the *deus omnipotens* of Neoplatonic metaphysical theology. These two notions, shall I say, rise or fall together.

I call this a novel solution because Daniel's move was nothing less than revolutionary. If Daniel were a Roman Catholic, the Inquisition would have toasted him for his heresy. The idea of an afterlife had been strictly prohibited. Adam and Eve got their walking papers not precisely for eating from the tree of good and evil but for fear that next they would set their sights on the tree of life, for wanting to be like gods and live forever. Death was not their punishment; they were punished for wanting to avoid death (Gen 3:22-24). Gods are immortal; mortals are mortal. God is heavenly; mortals are earthly. That's the way it is. That was basic Jewish theology, from right out of the gate of Eden. The idea of immortal earthlings was so horrifying to Yahweh that the very thought of it sent Adam and Eve packing, resulting in a very earthly life of earthly toil and earthly trouble instead of a life of easy innocence (and low sartorial expenses). So the novelty was not the idea of an afterlife. That was not "unknown" to the Jews before the book of Daniel. It was well known, right from the start—and strictly forbidden. It was denounced as idolatrous, like the Egyptians who worshipped their dead. The only spirit around is the Spirit of God, the one and only God, a jealous God who will tolerate neither other gods nor anything remotely resembling other gods, like demigods with everlasting bodies, bodies of glory, like surviving ancestral spirits that could only prove to be competition to Yahweh's sovereign unity and unitary sovereignty. The afterlife was at odds with monotheism. Until it wasn't.

The Jews were right to be sent back to the drawing board by this defeat and rethink their view of God, but, in my view, they drew the wrong conclusion. Instead of upgrading God's powers to include resurrecting the dead, they should have reconsidered this idea they had that God is a superbeing who will settle the hash of their enemies. They were right to ask themselves what this defeat reveals about God, but in doing so, what was first and foremost in their mind is that God does not lose. God is not defeated, which also meant, of course, that *they* are not defeated, which is not a minor point. God is about victory. That is what they *meant* by God, somebody who sees to it that victory is ensured. So, they decided, if God is defeated, which means that God's *people* are defeated (a very important inclusion), the defeat must be only *apparent*. God is *not* defeated, not *really*. Maybe they should have asked themselves, is God about winning? (Avoid economics.)

THE DOCETIC LOGIC

So we see the Docetic logic setting in. If God always wins, then God only appears to lose. The glory is always God's. The ones who think they have won have only won a Pyrrhic victory. They win, but only for a time. Ultimately, God will win, and that victory will be an everlasting victory. You would think that would have been enough for Daniel but he goes on. *And*—and this "and" is punishingly important—the ones who crossed their God will rue the day. Daniel could have had his God raise the just and allow the unjust to be deprived of resurrection. That would fix them. But Daniel wanted more. The glory of this apocalyptic scene is only complete if his God wakes the dead from their sleep to torment them, like waking a prisoner to torture him. They do not deserve to rest in peace, so Daniel's God resurrects them so that they could be punished forever. The art of torture is to keep the victim *alive*, so when God is the torturer, you have the advantage of resurrecting the dead and keeping them alive forever for the purpose of everlasting torture. Compared to a torture that lasts forever, the Roman torture and execution of Yeshua is small potatoes. Daniel is fashioning the greatest torturer the world has ever known, the very limit idea of torture, which is why Blake thought that the ideas of God and Satan were not always so easy to keep apart. This is economics gone mad. The Docetic logic and economics go hand in hand.

Suffice it to say that I think the line that Daniel struck is, in the words of Paul Tillich, "half-blasphemous and mythological."[18] The mythology is found in the big story of imaginary immortal mortals, of highly heavenly, very unearthly earthlings, of "resurrected bodies," let us say, of Docetic bodies, which had hitherto been strictly prohibited. And the blasphemy in turning God into history's most gifted torturer. Thereafter, there were two schools of opinion on this story, the Pharisees who bought Daniel's story and

---

18. Tillich, *Theology of Culture*, 25. I take this text as my touchstone in *Folly of God*.

made it a centerpiece, and the Sadducees, who practiced—to cite Lyotard's famous phrase—"incredulity about big stories" like this.[19] Yeshua and Paul belonged to the Pharisaical tradition. They accepted the resurrection of the body. Mark even constructs a rabbinical debate in which Yeshua puts it to the Sadducees (Mark 12:18–27).

Now let us return to First Corinthians, to Paul's breakthrough, that God is revealed in the defeat. We see that it is followed by a second chapter, which pretty much walks back everything that Paul said in the first chapter.[20] It turns out that even for Paul God is not defeated. It only looks like he was defeated. The defeat was temporal, temporary. Paul *apocalypsis* included a fiery apocalyptic glory. The people who crucified Yeshua will rue the day. Their human wisdom is nothing, a mere appearance of wisdom, compared to God's wisdom, which is the *real* wisdom. Human power only appears to be power; it is small potatoes compared to God's power, which is the *true* power. If these people had known this is God's anointed, if they weren't deceived by appearances, they would not have crucified him. As it is, they are "doomed to perish," but as for us, well, eye has not seen nor the heart conceived the treasures God has laid up for us. Both the Docetic logic and the economic logic (of rewards and punishment).

Then, in chapter 15, to cap off the Docetic logic, we are introduced to "spiritual" bodies. The bodies of glory are bodies without flesh and blood (15:50), completely incorruptible bodies, immortal mortals, heavenly earthlings, the desire for which earned Adam and Even a hasty exit from Eden. These bodies are incorruptible—no cells breaking down, so no need for sleep because they do not get tired, for eating because they need to replace lost energy, for reproducing because nobody is dying and in need of replacement. They never throw up, grow old, or get bitten by mosquitos. In other words, these bodies lack, in every way that *matters* (pun intended), the only things that make them worthy of *really* being called bodies. They will however—maybe for purposes of identification—look like (*docet*) bodies. These "spiritual" bodies are bodies in name only, having taken leave of real bodies—the bodies of flesh and blood, the bodies that are entangled in joy and sorrow, pleasure and pain, life and death, the earthly bodies upon whom Yeshua the earthman said the kingdom of God settles, *really* hungry, thirsty, blind, deaf, and imprisoned bodies. So Paul betrays his apocalypsis with apocalyptic fury when he unfurls its full logic in the second chapter. There he shows the real *logos* of the cross, the *whole* logic, the *real* logic. God is revealed in defeat, *but* the defeat is only temporary. In the first chapter,

---

19. Lyotard, *Postmodern Condition*, xxiv.
20. I spell this out in Caputo, "Weakness of God."

God is revealed in the defeat, but keep reading. In the next chapter, God wins, God's enemies rue the day. God is never defeated. Once again, Tillich: the half-blasphemous and mythological result of driving under the influence of what Tillich calls "supernaturalism," which I think introduces a theomagic into what is really a theopoetics.

GLORIFIED MUTILATED BODIES

Craig wants nothing to do with Docetic bodies. Even in glory this body is a "glorified carnality."[21] Or does he? This is where we differ. We have different takes on what sticking to Yeshua the earthman means, a different construal of what the theology of the cross and the corresponding theology of glory mean. I think his Yeshua, like his Kierkegaard, comes to him through Barth, and mine through Tillich.

Craig rejects the notion that the risen body is a Docetic body on the grounds of a genuinely interesting interpretation of what he calls the "glorified mutilated body" of Jesus.[22] In the gospels, in direct contradiction of Paul, the risen body of Jesus is said to include flesh, and Craig singles out the scene in the fourth gospel, in which Yeshua's glorified body retains its wounds (John 20:24–29). On the traditional interpretation, this proves to doubting Thomas that this is really Yeshua, the one they crucified and that, were Thomas's faith stronger, he would not require such proof. But over and beyond that, Craig says this represents a gesture of radical departure from the Greek ideals of integrity, of the harmony of the cosmos, of the harmony of the good, the true, and the beautiful in the life of the philosopher. That ideal made snub-nosed Socrates a paradox to the Greeks, who celebrated the unity of health, power, strength, and beauty. On the contrary, the wounds of the risen body of Yeshua are telling us that God's solidarity with the suffering, the afflicted, the wounded goes all the way down, that it extends beyond temporal life into eternal life:

> the hope of the hopeless, of the outcast and subaltern, of the child of death and damnation, of those who die knowing that they were never made whole, is precisely to be found in the glorification of a body that even in glorification, even in eternal life, is no less mutilated than it was in temporal death. . . . [This] is perhaps disappointing to the poster children of the good, the true, and the beautiful, but it is an *uncanny* good news to the poor. . . . The God who says "Yes!" to the peasant Jesus says

21. Keen, *After Crucifixion*, 29.
22. Keen, *After Crucifixion*, 18, 107, 189n75, 228.

"Yes!" to all the poor, to widows, orphans, strangers, eunuchs, Gentiles, terrorists, sell-outs, thieves, Roman collaborators, whores, the abused, the abuser, scum, the diseased, the dying, the dead, and the damned, so entangled in their lives is his, so entangled in their death is his, so entangled in the coming of the Reign of God is thus he and they.[23]

We can all be grateful to Craig for this construal, which I think is genuinely illuminating. But it is precisely here that I am left to wonder. Suppose the Romans departed from their usual customs and beheaded Yeshua? Would his glorified body have appeared beheaded to the disciples? Would the body of any history's innocents who were beheaded pass eternity "no less headless than it was in temporal death?" What about Ignatius of Antioch who was consumed by the beasts? What about those who were burned at the stake or blown to bits or horribly mutilated in an accident? What about missing teeth, speech defects, diabetes, cancerous growths, all the other maladies and mutilations that beset mortal flesh as it departs this world? All these mutilations will reappear in glorified form?

This is a can of worms we do not want to open. If we do, we will be inundated with conundrums—glorified digestive system taking a meal of fish? Will there be celestial waste? Will these deified bodies defecate? Does glorification, deification, stop at defecation? Heavenly waste disposal system? But then again why would an incorruptible body need to eat anyway? Or breathe—it obviously would not be exposed to suffocation? Why would it need *any* bodily organ? What will these organs *do*? What *work* would they do? What needs tending? What *work* is there to *do*?[24] If these glorified bodies are *real* bodies, will they require food, shelter, and clothing? Will they need housing, beds? There is no temple in the heavenly Jerusalem, but then again what is there?

As these questions roll off our lips—they have filled many libraries—we realize something has gone seriously wrong. Are we to understand that the author of the fourth gospel is reporting supernatural facts of the matter, that this language is representational, describing an objective occurrence, an appearance of the wounded but risen body of Yeshua, in some locatable place and datable time, one that, any casual passersby would also have observed had they chanced upon this scene? Are we to take this story "objectively," as if it bears metaphysical weight? Once we treat this story as a supernatural fact of the matter, a landslide of crazy speculations about bodies all appearing, not mutilated, but at their best, as thirty-somethings,

---

23. Keen, "Glorified Mutilated Body at (Intercessory) Prayer," unpublished paper.
24. Keen, *After Crucifixion*, 78.

so when you and your grandmother meet, you just have to adjust to being the same age.

At this point I am reminded of one of Woody Allen's quips, behind which I think lies a sound theology. "I don't want to live on in my children. I don't want to live on in my works. I want to live on in my apartment!" Is Woody Allen descended from the Sadducees?

Daniel and Paul meant that God would establish his rule on earth, unearth these bodies from their graves, and restore their life on earth, where they would live forever. But what happened in the history of Christian theology is that these gospel scenes, having passed over into Greek hands, have been absorbed by a metaphysical distinction between time and eternity that comes from "the poster children of the good, the true, and the beautiful"— Plato and Aristotle—which was grafted upon the distinction between the "everlasting" and the merely mortal in the Scriptures. In Corinth, where the seeds of a nascent Christian community were planted in a flourishing Greek city in no short supply of philosophers, the resurrection of dead bodies drew down a lot of ridicule and sarcasm upon the Corinthian Christians. Paul tried gamely to feed them a line—pace Kierkegaard, Paul was *both* a genius and an apostle—to give them some talking points.

The risen body, Paul said, is a *soma pneumatikon*, an answer that became the subject of a mountain of new questions—two thousand years and counting. The best explanation I have seen is offered by Dale Martin.[25] Paul, having never read the *Phaedo*, was not making a Platonic distinction between an immortal soul and a mortal body, but between two different kinds of bodies: a wet-earthy one (a "hyletic" body), which is corruptible, and a hot-dry-fiery one (*pneumatic*), which, like the heavenly bodies, is incorruptible. Of course, Paul did not know—how could he?—that the heavenly bodies actually are *not* incorruptible. Paul could not have known that the light of some of those stars he observed overhead on one of his many sea voyages had already burned out millions of years ago and that even the sun, expanding at an increasingly accelerating rate, is also burning out, on the way to becoming stardust, even as little planet earth is on the way to becoming ashes. Even the glory of the heavenly bodies is passing away, if they are *real* bodies that is.

HERMENEUTICS

I find two different suggestions in *After Crucifixion* about how to deal with these conundrums. The first is *apophatic*. The risen body is an apophatic body, a mysterious body, and so the promise of eternal life is "heartening"

25. Martin, *Corinthian Body*, 108–36.

but incomprehensible; it is an "unimaginable promise."[26] I love most things apophatic but there is a difference between a genuine mystery and a mystification resulting from conflating different levels of discourse, playing one language game with the rules of another, like calling "checkmate" in baseball. That's not a mystery; it's a mistake, which leaves the players on the field and the fans in the stands mystified, not steeped in mystery. I am all for the play of language, but this play merits an instant replay. To switch language games again, I think at this point, Craig is punting. As he says, theology is dangerous business, precarious, and it also is "perhaps delusional."[27] Sometimes we drive under the influence of theology, so we have to keep up our guard.

That is why I think the further suggestion Craig offers makes more sense, because it sorts out levels of discourse. We do not want to allow ourselves to get tripped up by the play of tropes, figures, and words, as we said at the beginning. Here the move is not merely apophatic but *hermeneutic*: do not literalize the tropes in which an *apocalypsis* is given words. Do not get carried out to sea by the drift of language "languaging," doing its thing as language. We do not want to make the mistake about the nature of apocalyptic discourse that is singled out in a citation Craig makes of John Collins, taken from the latter's *Apocalyptic Imagination*.

> The language of apocalypses is not descriptive, referential, newspaper language, but . . . symbolic attempts to penetrate the darkness, which provide[s] ways of imagining the unknown, not factual knowledge. The value of these imaginative ventures cannot be assessed by a correspondence theory of truth, but only by evaluating the actions and attitudes which they supported. . . . Apocalyptic language has a pragmatic aspect . . . it commits us to a view of the world for the sake of the actions and attitudes that are entailed. . . . The apocalyptic literature does not lend itself easily to the ontological and objectivist concerns of systematic theology. It is far more congenial to the pragmatic tendency of liberation theology. . . . The apocalyptic revolution is a revolution in the imagination. It entails a challenge to view the world in a way that is radically different from the common perception. . . . It can foster dissatisfaction with the present and generate visions of what might be. The legacy of the apocalypses includes a powerful rhetoric for denouncing the deficiencies of this world. It also includes the conviction that the world as now constituted is not the end. Most of all, it entails an appreciation of the great resource that lies in the human imagination to

26. Keen, *After Crucifixion*, 27.
27. Keen, *After Crucifixion*, 52, 59.

construct a symbolic world where the integrity of values can be maintained in the face of social and political powerlessness and even of the threat of death.[28]

To which Craig adds, "One might however, imagine as well a "systematic theology" that is not stuck in "ontological and objectivist concerns.""

I agree with this completely. I think "resurrection" is just such an apocalyptic trope, a work of the apocalyptic imagination, a way for the promise to assume an imaginative form, for it to be given a powerful rhetoric, adorned with striking images and stirring narratives. It is not supposed to represent a fact of the matter, to pick out a state of affairs. It is not supposed to have objective, representational value. It is not supposed to be an ontology of metaphysically risen bodies. It is, as Derrida likes to quip, not an ontology but an hauntology.

SO WHERE'S THE GLORY?

The problem is clear. If, as Craig insists, it is bodies all the way down, and if real bodies are earthly things, body of "flesh and blood" banned from heaven by Paul, often dirt poor and downright dirty, then just what is their *glory*?[29] After the theology of the cross comes the theology of glory, *so where's the glory*? How are bodies glorified? In this language game, that's the whole ballgame!

Bodies are "glorified" in Hollywood films with the aid of stuntmen and digitalized photography, in the celestial air-brushings and Photoshopping of the bodies in the world of advertising, and in animated cartoon bodies like "The Ice Queen" or the superheroes of summer action films. These are all apparent bodies that variously entertain, lure, or torment us. Why can't *we* look like that? Never fear. Nobody looks like that. Not even them. These are not real bodies but solely "for show," that is, Docetic bodies. Hollywood films glorify real people; they make a point by making them "larger than life."

The *real glory* of the flesh that Paul wants to ban from the kingdom of God is tied up with things of unconditional value, things *faith and hope and love*, or *justice* and *compassion*, things that do not belong to commonplace visibility or to digital technology, although we might catch sight of them in works of art (which the Reformation opposed!). The real glory is the glory of the unconditional, found in bodies touched by the power of the unconditional, responding to its touch. Bodies of love, like loving the flesh and bones of others in all their fleshiness, vulnerability, mutilation, and

---

28. Collins, *Apocalyptic Imagination*, 282–83.
29. Keen, *After Crucifixion*, 146.

mortality. What greater glory than to hold the hand of the dying through the night? Or to be in the presence of someone who dies with dignity and gratitude for life, more concerned with those she is leaving behind than for herself? If unconditionals like love and compassion are the rule, then we are best served to stick to this principle of earthiness and to the principle that the resurrection stories belong to an apocalyptic discursive form, that is, to a nonobjectifying figuration and that they are, as Collins says, ultimately of *pragmatic* purpose! To speak of spiritual bodies is to speak of spiritual practices. That is, these stories translate into *praxis,* into *theo-praxis,* the material practice of faith and hope and love, of mercy and compassion, right here on earth in earthly bodies. That is why, for all our differences, I think Craig and I are traveling down the same path, but we have different hermeneutic renderings of the name of the path.

The "good news" is not a newspaper report. The stories of the risen bodies found in the Greco-gentile staging of Yeshua several generations after his death are what Hegel called a *Vorstellung* (an imaginative presentation), and what Collins and Tillich called a "symbol," but as Tillich said, if you understand what a symbol is, you would never say "only a symbol." Why not? Because symbols transform lives. Symbols translate into a form of life, right here on earth. They translate into a theopoetics and theopraxis of faith, hope, and love, not into a mythical afterlife, not a mythical heavenly glory but a real earthly glory. They have a pragmatic impact, a prophetico-revolutionary one, enabling us to imagine life *otherwise,* to enable the poor and oppressed to imagine *not* being poor and oppressed—and to *do* something about it. God calls—*we* respond. God insists—*we* exist. To speak of a theology of incarnation is to say that Yeshua is a carnal event and that we are called upon to reincarnate him, each time we meet the poor, oppressed, or imprisoned bodies who populate the kingdom (Matt 25).

These stories enable us to imagine life *otherwise,* not elsewhere, not outside space, and to imagine the *future,* not something extra-temporal. They do not describe another world but a world to come, a coming time, right here in space and time. In this light, the figure of wounds in the risen body is significant, but it is a significant apocalyptic symbol, not a theological object or supernatural fact of the matter corresponding to a religious belief. Then what does it figure? Exactly what Craig says—that the God of Yeshua stands with the poor, the oppressed, the mutilated, all the way down, and that bodies go all the way down, including the fact that bodies are mortal and when they die they go six feet down. It is an exercise in Docetic imagination to imagine we can disconnect the cycle of life and death by which life is passed on from generation to generation. Our outrage that death is visited upon the victims of injustice cannot be translated into a rejection of the real, dead-as-a-doornail character of death without becoming a "revulsion" at flesh itself.[30] The unconditional affirmation of life includes affirming the mortality of the human condition.

We cannot "slip through the fingers" of the "entanglement" of life with death.[31] That entanglement is how life is perpetuated, propagated, diffused across the surface of the earth—*bonum diffusivum sui*—how Yahweh filled the air and the earth and the deep with life. The entanglement with death is what makes life so precious, what makes children blessed. We cannot sing hymns to the child and lament the suffering of innocent children without realizing that the child is the partner and the counterpart of death, that death and birth are partners along the path of life. Life passed on to life through the humility of death. I would not speak of the "conditional immortality" of the child but of the child's unconditional natality.[32] That is why the attachment of children and grandparents is so beautiful, so sacred. It is why, when two or three and sometimes even four generations are gathered together, we reach for our cameras to get a shot of this moment, made infinitely precious by its mortality and transiency.[33] We must not prove to be fair-weather friends of the flesh, glorifying a life that accepts pleasure but not pain, joy not sorrow, the high noons not the midnights, the life not the death. Binary oppositions are not undone by breaking one clean from the other, as in life without death, but in showing that the one side bleeds into the other, that this mortal life (*vita mortalis*) cannot be kept safe from a living death (*mors vitalis*).

TRANSASCENDENCE

So then what *is* the glory? I want to stand firm with the early Jews, before Daniel's distortion, and Paul's apocalypsis, that God is revealed in the defeat—in God's solidarity with the defeated. Then I go on to say that the dead *do* rise up again but not in mythological immortality, as in these Greco-gentile stagings of an apocalyptic event—but in the demythologized dignity, in the genuine glory of *justice, love, and compassion*. The risen body is a *body of justice*, and *a body of prophetic protest* against the injustice by which they were slain or mutilated or forced to live subjugated, oppressed, and impoverished lives. It was ever thus. Two thousand years and counting. History

---

30. Keen, *After Crucifixion*, 185–87.

31. Keen, *After Crucifixion*, 157.

32. Keen, *After Crucifixion*, 128.

33. This is the phenomenon of the "nihilism of grace" that I defend in *Insistence of God*, 223–45.

continues to run its bloody course. The year of the Jubilee does not belong to calendar time, and the risen body does not belong to some mythic place and period outside space and time. They are not, as Collins says, ontological objective supernatural facts of the matter. The risen body is a figure of hope, a *body of hope*, which *rises up in anastatic dignity*. Craig puts it perfectly: "Victory comes here not *instead of* defeat, but *in* defeat," in a "tale of martyrs, who wait, despite all evidence, for a *coming* redemption."[34] Although I would take some of the air out of any song to "victory," as we have enough of them already, I am doing nothing in this paper other than to hold Craig's feet to the fire of these words. Even when we disagree, we agree!

To that end, in the place of a Hellenistic hermeneutics of resurrection as celestial ascent, I put a more Jewish hermeneutics of a rising up that Levinas calls "trans*a*scendence," which is found in what Levinas calls "the impossibility of murder."[35] Of course, Levinas, a Jew imprisoned during the war by the Nazis who slaughtered most of his family, whose names he lists at the front of the book, knows better than most of us that you can kill someone, murder them in cold blood, in an objective-factual way. Then the victim is as dead as dead can be and the kindest thing you can do for it is to dispose of it respectfully. But, Levinas said, and this is the lesson he learned from the camps, there is something you cannot kill, the *visage*, which is immortal. The *visage* is not the visible face (*face*) but the invisible look issuing from the eyes of the other that *rises up* into a moral height, that comes to us from on high, like the face of God, that looks back at the killer in prophetic resistance and says "thou shalt not kill!" This command is a "weak force"— as witness to all the killing that goes on in bald defiance of this command. The command insists; we exist and are asked to respond, which we may or may not do. The command is Isaac looking back at Abraham—this on the Jewish telling, not the tale of the leap of faith of the hero prepared to spill blood woven by Kierkegaard—commanding the *end* of human sacrifice. This invisible *visage* cannot be killed. It will come back to haunt our days and nights, and if not ours, because we are hard of heart, then others, who will *remember* what we have done, what has been done. God is found *in memoria*, in the memory of the dead, in the "dangerous memory" of the mutilated body of Yeshua,[36] symbolized by wounds still visible in death.

---

34. Keen, *After Crucifixion*, 150; italics in original.

35. Levinas, *Totality and Infinity*, 35 and 35n2, where Levinas credits this term to Jean Wahl; on the impossibility of murder, 198, 232–33, 236. In response to "Deferral," Craig's contribution to Severson, ed., *I More Than Others*, 28–34, I would say my "insistence of God" is quite close to Levinas and that I keep my distance from the strong metaphysics of Whitehead as also of Tillich. Caputo, *Folly of God*, 65–71.

36. Metz, *Faith in History and Society*, 109–15.

It is this trans*a*scendence that also explains what took place with Yeshua and the disciples. The Romans killed him and they very likely left his body to rot, and nobody was there to witness anything or record the last words.[37] Yeshua was far too insignificant, a slumdog, to merit the dignity of a tomb. The story of Joseph of Arimathea is very edifying, but the reality was more likely much harsher. But his *visage*—the memory of his words, his deeds, his mission to the poor, the blind, the lame, the imprisoned, in short, his witness (*martyros*) and his *promise*—would *not* die. How can he be dead, the disciples asked, if his invisible *visage* is with us now, if we can feel in our hearts the invisible breathing of his spirit, if he is doing all this to us now? Why do we seek the living among the dead? This is the earthly business of Yeshua the earthman, his earthly Easterly transascendence. It all takes place on earth, in flesh and blood, in Aramaic, and it is all about the earth, about real bodies, and it all takes place among mostly illiterate peasants, who live under a punishing rule, all the while the hoping, praying, dreaming of the way the world would look if God ruled, not Caesar.[38]

But—and here is where we must resist "revulsion"—will those who have been oppressed and persecuted, or will infants born with terrible birth defects and consigned to an early death, receive justice? Can we count on this happening? No. Of course not. Life is beautiful and life is cruel. Both entangled together; not one without the other. Even if we make something good come of their suffering, does that restore justice to the dead? No. Of course not. Life in time includes ruined time, time that cannot be made whole. Life, our life in space and time, the life of flesh and blood, that is to say, our life, *simpliciter*, is both beautiful and cruel, not one without the other, in just the way there cannot be a promise without a threat. None of this can change the past—although that was part of the apocalyptic imagination

---

37. Caputo, "Undecidability," 220–48.

38. The Sadducees were wise to decline resurrection and to stay with the older Jewish tradition, where the Torah was all about land and children, about real bodies, all the way down. The prophetic imagination is not about imaginary bodies that were devised to answer the question, how could Yahweh let this happen? Yahweh's job is not to ensure victory but to call for justice; the rest is up to us. I am dubious in the extreme of the criticism of the Sadducees voiced by N. T. Wright. Is Craig citing this with approval? Wright applauds the greater willingness to be martyred, the encouragement it gives to "young hotheads" to attack religious symbols, when these young hotheads are confident that they will live forever in a better place. Keen, *After Crucifixion*, 157n96. Really? It is too late to tell that to Khaled al-Asaad, the eighty-one-year-old curator of antiquities at Palmyra, who was beheaded rather than surrender the treasures of that ancient city to the "young hotheads" of ISIS who were sure they were headed for paradise. I agree that belief in resurrection encourages violence, but is that supposed to be an argument *against* the Sadducees?

of Peter Damian[39]—but we can change the *meaning* of the past. We can see to it that these dead who have died unjustly have not died in vain.[40] For two thousand years and counting, these stories of Yeshua the earthman have solicited us; they insist, while we exist. We are, like the disciples, stationed between his memory and the promise. Theopoetics is theopraxis. The call of the event is a call to action, to make all things new, to make the impossible possible. The name of God is the name of something to *do*.

The dead have been reduced to ashes but they rise from their ashes, from the traces they have left behind, like the *gramme* they scratched out on a scroll, their memory soaring over us, coming to us from on high, urging us to finish the business of their unfinished lives. They call to us to mourn them, not in airy words and stone memorials, but in flesh and blood testimonials, in deed and in truth. From their ashes rise the promise of future. The promise of theology is the promise to remember, to recall the dangerous memory of the crucified Yeshua, of every crucified and mutilated body of which he is the icon. Our task is to make that promise come true, to give their past, which we cannot change, a different future, and to do this in memory of Yeshua, for any least member of the kingdom whose coming he calls for and promises. That, I think, is what *After Crucifixion* is all about and why I think my disagreement with Craig is part of a deeper agreement.

I am alluding to Matt 25. Remember the twofold injunction. Avoid making what happens to bodies merely apparent (Docetism) and avoid the economics, the logic of reward and punishment. Craig makes every effort to steer clear of this implication and to prevent the event that takes place in Yeshua from being reduced to an economic exchange, which would destroy the gift. But in my view once you ring the bell of a really resurrected body it is impossible to unring the economy of rewards and punishment. A good case in point is Matt 25. There we find an exquisite figure of the way things work when God rules, not Caesar: whenever you have fed the hungry or visited the imprisoned, you have done this to Yeshua. This is pure, disinterested, *unconditional* love—of loving without why, without having any idea that this was the Lord or that there was anything in it for us. All the righteous had in mind was to feed the hungry because they are hungry, which is pretty much the Derridean notion of the pure gift, the gift given unconditionally, the expenditure without return.

But these works of mercy are then inscribed within an utterly merciless scene. The "Son of Man"—which hitherto would have meant an earthman,

---

39. See my analysis of Peter Damian in Caputo, *Weakness of God*, ch. 9.

40. I am writing this on Memorial Day weekend, 2016, and in this morning's paper I read about an inscription on the base of a war memorial in South Boston: "If you forget my death, I have died in vain." Weston, "Graves of the Men I Lost," 2.

a merely mortal man, born of the earth—"coming on the clouds of heaven with power and great glory" (Matt 24:30)—that is what has become of Yeshua the earthman—sends out his police force (a host, as in hostile, of angels) to carry out a roundup of the nations, of a no doubt terrified population. Then, aided by his heavenly police, the Son of Man, like a merciless executioner, proceeds to separate the sheep from the goats, those who will inherit the kingdom—this is their reward—from those who will be consigned to eternal fire. On the telling of the Sadducees, the works of mercy *are* the kingdom of God, that is what it is like when God rules, not the Romans. But in Matt 25, the kingdom of God is a *reward in heaven* for performing the works of mercy, while failing to be righteous merits eternal punishment. That may be another reason, maybe the real reason, Matthew prefers the expression "kingdom of heaven" to the "kingdom of God." The "unimaginable promise" goes hand in hand with an unimaginable punishment![41]

INTERLUDE

In the place of a conclusion I offer an interlude, meaning the road still stretches far ahead, the journey continues, the music of theology is still playing, the dance goes on, far into the night. The kingdom is always, structurally, to come. Until the night overtakes us, escorting us both, Craig and me, and you, in case you thought you were simply an observer, back into the earth from whence we were drawn.

The promise of theology is the promise itself. Theology is one of the ways that the promise comes to words. Theology is theopoetics, a robust symbolic, a vivid *Vorstellung*, of the promise. The promise of the theology is the promise of hope, the hope of a promise. The hope is real; it is for the children, for the future, down here on earth, hope for what is to come.[42] Yeshua the earthman is the figure of this hope in the world. The promise of theology is the promise of the world, the promise of the earth, of what is coming, of the event. That means that God is revealed in the death of a child, not because of some obscene idea that "God has a plan"—tell that to the parents—or because of the glib used-car sales pitch that God writes straight with crooked lines, or that there is a heavenly banquet in store for

---

41. The expression "without why" was coined by Marguerite Porete (d. 1310), who was trying to avoid economics, to find a way beyond this economy of virtue, to bid "adieu to the virtues," as she put it. Like Meister Eckhart, she recommended we love God so unconditionally as to prefer hell to heaven were it God's will she be damned. For that pure thought, the Inquisition burned her at the stake. See Keen, *After Crucifixion*, 179. See Caputo, *Hoping against Hope*, 63–80.

42. Keen, *After Crucifixion*, 152.

their emaciated bodies in the fiery-airy bodies they will have in the afterlife. God is revealed in the defeat in the sense that in the deep, dark injustice of this death, the call for justice rises up in protest from these bones. The future is open. Justice is always to come, structurally to come. There is more time, time to make something good come of this terrible tragedy, something that will not justify it, or change it, but give it a new meaning and so give hope, which has no place to lay down its head, hoping against hope.[43] It is always possible to give things a new meaning, as long as there is time.

The promise of theology is a theology of promise, of the name of God as the name of a promise, one of the names we have come upon to name the promise life holds. The name of God is the name of our hope in the event, which may turn out to be a disaster, which is why we hope against hope. The name of God is the name of an elusive promise, where nothing is guaranteed. The name of God is the name of a perhaps, not an evasive, fence-sitting escapist indecisiveness, but a dangerous perhaps, of a "dangerous caregiver."[44] Theology ventures to affirm the adventure of the coming of what we cannot see coming. That is why Craig rightly says theology is a precarious and dangerous business.[45]

The apocalypsis is that God is found in the defeat, that God stands with the defeated, not in such a way as to give them victory but to give them hope. Theology does not promise we will win. Theology is not about winning or making things even in the end. God does not guarantee victory in the long run. God gives hope. The might of God lies not in the omnipotence of the super-being who is going to make our enemies our footstool or makes things even in the afterlife or somehow or another rescue us. The genuine might of God lies in the might-be of God, and the being of God lies in the may-being. If you think that is playing with words, think again.

---

43. Keen, *After Crucifixion*, 142, 149.
44. Keen, *After Crucifixion*, 132.
45. Keen, *After Crucifixion*, 52, 59.

PART II

Bodies

5//

Corpus Christi

CHRISTINA M. SMERICK

WE SERVE AN EMBODIED God. Or rather, God in Christ *is* a body, and not in some universal way, but a *singular*, particular body. Us westerners, however, are far more comfortable in the air of abstraction rather than the mess of the flesh, and so most of theological history has focused upon the intangibles—the mysteries of the Trinity, the Spirit, the rules and orders and laws that God creates and/or is bound by (see process theology). How funny is it, how strange, that human beings are so drawn to incorporeality, when we spend our lives 24/7 not simply enfleshed like some ghost in a machine but existing *as* flesh. We are bodies. The language of the west tries to soften this via possession, saying "we *have* bodies"—but what is this possession? What is the "we" here, existing separate from and outside of the flesh? A Platonic haunting, a Cartesian fantasy? Does something like a spiritual nonembodied soul exist? That is a question for the western theological imagination to distract itself with. In the meantime, it is quite evident that we are bodies—about this (setting aside "brain in a vat" philosophical dilemmas) we have no doubt, Descartes not withstanding. More radical is that we, again, serve a God who is a body, *a body*, not the body universal, nor all bodies, but a particular, fleshy body.

Two men have shaped my theological wrestling over the past few years (well, truly, Craig has taken up residence in my mind and heart and life for half my life now). Two men, both of whom have had their chests cracked open by modern medicine, who have had medical miracles performed upon their very hearts. Jean-Luc Nancy has another's heart lodged within his body. Craig Keen has had his heart reconstructed and has become, surprisingly, a jazz musician as (I think) a direct result. Their bodies have been sites of opening. Their works, for longer than that, have been sites of opening, of seeing anew.

If there is an underlying theme to Craig Keen's work, or more appropriately a recurring riff, it is the body of Jesus (and with this body our bodies). What happens to this particular body, what is done to it, what is undergoes, is the heart and life and blood of the Gospel. In returning again and again to the body of Christ, Keen fights against the tide of western theology, which seeks again and again to sweep us out away from bodies toward debates about the nature of God. He resists the rip current that pulls us away from this body. His work seeks to cradle the fragile body of Christ as Mary does in the *Pieta*, as Mary Magdalene longs to do at the tomb. Resisting theories of atonement and arguments regarding free will, resisting all the many ridiculous things Christians love to debate, Keen gestures, with increasing urgency, toward the scrawny, tortured, middle-aged body of Jesus—because it is there, together with this body, that our salvation works and rests. "My calling as a theologian is to do my word-work down this path . . . a body-part of a journeying body."[1]

More particularly, Keen draws us to the resurrected body while refusing to abandon the crucified body, even for one second. Indeed, the resurrected body of Christ does not abandon the crucified body, does not leave it behind or replace it, but *remains*. This focus—this hammer driven home again and again in Keen's work—is again working against the pacifying, numbing tendencies of modern western Christianity, tendencies Søren Kierkegaard railed against as well. These are the tendencies to take this crucified one and make him palatable, clean him up a bit, cover the wounds, perhaps put him in a nice suit with a tie and pocket square, to make him presentable to the nice, middle-class congregants of middle America. Western Christianity in both its academic and political institutions prefers a "floaty" Jesus, a disembodied Spirit, or at the very least a *winning* Jesus rather than the actual, beaten-down resurrected body of Christ. That this body *as beaten, as tortured, as bloody* is glorified (without thereby glorifying the violence that caused such wounds)—this is too difficult, it is argued, for middle-class Christians to deal with. Better to get them to Christ via the easy road. In books and essays

---

1. Keen, *After Crucifixion*, 29.

and chapel addresses, in classrooms and meetings and public forums, Craig Keen has devoted his life to pulling our gaze away from our comfortable fictions and toward the only hope of salvation we have. We tend to prefer to put our gaze upon simulacra of violence and the fictive bodies enacting and undergoing it rather than place our lives together with other real bodies undergoing real violence and pain. Craig's work is a sustained riff upon this theme. So how about we stop letting Craig riff alone?

I imagine that us academic types in this volume on Craig Keen's work are here to add our own riffs and rhythms, here to repeat his phrasing such that perhaps, just perhaps, we may evangelize our own people to salvation. It's risky, folks. Ask Craig about some of the consequences. But it's only risky if you're secretly convinced that your salvation lies in your reputation rather than in the body and blood of Jesus Christ. Those of us who write about or upon or with Craig's work, who try to think along with him, are trying to learn how to walk with Jesus by adding our own voices, scans, and scats (in its various definitions) to this theme, to this aching minor-key melody Craig has been whistling his whole life.

So here's my riff. I do a lot of reading and writing and thinking about Jean-Luc Nancy. Nancy, for those not in the philosophy business, is one of those dreaded and feared continental philosophers—he's even French!—who has inexplicably found western Christianity a fascinating course of study in recent years. Like Jean-Luc Marion and even Jacques Derrida, Nancy is drawn to philosophy of religion. Like Derrida, he remains outside the faith he studies, but his reflections on Christianity are not unsympathetic. He seems at times fascinated by what we try to pull off. More to the point of this essay, Nancy's work echoes Keen's to a surprising degree, especially given their rather different points of orientation. My riff, my meager contribution to the extended jam of Craig's work, is to let Nancy and Keen resonate with each other. Two such creative and original thinkers discovering again the weirdness of Christian thought from such different perspectives seems too good not to point out.

For thinkers who (as far as I know) have never read each other, Keen and Nancy share an eerie resonance—even down to echoing the other's phraseology at times (which, given that both are careful writers who seek exhaustively for the best way to say things, is a bit creepy). For example: Nancy writes, "In truth, the body of God was the body of man himself: man's flesh was the body God gave himself. . . . Bodies are the exposition of God, and there is no others—to the extent that God exposes himself. Thus, indeed, he's the one who's exposing himself *dead* like *the world of bodies.*"[2]

---

2. Nancy, *Corpus*, 61.

Keen: "[Christ] has not gotten better. He has not been resuscitated. His stripes are not healed. His body yet carries the cross.... He remains the lamb slain."[3] Nancy's *Noli Me Tangere* in particular uncovers the presentation and representation of the resurrected body of Christ in paintings, particularly focusing upon the "don't touch me!" of Christ's initial encounter with Mary Magdalene. He reads this prohibition on touching as a significant moment for understanding resurrection. Keen's theology, on the other hand, emphasizes the intimate—the "don't touch me" dissolves into an invitation to touch (given to Thomas, for example). Nevertheless, the rupture of boundaries—of body, of wholeness, of exclusivity—that Christ's body performs and presents haunts the work of both thinkers, and provides fruitful ground for an articulation of the body of Christ that undoes the boundary between continental philosophy and theology.

First, let me begin with a more general account of Nancy's writings upon and about the body. The author of *Corpus* and *Corpus II: Writings on Sexuality* can hardly be accused of avoiding the topic. In the aforementioned works, as well as in personal essays reflecting upon his own health crises, Nancy wrestles to free the body from the suffocating abstractions of western thought. We tend to import to the body's "mind" or "self"—when we're not reducing the body to a kind of machine or tool. Nancy reads (or inscribes) the body as having neither "head nor tail"—the body is not intelligent in the way we want to use that category. It is not thinking. Likewise, the body does not have a self, an autos. It is silent and lacks the making-sense that we ascribe to thinking subjects. It is mute and closed, but not *stupid*. The body resists performing in ways that fit our categories of intelligence, yet it is or contains a kind of knowing that escapes conscious thought. He writes, "Bodies aren't some kind of fullness or filled space: they are *open* space, implying, in some sense, a space more properly *spacious* than spatial, what could also be called a *place*. Bodies are places of existence, and nothing exists without a place, a *there*, a 'here,' a 'here is.' ... The body *makes room* for existence."[4] Our bodies are the sites of our existence, as much as we wish to deprioritize them, fetishize them, manipulate and humiliate them. They allow us to be, and yet they resist our machinations, mutely.

Bodies are also always about to leave; they are precarious. "The body is *self* in departure, insofar as it parts—displaces itself right here from the *here*." And again, "The body is the being-exposed of the being."[5] There is no continuum within the body itself—even the senses of a single body are

---

3. Keen, *Transgression*, 15.
4. Nancy, *Corpus*, 15.
5. Nancy, *Corpus*, 33, 35.

disjointed, all the way down. Our cells are in a constant state of dying and rebirth; our guts house a world of microbes. It is only our conscious mind that constructs and links this disparate flux into a kind of fractured whole (think of Kant's regulative idea of the self and you can see that Nancy is aligned with western thought even as he critiques it). Our parts have parts, and we are always already in a state of decomposition. We are, as bodies, "a disseminated and endlessly renewed break-up of the utterly initial assemblage/uncoupling of cells whereby 'the body' is born."[6]

Perhaps it is understandable, then, why western thought seeks to objectify, to *other*, the body, or to avoid it. There is something altogether too vulnerable, open, and changing about bodies, making it more pleasant to remain in the far more manageable realm of ideas. Nevertheless, Nancy's articulation of the body helps us wrestle with the body of Jesus and with Keen's writings upon it, precisely because Nancy exposes the conundrum of the flesh so evocatively. Nancy sees this discourse regarding bodies as a new way of 'seeing' the world, or a new way of incorporating the world, understanding the world. Historically, Western thought has moved from the standpoint of an ordered cosmos fashioned by gods, to a mechanistic *res extensa* fashioned by modernity, a dichotomous construction of mind and matter. Now, we move toward the model of the "modus corpus": "the world as a proliferating peopling of [the] body['s] places."[7] This is a "world of non-generality, a world offered not to 'humanity,' but to its singular bodies."[8] Rather than a universal generality (or that word Craig hates so much, a "worldview"), we stand on a cliff edge, gazing upon and caught up in a worldwide multiplicity of singularities.

And this worldwide multiplicity of singularities touches us, touches upon our bodies, and cries out for justice. Nancy's modus corpus incorporates justice. He writes, "Bodies are evident—and that's why all justice and justness start and end with these. . . . Injustice is the mixing, breaking, crushing, and stifling of bodies, making them indistinct."[9] Here, too, Nancy's work on bodies resonates with Keen's, for ultimately what is at stake in Keen's writing is not only salvation in and through and *with* the broken body of Jesus, but salvation in and through and *with* the broken bodies of neighbors and strangers, particularly of the poor and destitute. Nancy recognizes and heeds the call of bodies to a kind of justice for the body, justice only *as* justice for the *body*. The suffering body is never an object, but always

6. Nancy, *Corpus*, 33, 35.
7. Nancy, *Corpus*, 39.
8. Nancy, *Corpus*, 41.
9. Nancy, *Corpus*, 47.

a subject, and with every blow one strikes, one *never* makes that body an object, but only reaffirms, again and again, the subject-ed-ness of the body. No Being, no Essence, no Other World than this, no Body but only bodies; no single unity but only plurality, multiples, Multiples that *share*. Bodies are what we share, and we share bodies in that we are each a body, discrete, unknowable, only traceable, vulnerable, here, now. We share these qualities by virtue of each of us, singly, living them. The trickiness of language beguiles us into believing our categories are real, when the only real is this plurality, this community of bodies. And for Keen, and for us, Jesus *is* and is *with* this community of bodies. Nancy himself refuses to turn this into mysticism, to allow us to make this holy Other, Wholly Other, ineffable, "elevated, refined, secret, sublime."[10]

Nancy writes, "*Bodies are the exposition of God, and there is no other— to the extent that God exposes himself.*"[11] Bodies are not images *of*, not representations *of* a godly idea; bodies are the coming to presence from nowhere. Again, bodies are not derivative, or projections, or means by which we get at something, or precursors to future glory or reminders of past glory, but rather bodies are the coming, the coming that never ends, because what we have is the present, the constantly arriving present, and the present is always local. The body, in this vulnerable always-arriving and never-arrived, is, ultimately, a *wound*.

The body is a wound in Keen's theology as well; the wounded body of Christ ushers us into a new creation, a creation that is not whole, but is redeemed, however paradoxical that may seem. Keen writes, "the glorified *carnality* of the body of Christ calls out to us."[12] And again, "By entering into the body of Christ, the discarded bits of decaying tissue that litter hell are stitched together to make that body's vital organs, they there partake of its glory."[13] Our salvation comes from nowhere else, to nothing else, than ourselves as bodies, together, in hope. The deadening effects of middle-class industrial nationhood numb us to the precariousness of bodies, a precariousness known all too well by those living and breathing and arguing and dying near Jesus. Yet no matter how we medicalize, desensitize, or objectify the body in western culture, the body remains "permeable; others get in."[14] And Christianity, or rather Jesus, rides here on and in and with

---

10. Nancy, *Corpus*, 47.

11. Nancy, *Corpus*, 61; italics added.

12. Keen, *After Crucifixion*, 29.

13. Keen, *After Crucifixion*, 29.

14. Keen, *After Crucifixion*, 130, referring to Berquist's *Controlling Corporeality*, 135–36.

our bodies, for "grace . . . comes to bodies entangled in a bodily world, a world . . . of backs and hands and bellies, of the beaten and the exhausted and the hungry. Therefore, the Spirit comes to us calling us not out of embodiment, but to it."[15]

Keen refuses to separate the cross from resurrection; more so, he refuses to separate the resurrection from creation or from annihilation. While Nancy's reading of the resurrection accepts the emptying of the tomb, it also empties the resurrection of its hope. Nevertheless, almost in spite of itself, Nancy's writings on resurrection echo Keen's far more than they echo any other secular philosophical exploration of Christian doctrine (if such a thing has been written at all—for who would bother?) The crucified/resurrected Jesus is mutilated and wounded still; Jesus, in Craig's work and in truth, has been emptied of all life, dead, crushed. There is no secret truth, no seed of life still present waiting to be resuscitated. Likewise, Nancy also reads the resurrection as non-resuscitation: the body remains dead, is "not returned to life. It is the glory at the heart of death: a dark glory, whose illumination merges with the darkness of the tomb."[16] Both Keen and Nancy read the resurrected Jesus not as a return to the life interrupted, and Jesus's death not as a pause or interruption but a real ending, and the resurrected Jesus is in both cases not made whole, not fixed or healed. Both see the resurrection as a kind of passivity—Jesus is helpless, dead as a doornail, without activity, without potential. Resurrection is received by a dead thing, and that dead thing, still wounded, is made to stand up. For Nancy, however, this starts to read as some sort of zombie story, whereas for Keen, this body that was dead is now *alive*, and all that is or was or will be dead is alive with it. It, and thus the whole world, is a new creation. For Nancy, who also writes extensively on creation, Jesus is as empty as the tomb—what is revealed in the resurrection is nothing *but* emptiness, absence, an utter lack. So, too, for Keen is there emptiness in the tomb and even the resurrection—but this emptiness is directed, is emptiness of a certain "thing." *God* is not absent—what goes missing is only an *idea* of god, an onto-theological understanding of divinity. What is revealed to be lacking all presence, all realness, is the system of the world itself—the powers and principalities, the logics and ideologies, the structures and institutions. All such structures are revealed to be already dead, already empty. What stands up in the space of that emptiness is not a new structure or "true" theology, but a person . . . specifically a dead person now alive, a wounded person whose very existence is that of wounds, not wholeness. Nancy writes, "The 'good' life . . . is that which, in this very life

15. Keen, *Transgression*, 57.
16. Nancy, *Noli Me Tangere*, 17.

and in this world, keeps itself in close proximity to what is not of this world: to this outside of the world that is the emptiness of the tomb and the emptiness of god, the emptiness opened up with god or as 'God' by the birth of man, by the birth of the world."[17]

Keen would say yes up to the last clause, I would think. Life in Jesus is a life that keeps close to what is not of the order of the world (powers, principalities, etc.). This life in Jesus means keeping *close* to him, he who is this wounded opening to a new creation, this birth canal of a radical new life that is particular all the way down. There is no foundation, no universality, hidden at the foot of the man Jesus, upon which he stands. When he stands up, indeed he stands upon nothing, upon emptiness, in that he stands upon nothing this current world can understand as foundational, universal, unmoving. He does not stand upon onto-theology. And if God, as God, opens up this wound, this opening, then it stands to faith (not reason) that perhaps "God" is not Being. Nancy writes that resurrection is the "last word" of a revelation that reveals "that there is nothing to show, nothing to make appear out of the tomb, no apparition, and no theophany or epiphany of a celestial glory. Thus there is no longer a last word."[18] And also: "The resurrection designates the singular of existence."[19] Keen would say . . . yes. But do you have eyes to see? Ears to hear?

And what is to be done in the face of this wound through which we may live a new life? Both Nancy and Keen write about love (and how trite, how annoying, that little word is. Nevertheless . . .). Nancy writes, "The impossibility of Christian love could be of the same order as the impossibility of the 'resurrection.' . . . It is a matter of holding oneself in the place of the impossible, without making it possible but also without converting its necessity into a speculative or mystical resource. . . . This place can only be a place of vertigo or of scandal, the place of the intolerable at the same time as that of the impossible."[20] Keen writes, "The course to be taken in this transformative enterprise [transforming culture by the very existence of the church's people] must follow the lead of what emerges in the cross and resurrection of Jesus Christ. What emerges there is 1) the nihilation of everything that is, and 2) the embrace of everything that is. What emerges is redemptive love in the midst of absolute loss."[21] This love must itself be cast away from the trite, simpering surety of modern "love" as a sort of

17. Nancy, *Noli Me Tangere*, 39–40.
18. Nancy, *Noli Me Tangere*, 45.
19. Nancy, *Noli Me Tangere*, 46.
20. Nancy, *Noli Me Tangere*, 52.
21. Keen, *Transgression*, 180.

sentimental affect(a)tion. Again, as we stand upon a cliff edge, viewing and caught up in the multiplicity of singular bodies, each with wounds visible and invisible, each dying and living, gasping and gulping, eating and drinking and defecating and dying, and as we call out for justice for each wound, each gasp, we find that justice and love kiss. Christian love can be nothing else but "holding oneself in the place of the impossible," clinging to Jesus as that impossible place, a place that is no place but an opening.

We academic types are drawn to debates and arguments regarding abstract ideas like justice and love and salvation. At times, we mistake our ideas for reality, our broken simulacra regarding God for Godself. This occurs most often when we forget that embodiment is not an idea among ideas, but an inescapable, if equally mysterious, fact of existence, our "own most possibility" or "facticity," to borrow a few fancy words from Martin Heidegger. If repentance involves a returning, a swinging repetition, then part of our repentance must be a return, again and again, to the body of Jesus of Nazareth. And that means that our debates about justice must return to the body. Our debates about love return to the body. And our debates about salvation, most of all, or inseparable from the former, must return to the broken, bloody, glorified body of Jesus and therefore to those bodies, here and now, that lie tired, bloody, and broken. If "our salvation is built on nothing less than Jesus's blood and righteousness," that blood, that justice, can be found nowhere but now, here, with each other, with our neighbor, in suffering and in hope of the resurrection.

6//

Knowing an Unseen God

Thoughts from Neuropsychology

WARREN S. BROWN

IMAGINE THAT YOU ARE walking late at night along a city street with no lights other than the occasional light from a window. You see, dimly, what appears to be another person walking toward you. The person's face is dark, shadowed by a hat, and the person's gait seems unusual ... somewhat rushed. Arising in your body is a sensation of fear (... and perhaps the urge for some self-calming whistling). The emotion-rush is due to the uncertainty and the desperate task of inferring based on incomplete information what sort of person is rushing toward you ... is this person male or female, old or young, someone I know or a stranger, a threat or friendly.

This scenario illustrates the nature of a process that we face commonly—our need to infer the intentions, emotions, perspectives, personality, and character of the other person with whom we are presently engaged. We must take a complex matrix of rapidly unfolding information and infer the nature and state of this person—information that is never sufficiently complete for our inferences to be certain. What we infer about the nature of others is not without some grounding in experience, but it is nevertheless based simply on that—an inference. Clearly this problem gets more tractable when encountering someone we know well, allowing us to draw deeply on past encounters. We have a large bank of experiences to ground our inferences about the personalities and characters of our friends—but even here we are sometimes wrong.

In this chapter I will discuss the nature of social inferences as they occur in our everyday lives. I will particularly attend to research in social cognition and social neuroscience and what these fields tell us about how we make inferences of the personhood and mind of other individuals. I will suggest some parallels between these inferences and what is a fundamental process in theology—inferring the person and nature of God. While not ungrounded, this critically important process leaves us sufficiently uncertain such as to elicit some self-soothing whistling.

AUTISM AND DEFICIENT SOCIAL INFERENCE

My students and I study persons with a congenital brain malformation called agenesis of the corpus callosum (ACC). This brain disorder involves a failure in the development of the primary connection between the cerebral hemispheres called the corpus callosum. The behavior and cognitive capacities of these individuals have a certain similarity to high-functioning persons with autism, particularly with respect to deficiencies in their capacity to understand the minds of other persons. Persons born with ACC may, in many cases, have basic intelligence within the normal range, but nevertheless have problems understanding subtle aspects of social interactions, particularly what might be in the mind of the other person that motivates what this person says or does. While this is similar to deficiencies in social awareness seen in high-functioning persons with autism, it is typically less severe in persons with ACC.

There is a test procedure that is used to observe and measure capacities for social inference that is used to study autism and that we have used in our studies of ACC. In this test, persons observe very simple animations involving two triangles moving around on a computer screen. After viewing one of these two-minute animations, the person being tested is asked to tell what they saw.[1]

For example, in one of the animations there is a box with a closed flap on one side (usually inferred to be a "door"). At the beginning, one triangle is inside the box. A smaller triangle enters from the side, goes up to the flap and taps one its corners on the flap ("knocks at the door"), then moves around to an adjacent side of the box ("hides"). The larger triangle (the "adult") inside pushes the flap open ("opens the door"), moves into the

1. Castelli et al., "Movement and Mind."

doorway, and its triangle peak is distorted side-to-side ("it looks back and forth"). Then it moves back into the box and the flap closes. The previous process is repeated with the little triangle (the "child") initiating action by again tapping on the flap ("knocking at the door"). However, this time when the large triangle begins to go back into the box, the smaller triangles moves quickly from the side of the box, taps the larger triangle, and creates a slight jump in the larger triangle ("the child surprises the adult"). Then both move into the box, the flap closes, and the two triangles touch each other peak-to-peak, then move side-to-side, and wiggle ("they go into the house, and kiss and hug each other").

Non-autistic individuals, when asked to describe what they saw in the animation, inescapably infer much more than triangles moving around the box with a flap. They infer that the triangles are animate and tell a story much like the text in quotes within the parentheses above. The triangles are inferred to be person-like, the box to be a house with a door, the intention of the little triangle (the child) to tease and surprise the larger triangle (the adult), the larger triangle to be initially fooled by the knocking, the jump to be a reaction of surprise, and the interactions of the triangles at the end to be hugs and kisses (to me this is the game of "ring-and-run" we used to play as children).

Obviously, such inferences go well beyond the information available in the video. Most importantly, to impute person-ness, minds, emotions, and intentions to the triangles is an almost inescapable inference for the non-autistic human mind.[2] Once the actions and interactions begin, one cannot help making imputations of agency, emotion, and interpersonal relatedness to these interacting triangles. When shown these animations (without prior explanation) the students in my graduate classes always laugh at the "teasing," and go "awww" at the "affection" shown at the end of the animation. Sadly, persons with autism tend not to infer these qualities, merely telling about the physical movements of a larger and a smaller triangle.[3] Persons with ACC tend to get the basic social nature of the animations, but relate stories that contain many fewer words indicating emotions and intentions—similar to autism, but less severe.[4]

The process of inferring the intentions, emotions, knowledge, and perspectives of other persons is referred to in social cognitive psychology as indicating a "theory of mind" or as "mentalizing." The test described above

[2]. That is "normal" among modern Western persons. Such inferences would be culturally conditioned and thus the animations might lead to different stories in persons from other cultures.

[3]. Abell et al., "Do Triangles Play Tricks?"

[4]. Renteria-Vazquez, "Topic Modeling."

is only one of many that attempt to understand, describe, and measure the process by which individuals make inferences about the mental processes of other persons. The capacity to mentalize is obviously critical to the flourishing of social and relational human life.

This process of inferring the mental processes of other persons, and doing so with reasonable accuracy, is a developmental achievement. By about age two children begin to understand the minds of others—for example, differences between what different people want or feel. Around age four, children begin to realize that other persons can believe things that are not true. From there on they continue to be able to infer with greater depth and accuracy what others believe, think, or intend. The rate of development of the capacity to mentalize is influenced by factors such as interactions with parents and siblings, participation in pretend play, and storybook reading. As can easily be imagined, children with a more developed capacity for mentalizing have greater social competence and get along better in school.

SOCIAL NEUROSCIENCE AND THE ROLE OF MIRRORING

The process of knowing the mind and intentions of other persons is thought to be related to the capacity to *mirror*, the physical and mental states of others within our own brain systems. A remarkable advance in recent neuroscience was the discovery of the existence of mirror neurons. Researchers serendipitously discovered that some neurons in the *motor* areas of a monkey's cerebral cortex fire not only when the monkey is performing a motor activity, but also when that monkey *sees* someone else performing the same act. It was theorized that the monkey was simulating the activity *seen* using its own *motor* system in order to *understand* the meaning of what it was seeing another monkey (or person) do.

Further studies have demonstrated that similar sorts of neural mirroring occur in the human brain. Using techniques for imaging brain activity (i.e., functional magnetic resonance imagine, or fMRI), it was found that, in humans as in monkeys, observing the actions of others looks much like performing the act oneself.[5] Further research has shown that this neural mirroring becomes a basis for understanding not only the actions, but, more importantly, the *intention* of the actions of others. Observing the actions of another causes persons to implicitly imagine themselves doing the same act

---

5. Research on mirroring the neural activity of the actions, sensations, and emotions of other persons is reviewed by Keysers and Gazzola, "Towards a Unifying Neural Theory."

and, thus, to experience having the same intention to act. Research has also shown that we mirror the action-implications of what we *hear*. For example, an accomplished pianist shows strong activation of the hand areas of the motor cortex while listening to piano music, while the brains of nonpianists are primarily active in brain areas involving auditory processing.[6]

Thus, our brains allow us to understand the actions of others by simulating what it would be like to do—and to intend to do—the same action ourselves. Such mirroring is believed to be the basis of not only comprehending the actions of another person, but also of other important interpersonal processes, such as anticipating actions that might take place, feeling the emotions of others (empathy), and inferring what another individual is thinking ("mentalizing" or "theory of mind").[7]

This sort of understanding-by-mirroring is one indicator of the embodied nature of the human mind. The concept of embodiment is not simply a recognition that the processes of mind take place in the brain, but also that these processes involve implicit simulations of past activities of our own bodies. Mentalizing is just one of many ways in which we use records of whole-body actions to think.[8]

STORIES AND THE INFERENCE OF PERSONHOOD

Much like the accomplished pianist who comprehends piano music by mirroring (simulating) the motor movements that would accomplish the musical sounds being heard, we mirror the actions described in the stories that we hear or read.[9] Understanding the actions of persons in a story requires that the systems of our brain that form our intentions and control our own behavior become engaged in a process of internally simulating the actions that constitute the story. We understand the narrative by imagining what it would be like if we were doing what the hero, villain, or victim in the story is described as doing. We do not passively comprehend stories. The mere act of hearing sets our action systems going (offline) in order to comprehend. The result of this process is not simply a memory of the abstract details of the story, but rather a memory of the feeling of doing—a behavioral residue of comprehending the story using the neural processes by which we organize

---

6. Bangert et al., "Shared Networks."

7. For an excellent summary of mirror neurons in humans see Keysers, *Empathic Brain*.

8. Gibbs, *Embodiment and Cognitive Science*.

9. Gallese, "Embodied Simulation Theory." See also Zarr, Ferguson, and Glenberg, "Language Comprehension."

our own actions. Via internal simulation, we live into the events of the story. We cannot be passive and still comprehend.

As a consequence of our action simulations, we also infer a great deal about the actors in the story. We infer their personality, character, and mental processes. The more we read (or hear), the more the characters become known to us as persons as we embody their mental states, thought processes, and emotions. Through all of this, we come to infer the existence of a person, even when that person is known to be pure fiction. Like the inescapable inferences of personhood in the case of the animated triangles described earlier, we inescapably infer a real person from the accounts of the actions of characters in stories. Of course, the better the writer, the stronger the inferences.

Perhaps you have also had this experience. I occasionally like to read Craig Johnson murder mysteries (my preferred form of "brain candy"). The central character in these stories is Walt Longmire, sheriff of a rural county near the Bighorn Mountains of northern Wyoming. After reading a number of these books, I saw an episode of the *Longmire* TV series. Of course, it was all wrong. The Longmire in the TV series was not the person I had come to know (infer) from reading the stories. There was in my mind a real Walt Longmire, and the person on TV was experienced as an imposter. Despite our rational knowledge to the contrary (i.e., "This is pure fiction"), there is a felt reality to our inference of personhood from stories.

Our capacities to experience (simulate) events in narratives is dependent to a large degree on our own past experiences. Remember that an experienced pianist hears piano music in a way that involves more robust motor simulations than nonpianists. A similar experiment was done with male and female ballet dancers. When viewing dancing while their brain activity was being scanned, both males and females showed robust motor mirroring to dance moves made by both male and female dancers. However, females mirrored significantly more intensely moves made only by female dancers, and males mirrored more intensely male moves.[10] They could imagine (mirror the bodily movements) more clearly the moves they were used to doing themselves. Thus, the capacity to mirror is, to some degree, based on the viewer's past experiences. Neuroscientist Christian Keysers talks about "broadly congruent" and "specifically congruent" mirroring, such that activities novel to us are only broadly mirrored, but activities we know well can be more precisely and intensely mirrored.[11]

---

10. Calvo-Merino et al., "Action Observation."
11. Keysers, *Empathic Brain*.

THEOLOGY AS NARRATIVE AND INFERENCE

The work of theology is to understand the nature of God. As a systematic endeavor, theology is constituted by rational discourse about God that is focused on propositional and relatively abstract concepts—so much so that some have even presumed it to be a "science." Rational and systematic discourse has value in clarifying our thinking *about* God (. . . hopefully), but generally such discourse contributes little to *knowing* God. Narrative theology takes a somewhat different course in suggesting that the Bible needs to be understood as a story about God and his relationships with his people, not a text from which one extracts propositions for discourse. What is theologically important is the overall meaning of the story throughout Scripture, as well as the meanings of particular stories in the Bible. Implied in this view of theology is that some of what is known from a story is tacit, and the task of the theologian is to try to make more explicit what is tacitly known through story comprehension.

The implications of how we know (infer) the personhood of other human beings through observation and mirroring of their actions, or through hearing or reading stories of their acts, adds an important wrinkle to narrative versions of theology. The discussion in this essay about the processes involved in the inferences of the minds and personhood of other humans—including the role of mirroring in the comprehension of the intentions behind actions that we observe, and the action-mirroring involved in story comprehension—suggest that God can also be known as a person through our observance of what he does—acts apparent in stories or in the life of a community.

Stories in the Bible involve God as an agent and actor, causing us to mirror the acts of God, and consequently to infer the nature of the person whose actions are described. Through such mirroring, God is encountered not as an impersonal force, but rather as a relational agent—a being who loves, cares, admonishes, punishes, and extends the possibility of personal relationship to Israel, and ultimately to the church. While the information available in biblical stories is necessarily incomplete (given the transcendent nature of God), it is nevertheless sufficient to prompt an inference of his personhood and character.

Throughout the Bible God speaks, acts, and interacts. Biblical stories of God's very direct interactions with individual persons—e.g. God's self-revelation to Moses in the burning bush, or Paul's encounter with God on the road to Damascus—are particularly important. In these stories, inferences of personhood are readily made and are pretty deeply grounded. To read the story of God's intervention with Saul on the road to Damascus—Saul who was actively persecuting the church and denying the Lordship of Christ—is to infer something of the mind, intentions, and character of God.

The Gospels and the accounts of the life of Jesus are most critical and central to our inferences about the nature and character of God. The incarnation is a full revelation of God to us in that we have stories of the actions, conversations, teachings of the divine Person among persons. Our powers of mentalizing and mirroring are robustly engaged in reading and hearing these stories. Viewed through the lens of incarnation, in Jesus the personhood and personality (character, intention, emotion, love, etc.) of God become more clearly apparent.

Craig Keen relates a story in *After Crucifixion* where he recounts trying to explain the trinity to junior high school students. He wishes them not to view each member of the trinity as some "guy," but to think about primary qualities like "mystery," "story," and "life." Thus, for Craig, the Son is thought of in the context and semantics of "story." Keen writes, "This life story with mystery all over it does not put an end to all understanding, but gives understanding a future—precisely as it forever eludes resolution."[12] One part of the future of this story is its ability to reincarnate this life as it is embodied in us though our behavioral mirroring. And if told truly, what sort of story reincarnates itself in us? As Keen suggests,

> The story of Jesus is the story of a light that shines to the far side of darkness. It is the story of a life that ceases to be threatened by death, because it has outbid it. It is the story of a life free to undo competition, a life whose abundance makes useless both the claim to "mine" and to "yours." It is the story of an excessive love given freely both to friends and to enemies. It is the story of the forgiveness even of great debt, of the emptying of prisons, of the feeding of the hungry, of the renewal of the strength of atrophied legs and blind eyes, of the coming of peace, of the awakening of a righteousness that will not be defiled by contact even with what is most unclean. It is the story of a sanctity that comes to dwell among even the vilest of criminals, humbly and invitingly. And it is the story set inseparably in the context of the kind of grueling life that the great majority of the human race lives, has lived, and will live for as long as we can imagine. That is, it is good news only where news, more often than not, is bad.[13]

Of course, this revelation of God in his acts does not end with the last period on the last sentence of the authorized books of the Bible. Acts of

---

12. Keen, *After Crucifixion*, 52n42.
13. Keen, *After Crucifixion*, 75–76.

God can be detected in the history of the church and the lives of Christians though the centuries. Of course, some of what we read in these histories seems like acts of the God of the Bible, and some of it does not. For example, much is to be inferred of the nature of God in the life St. Francis of Assisi (however imperfect the life), particularly in his commitment to the poor.

Equally important are contemporary and local stories—stories we tell each other—in which God's work can be seen and his character inferred. About a year ago our church decided to write some of our local stories. In the end, about ninety difference stories were contributed by sixty different persons.[14] Through these stories we can see something of the working of God in our community, and can perhaps refine our inferences regarding the person and character of God. The book's subtitle, *Memory for the Sake of Hope*, signals the role of such stories in our understanding of, and hope in, God. However, there is a caution to be recognized in our process of storytelling. We need to be careful and discerning about how we narrate the stories of God's work in our midst lest we misrepresent God, causing ourselves to infer a god that is not the God of Israel. Biblical and communal discernment is necessary to adequately narrate the work of God within a community of believers and in the world.

Finally, there are experiences that strike us as evidence of the immediate presence and movement of God. Often these experience are not easily conveyed in narratives (". . . you should have been there"). These events and experiences also cause us to infer the activity, and thus the personhood, of God. Occasionally, in a time of worship, a moment in prayer, during a conversation, or while serving together, one can discern something of the activity of God. Again, it is the acts of God, however dimly seen, that allow us to infer the person of God.

CAVEATS AND CONCLUSIONS

The level of explanation of our knowledge of God proposed in this essay is, of course, humanist. That is, it employs knowledge of brain processes that undergird human cognitive and social capacities to describe our process of inferring the personhood of God. It also implies a view of human nature and Christian life as embodied (rather than implicating a nonmaterial and disembodied soul).[15] Therefore, missed out in this brief essay is any treatment of more transcendent and nonmaterial perspectives on revelation of the nature of God.

14. *Mountainside Perennial.*
15. See review by Teske, "From Embodied to Extended Cognition."

A hazard of describing the human side of our theological understanding is opening the dialog to deconstruction of the knowledge of God as a misapplied human cognitive process—that is, nothing but human cognitive processes gone awry. Logically, this perspective is reasonable and not incoherent. Those who would advocate this position can point to contexts in which a person's judgment of personhood is mistaken. Here I am reminded of the Turing Test, suggested by Alan Turing, inventor of the first general purpose electronic computer. The test is passed if a third party observing a text-based conversation between a person and a computer cannot tell them apart. At this point, the computer can be said to have mimicked human intelligence. The test presumes that a convincing conversation will cause the observer to infer personhood to the computer. The test was passed in 1966 by a program called ELIZA which carried on convincing conversations with persons, the responses patterned after Rogerian nondirective psychotherapy. As we have already seen, in many contexts we almost inescapably infer personhood even when we know the inference to be false, such as my inference regarding Walt Longmire. Ventriloquists lead us into the inference that the puppet is a person even though the puppet is known, on another level, to be merely wood and cloth. Anthropomorphizing by extending personhood to animals, particularly household pets, is not uncommon.

Here I would like to return to our test of mentalizing involving the animated triangles. At one level it might be said that the inference, though compelling, is wrong. One is not seeing interactions of agents with human qualities, but merely moving triangles. However, there was in the creation of the cartoons a human person who shaped the action of the triangles. Thus, while the inferences of the personhood of the animate triangles themselves are obviously incorrect, it is a perfectly adequate inference about the mind that created the animation. This is also the case of ELIZA, ventriloquist puppets, and Walt Longmire. There is a human mind behind the creation that has orchestrated the action. In the case of animals there is animate and moderately intelligent action that we, rightly or wrongly, presume to signal the output of a mind somewhat like ours.

Often it is easy to say, "well, that event was only circumstantial" or "that experience was not what you make of it." But, within the context of Christian belief, it is also not unreasonable or incoherent to infer a divine mind behind events. We do this regularly in other contexts and our powers of inference are usually reasonably accurate. One cannot easily negate our knowledge of God on this basis. Of course, as with stories, it is necessary to be discerning regarding where one sees evidence of the acts of God and what sort of god we presume to be acting, lest we deceive ourselves and impute events to the actions of a god that is not God.

EUCHARIST

Arguably, the central event of the life of a Christian community is celebration of the Eucharist. In this practice we enact a story—the story of Jesus' last meal with his disciples—including our reflections on its meaning as made clear in the story of the crucifixion. In participating in the Eucharist we actively dwell in this story—our mirroring is expressed and enhanced in a physical and communal act. What we do physically causes us to remember (and mirror), and in remembering deepen our inferences regarding the personhood, character, and love of God.

Craig Keen "whistles" a similar thought in the preface to *After Crucifixion*. He writes,

> To eat and drink the performance of the will of the Father is to pray that we would be in-scribed into the particular story of Jesus. It is indeed to hunt and gather, to build and sculpt, to speak and think—all week long. It is to breakfast, dine, and sup. But as written into *this* story, a week's meals and work become free acts of abandon. One carries them ("carries oneself") to that altar at which a gathering of people is taken into the history that on Good Friday is totalized to death and on Easter Sunday is loosed to life. We might call this history, which is simultaneously crucifixion and resurrection, "a living sacrifice."[16]

"For whenever [we] eat together this bread and drink this cup, [we remember, mirror, comprehend, and] proclaim the Lord's death until he comes" (1 Cor 11:23–26, NIV).

---

16. Keen, *After Crucifixion*, 17.

7//

Precarity and Disruption

DAVID REINHART

Although I am insisting on referring to a common human vulnerability, one that emerges with life itself, I also insist that we cannot recover the source of this vulnerability; it precedes the formation of the "I." This is a condition of being laid bare from the start and with which we cannot argue.

—JUDITH BUTLER, *PRECARIOUS LIFE*

To pray is to place oneself at the mercy of an other. It is to seek the favor of this other and to wait. It is to voice one's concern and to listen for the other's reply. It is to forsake one's rights, to yield to the other, and there to abide. Prayer has no certain outcome. Since one makes no demand and claims no privilege, its end is from the perspective of the supplicant completely out of control.

—CRAIG KEEN, *AFTER CRUCIFIXION*

To posit the transcendent as stranger and poor one is to prohibit the metaphysical relation with God from being accomplished in the ignorance of men and things. The dimension of the divine opens forth from the human face.

—Emmanuel Levinas, *Totality and Infinity*

In 1988 on a cold Sunday morning a prayer service was held in the Auschwitz crematorium. The steel tracks leading into incinerators constructed for efficient disposal of hundreds of thousands of human bodies provided a gathering place, where priests and a rabbi both prayed aloud for the dead. Then, in the distance, church bells rang from outside the camp. Down the road a parish church was celebrating Sunday mass. Hearing both the distant church bells and the prayers from inside the crematorium, Robert McAffee Brown was shaken. "My mind involuntarily and instantaneously took a leap back forty-five years. I reflected that at that time real guards would have been in the room in which we are now standing, thrusting real corpses into real ovens heated to temperatures extreme enough to dispose of corpses quickly, and that the same guards who were burning those same bodies would have gone out of that same camp, walked a few hundred yards to that same church, been absolved from their sins, received communion, and returned that afternoon or the next morning to continue the same grisly occupation—quite unaware of any contradiction between receiving the body and blood of the Jew Jesus, and destroying the body and blood of millions of other Jews."[1]

How does one address such breaking and broken bodies? Fragmentation that is both disposing and disposed, armed and disarmed, bodies of faith and bodies burned to ashes. The thesis of all prayer may be that none of these bodies are exclusive of each other and all were broken and thus intermingling. Discourse that may be more about my disruption than my knowledge, that comes from constant vulnerability as the basis of social responsibility or in other words responsibility for the other, to be opened by their alterity.

One asks whether prayer opens or closes capacities for relating for others. In the prayers at Auschwitz, McAffee is radically disrupted by the tension between inside and outside. Prayer that is a kind of opening, as much evasion as also confession, a kind of precarious listening, listening to alterity already gone by, at best in this kind of solidarity with all.

1. McAfee Brown, "Can Memory Be Redeemed?," 200.

Craig Keen calls for an *abiding*, listening actively as a way of life, listening to the dead, continuing after crucifixion, a life offered as a prayer and as concretized gift. This could be discussed as a dispossession of a consistent ontological framework, dispossession of a set structure or discourse, neither forming identities nor mechanisms of becoming. Keen describes precarity as more basic to life than knowledge.

> Therefore, the customary posture of prayer is kneeling with one's head bowed and one's neck exposed and vulnerable. One gives oneself to the possibility of a fatal blow from the other, over whom one has relinquished all rights. It is therefore no small wonder that our English word "precarious" has been derived from *precarius*, the adjective form of the Latin *precari*.... Let us for once be humble enough to admit that none of us is *homo sapiens*. Let us for once be humble enough to admit that we are created not as something in ourselves, but as something for God; that you are and I am *homo precarius*.[2]

Are we *homo precarious*? Is this possible? To be laid bare, exposed and vulnerable to the other? Praying with no certain outcome and with no demands or privilege, in other words prayers of no certainty and ideology. One would have to say that more metaphysical approaches to God are problematic to solidarity—for the sake of listening to the stranger and the poor and the executed innocents throughout time. Keen's work might then be characterized as a thoroughly socialized yet pragmatic ethic of nonviolence. Seeking to be responsible, it works within descriptions of sociality, is vulnerable to sociality, and especially the relation between the saying and the said—vulnerable to openings of *ipseity*. The prayer at Gethsemane, your will be done, accepts vulnerability in a way that rejects reliance on metaphysical beliefs that shrink our field of vision and ability to listen. What Keen might call holiness is more of a social responsibility that accounts for one's own ideological roots or ethnic and religious violence. Abiding with and not abandoning the tradition's better angels, he hopes for the messianic possibilities of a tradition best lived in precarity.

PRECARIOUS LIFE

John Dewey said the combination of both stability along with precarity is the path to the love of wisdom.[3] Later, Richard Rorty criticizes Dewey

---

2. Keen, "Homo Precarius," 147–48.
3. "We are here concerned with the fact that it is the intricate mixture of the stable

for the perceived metaphysical character of this binary. More recently, this led to debates over the status of naturalism in Dewey's pragmatism and in response whether Rorty gives an accurate reading of Dewey. For now let's say that Rorty takes issue with reductions of scientific knowledge to the correspondence of industrialization and democracy and generally agree that this is a fundamental issue in our time; organizing society by coordinating the variations of the environment and individuals in a constant attempt to navigate or coordinate precarity with stability.

Without delving too deeply, this debate over precarity reconsiders a collective confidence of the first half of the twentieth century, often intensely critiqued since then. Especially after further neoliberal entangling of the common good with economic interests, since the time of Keynes, seems to become the Gordian knot of globalism. Still Dewey's investigation of everyday experience helps inform Rorty's emphasis upon human conversation and epistemological behavior. According to Rorty, philosophical conversation is "not to find out what anything is really like but to help us grow up—to make us happier, freer, and more flexible."[4] While Dewey points to a back and forth relation with the world, that provides a capacity for change but also emphasizes that change is always also "potential doom." Dewey writes, "Knowledge is partial and incomplete, any and all knowledge, until we have placed it in a future that can not be known."[5]

Precarity and stability are fundamental to Dewey's philosophy of education, democracy, and the love of wisdom generally. For Dewey, democracy is important as a way of providing for individual variation (so often precarious) within public institutions and thereby providing stability. Society progresses by recognizing the uniqueness of individuals, which Plato failed to do, while also recognizing the stability that arises from an embrace of change.[6] Education may work with the individual, treading as lightly as possible upon human uniqueness and logic, in a way that equips each person with skills that increase scientific investigation, personal initiative, and adaptability. As Dewey writes, "After greater individualization on one hand, and a broader community of interest on the other come into existence, it is

---

and the precarious, the fixed and the unpredictably novel, the assured and the uncertain, in existence which sets mankind upon that love of wisdom which forms philosophy" (Dewey, *Experience and Nature*, 59).

4. Voparil and Bernstein, eds., *Rorty Reader*, 198.
5. Dewey, *Middle Works*, 48.
6. Dewey, *Democracy and Education*, 95–96.

a matter of deliberate effort to sustain and extend them."[7] Dewey alludes to this effort as "nominally democratic."[8]

To some, nominal democracy may seem a harsh term as opposed to real democracy that is responsive to the needs of people and holds elected officials accountable, fostering public deliberation by rule of law. Nominal democracy admits partiality, prejudice, and violence, are part of it all. Nominal democracy expresses an incomplete or superficial democracy that does function adequately for the people. I might say that all democracy is announced by name prior to actualization. Indeed, democracy was born in the United States nominally, and continues today nominally. Declarations of universal rights and human freedom were declared loudly within a time and space made possible by the American constitution that gave partial birth to a bill of rights. Dewey has reason to say that democracy is precarious, even doomed, at best moving from the actual toward the ideal. Promoting an effective distinctiveness, with the fewest barriers to communication, engaged in joint projects and inquiry, while avoiding violence. Dewey argues that the fundamental principle of democracy is that its ends, freedom and individuality, can only be attained by means in accord with those ends. This grows from his early observation that "the 'ought' is the 'is' of action."[9] There is no final fixed goal but progress by means of an end, not a Telos but the end that is ongoing, formation and growth. Throughout his career he continued to hold that democracy was the mediation of social transition through nonviolent means. Thus, the grand importance of education and critical inquiry liberated from habituated patterns of human community and more upon "foregrounded" joint activities. Dewey, like later theorists Gadamer and Habermas, later turned to the importance of symbols for sharing meaning, recognizing that the transfer of knowledge is potentially an oppressive enterprise when not risking participation in shared meanings—thus open to divergent interpretations.[10]

So while an overly rigid definition of democracy ignores the ongoing formations, it has neither the political will for compromise nor even the capacity to exchange multiple viewpoints. When imagination is lacking and public will is not available, then polarization and rigidity inevitably contribute to social paralysis, disillusion, and eventually acts of violence.

---

7. Dewey, *Democracy and Education*, 93.
8. Dewey, *Democracy and Education*, 328.
9. Dewey, *Early Works*, 108.
10. Schultz, "John Dewey's Conundrum." Angela McRobbie comments that precarity comes with feminism "preinstalled."

Not only is there a propensity to vilify adversaries but also to objectify them in democracy. The major problem of neoliberalism today is the way in which production and human flourishing are appropriated for a few. Society forgets the ultimate aim of production, as Chomsky often quotes Dewey, "not production of goods but the production of free human beings associated with one another on terms of equality."[11] By flipping these categories, making the production of things a higher good than the real life found together in meaningful ways, making things more valuable than the maturation of human beings, social anxiety deepens and increases the possibility of violence.

Yet the violence of democratic structures over time is often variegated: both systemic and individuated. Keen learns from Dewey not to move beyond an immediate concern with people, to work with the outsider, the stranger, the immigrant. Yes, social structures are nominal, unresponsive to abjection, precarious at best, and that is where Keen wants to begin and end his journey.

Similarly, Judith Butler helps us to "rethink the question of precarity as the lived experience of abjection even as we probe the possibilities of performative agency from and against precarity."[12] It becomes important to recognize how precarity is questioned, as a deepening of moral critique that engages social structures as well as self-knowledge. It is a notion of the vulnerability of an "I" as the outcome of relations of power. I am both within power structures and perhaps also capable of resistance.

Judith Butler remarks upon the precarious life by discussing the art of Regina Jose Galindo, whose work is *performative*. She practices the vulnerability of self-critique. In one public performance Galindo wears a black dress, carries a white porcelain basin filled with blood through the streets of Guatemala City—collecting curious followers as she walks. The sight of a basin filled with blood indeed attracts curious followers. She stops from time to time, puts down the basin, and dips her feet into it. Leaving on the concrete red footprints that lead to the National Palace. Butler calls this Galindo's "processional." The blood-soaked footprints are the way Galindo "signs her work, mounts a political protest, and dedicates a fierce memorial to the dead."[13] Butler discusses how Galindo's performance art represents precarity. She breaks down the preferences of her audience, which makes her even more vulnerable to them. Her body itself becomes part of a social history, "memorializing those forms of suffering and loss against the lure

---

11. Chomsky, *Chomsky on Miseducation*, 38.
12. Butler and Athanasiou, *Dispossession*, 167.
13. Butler and Athanasiou, *Dispossession*, 169.

of forgetfulness."[14] Her body is a memory come alive to die in solidarity with the murdered, a living sacrifice, inviting a possession of sorts, taken up and thrown down by a power too strong to counter. She, or her performance, resists any and all who would desire to erase the violence of the past. Galindo's art expresses a fundamental refusal to be disposed; she will not go away or be easily swept away.

The performance of precarity is agency formed by and within norming relations characterized by uneven powers. Everyday solidarity is with the stricken, more vital than any neutrality. It is *precariousness* that transcends identity processes and provides a space where an alliance against violence begins by walking together and making gestures of resistance along the way.

There is a patient and constant questioning of self-attachment, often social norms that decide in advance who will and will not become a subject. "Power attaches a subject to its own identity. Subjects appear to require this self-attachment, this process by which one becomes attached to one's subjecthood."[15] This sociality, that precedes and presumably will exceed me, is an inseparable context of any potential identity and therefore any potential resistance.

Butler's remarks about Galindo and her gestures of resistance also bring us to Keen's performative theology. If one sees the performative intentions of Keen's work, and how he performs precarity, we may see him walking in Galindo's procession, carrying another container of blood. Keen's chapters/lectures are like a mosaic of meditations. He also writes interludes placed between the chapters that remind me of Galindo pausing to put her feet in the basin she carries, gathering onlookers while soaking in the blood: =pause= Readers who have personally heard Keen speak have an advantage, I think. Anyone who hears him read a research paper at an academic conference, normally dry affairs, knows that Keen writes and performs his reading almost like a beat poet. Using his woofing tone and bluesy rhythm for a pathos that moves and is moved. The experienced reader may also hear the subtle tones of voice in the text as well.

Keen's way of theology is not the usual systematic coherent method of thought, bloodless and sometimes alienated from the earthiness of the everyday. He tries to call the reader to participate, to join in his aerobic activity, to inhale the apophatic and to run alongside this chariot of a book. Keen offers reconciliation like Philip who runs to hitch a ride with the Ethiopian eunuch, a treasurer of the queen, who is turned away from the temple. A

---

14. Butler and Athanasiou, *Dispossession*, 172.
15. Butler, "Bodies and Power Revisited," 190.

Philip(ian), a thinker of kenosis, that teaches the meaning of the prophets. Refusing to forget the blood of the innocents.

PRAYER AS PRECARITY

Yet Keen wills to go deeper and farther within sociality, unsatisfied with identity-making and distrustful of said authenticity. His questioning strives to encompass entire regimes of truth, their social network of values and disciplines. Both Butler and Keen question the status of a subject already formed and are open to discuss the dynamics of an unfinished process. Like Butler, who writes, "I am not outside the language that structures me, but neither am I determined by the language that makes this 'I' possible."[16] For Keen the language, the norms, are already in ruins. There is no continuing project of construction, not even if it's the project of critique and deconstruction. He writes, "I cry out 'Violence!' is the prayer of subjugation. Untamed, chafing under the yoke it may take on apocalyptic overtones."[17] He compares this, but does not identify it with the apocalyptic genre—but rather a coming of God that he personally witnesses to in the Christian Eucharist. Akin to the little house churches of peasants who prayed to the felled peasant they called Lord. In each case the liturgy is a performative artwork of bodies broken and blood shed for him, where one is acted upon and works in response, teaching the prophets as he says. He would claim that rather than a narrative of a neat divide between sacred and profane, there is the transgression of the integrity of God in each performance. His saying is an unsaying.

In both Butler and Keen the discussion is about the embodiment of criticism by remembering the bloodiness of the past, listening for the absent in the midst of principalities and power relations. To speak against them by avoiding the disconnection of phenomenology from hermeneutics that demarcates so much authenticity—that puts itself in a privileged position speaking for the subaltern or the dead. There is no transcending, no process, nor even a process of demythologizing and remythologizing. The placement of the dead along this *path* that is persistently, ferociously heterotopic; where orthodoxy is transgressively unorthodox and all containments are instead openings.[18]

16. Butler, *Gender Trouble*, xxvi.
17. Keen, *After Crucifixion*, 122.
18. Michel Foucault describes heterotopia as "simultaneously mythic and real contestation of the space in which we live, this description could be called heterotopology. Its first principle is that there is probably not a single culture in the world that fails to

This is perhaps why Keen's own advisement is often for going slow, advice given early and often throughout after crucifixion. At points the words are chosen to slow down the reader. A slowness that listens far more than speaks past the other, a slow burning passion that waits rather than questions, and this may be an important distinction between Keen and Butler. As Keen writes, "It may only be that we have pressed ourselves upon her too hard, that we have been too swift to make determinations" and this means to pray *with* each other, listening for an always broader responsibility. "We might walk with her, as she prays. . . . In time we might come to suspect that they and she are connected in ways we had not in our haste previously imagined."[19] This theological version of precarity that he says calls for the lightest touch, a sensitive listening and leaning-in slowly and gently. He asks whether the overheard prayers "were *less borne by her* and *much more have borne her and bear her still*, so far from home."[20]

For example, consider here suppliancy within Keen's notion of prayer. A supplicant is one who petitions or pleads, to be a supplicant always entails a larger narrative, a sovereign promise or ordering. Usually there is a pledge already implicated in a "prayer that remembers the questions and answers in the temple of the holy, holy, holy One high and lifted up."[21] This could be a primal discourse of the house of the Holy One. A temple that provides for discourse that nonetheless makes room for each. Leaving you and I with more to say than can been said. This space of hospitable discourse would always invite the other to speak, eat, and live. Dispossession, with no claim to privilege, making no demand except for justice. For Keen these are words and action that at best are given to cultivate a species, *homo precarious*. This unheard-of species is his version of an imitation of Christ—that seeks to evade, criticize, and avoid the rut-laden metaphysical road of social ethics. He does not always invoke Thomas à Kempis who prepares for the Eucharist by way of meditations upon one's transgressions of God and thereby following the way of the cross—but there are parallels indeed between these two. Kempis's *Imitation of Christ* does not lay out a systematic path for Keen but is instead more musical, event-centered, and liturgical.[22] That one is liv-

---

constitute heterotopias. That is a constant of every human group." Examples include traditional gardens and cemeteries. Although Foucault distinguishes heterotopias of crisis, deviation, a real space meant to be a microcosm, time and its ravages, heterotopias of ritual, and the space of illusions (Foucault, "Of Other Spaces").

19. Keen, *After Crucifixion*, 3.

20. Keen, *After Crucifixion*, 3; italics added.

21. Keen, *After Crucifixion*, xiv.

22. It is relevant that religious traditions can hold objects like texts and institutions as primary, and then subsequent events as accidental. From the stranger's perspective, this may be reversed.

ing not for oneself, or ultimately in oneself, but is capable of living within the self-emptying love of God. Quoting John Wesley, "God worketh in you; therefore you must work; you must be workers together with God."[23] As Keen explains, the work of love is the movement of Spirit, an exchange between God and humanity that then brings "an unmixed state of holiness and happiness."[24] In this way, suppliancy is also the breathing-in of an apophasis, remembering what it is not, by transgressing any so-called self-sufficiency or integrity. In this way supplication is inextricably linked to precarity.

What some call weakness Keen calls hope; he offers a full-throated alternative eschatology. For him, history of the responsible is a history of martyrs, a history of any who take bread from their own lips to give to the hungry, a history of nakedness like Francis in the bishop's courtyard, or Galindo walking with bloody footprints through the streets of Guatemala City. Illeity that is not an *arche*, nor a foundation, is an alternative path of history, more an anarchy in the sense of being out of control. Perhaps Keen is further down the road than I, when he writes, "Hope is the joyful wound of the eschatos, not the meeting of the need of the telos."[25] Naked, wounded, bloody, are the adjectives of the holy, the third space that is illeity. In other places he speaks of the roomy wound of Jesus as the opening for inclusion of others.

This is a disrupted and moving space for questions, where all are invited to poke around with sensitivity for all that ultimately cannot be ignored nor finally answered; in fact all this is proximity. As Levinas will write of the neighbor, the invoked is not what I comprehend but the God who comes to mind in the face of the other. In Keenian terms, to live is to live in an apocalyptic awareness, "members of the body of the one who forevermore hangs in solidarity with a world plummeting into the abyss."[26] This apocalyptic awareness is like a prolegomena for a liberation theology, the principle of mercy that takes the crucified peoples of the earth down from the cross. If the later could be called an ultimate dispossession, for Keen the penultimate dispossession is crucifixion as solidarity with the all who hang together. It is this sense of responsibility for all that permits one to abide with others. What one can know is how easy, how willfully, most humans prefer to miss, to ignore the face and keep possession of oneself. Not accepting an enculturation that defaces the other. "Praying that it might recognize . . . a

---

23. Wesley, *On Working Out Our Own Salvation*, 709–14. Keen develops many discussions of Wesley throughout his works. See especially Keen, *Transgression*, 30–32.

24. Keen, *Transgression*, 30–32.

25. Keen, *After Crucifixion*, 143.

26. Keen, *After Crucifixion*, 35.

way of life very different from the way of principalities and powers."[27] His life of prayer does not turn away from philosophical questioning, quite the contrary, it is the deepening of life lived. I take it as prayer that is multidirectional, life lived within aporia so that the field signified by the political is not an abandonment of obligation. Not self-aware of infinite obligations, heaven forbid, but then listening intently for them among the trampled and defeated. One cannot miss the radical albeit tenuous and unkept promise to work, to pray, to recognize, to hang in solidarity with the damned and the dead in all the laboring of cultivation—in so much proximity with all.

One hears an indictment of all parochialism, theology that is ultimately satisfied by any exclusionary truth. In tension between past and future, one may begin to learn to pray as a mutually critical discourse that opens critical perspectives to the other, to the face of the neighbor. It is Keen's autobiography when he writes, "The theologian remembers for the sake of hope. . . . For a theologian to receive what has been passed on is for her to wait intently for her elders to lead her to prayer and for them to wait for her to lead *them* in prayer. And so traditions include creeds, technical commentaries and speculations."[28] Prayer is a viable mode of exchange in the presence of a third, precarious all the way down. One might say that living a life that is precarious is living as a prayer, and so the word *After* in the title of *After Crucifixion* has the character of a traveller, pilgrim, untied and inviting. The person, and anybody who prays without ceasing, performs like a "liberation that does not need to survive . . . for the schema of this world are passing away."[29]

It is helpful to notice a quote that occurs in an early footnote of *After Crucifixion*. In footnote 12 there is a quote that I want to dwell with patiently. If it is Keen's concern to avoid a bloodless theology, then this is the marrow. Here is the soft propagating core, the rich cultivated soil found underfoot, underneath the text. The footnote cites Genesis and John, two texts about origin, then quoting Emmanuel Levinas.

> Responsibility for neighbor is precisely what goes beyond legality and obliges beyond contract. It comes to me prior to my freedom, from a nonpresent, from an immemorial. Between me and the other there gapes a difference which no unity of transcendental apperception could recover.[30]

27. Keen, *After Crucifixion*, 35.
28. Keen, *After Crucifixion*, 56–57.
29. See Keen's response to this seminar, in Keen, *After Crucifixion*, 3.
30. Levinas, "God and Philosophy," 71. Keen cites this text in the prelude of *After Crucifixion*, 3.

Here, to have some sense of responsibility that comes to me prior to freedom, it may be helpful to know Levinas's biography. As a student of both Edmund Husserl and Martin Heidegger, his doctoral dissertation combined ideas from both. He translated some of Husserl's work and at that time attended the famous debate between Martin Heidegger and Ernst Cassirer in 1929. Later he became a naturalized French citizen before the war, later captured as a member of the French army. Unable to help his family during this time, his parents and extended family were killed in the Holocaust, while his friend Maurice Blanchot helped hide his wife and daughter in a monastery throughout the war.

Given this background, how does one even imagine the nature of responsibility, as a philosophical theme that goes back to the Greeks as well as the prophets, and seems itself guilty of so much irresponsibility. Levinas tells us that responsibility is not chosen [qu'elle n'a pas choise]. "Unreplaceable in responsibility, I cannot, without defaulting, incurring fault or being caught up in some complex, cannot escape the face of a neighbor; here I am pledged to the other without being able to take back my pledge."[31] Responsibility is immemorial, ungraspable, it is more like being taken hostage. There is no riddle to solve, no magic ontology nor ontology of magic, no metaphysical unveiling of truth, except in response to the other. "I cannot avoid the face of the other, naked and without resources. . . . Responsibility does not come from fraternity, but fraternity denotes responsibility for another, antecedent to my freedom."[32] Levinas is also an influence of Butler when he explains how "I" am always late, describing responsibility as beyond legality, before and beyond contract, prior to rights and protected freedoms. This vein of description considers how goodness is liberated from the I of egoism. This is also a challenge to the Hegelian approach that all events are moments in the unfolding of reason. Responsibility is first to defend the otherness of the other rather than swallow one's relation in reason. One sees similarities with the above discussion of precariousness.

So there is a question I would like to pose on these last pages. What is the relation of Keen's prayer and Christian liturgy? I am troubled to the degree that prayer seems to remain the exclusive domain of a Christian discourse, if it does for Keen, or even if it's the prayer of a person, finite and waiting for Christ's coming. How does one pray with, alongside, the many other forms of praying in this world? There are both prayers that pray to listen to the other, and prayers that pray to seek revenge. Prayers of various spirits and nonspirits. Indeed there are some (myself included here) who

---

31. Levinas, "Manner of Speaking," 181.
32. Levinas, "Manner of Speaking," 181.

pray within the Christian liturgy because of non-Christian saints far away, who would not pray particularly in the same way.

This questioning may be ecclesial—even if *After Crucifixion* develops theology like the church that does not exist for itself but rather is a way of dying—maybe one could say it is precarious first responsibility to the other. "Its method leads to the cross and from the tomb out into the future coming of Jesus Christ in glory . . . a peculiarly wayward life and truth—one that is sent to the lost and forsaken."[33] Might not the proclamation of the gospel as a way of seeking meaning, also include prayers articulated, chanted, meditated outside Christian or even ecclesial boundaries?

Let us consider an interlude near the end of *After Crucifixion*, the story of young Keen he tells about himself. On a trip to England with a college choir, he finds DOMINUS unofficially carved on the window stone outside his dormitory room at Oxford. It is unknowable, it seems, who carved it. I would say that it performs for Keen as a generative symbol—operative as the meeting of the inside and the outside, indelible indeed. Dominus (translation of lord, adonai, kyrios) may represent a third space from which to work for the other, the one who is always outside any given system. For Keen this is the import of waiting, abiding, walking with, to watch for this performance of dominus. The mistake to avoid is a tourist's hastiness, like a choir tour overly protected, unruffled, perched upon a capital, shielded, in a sense with walls uninterrupted by windows, where there is no deferment, only defacement. (Providentially, perhaps, Keen was permitted to set out as a hanger-on and thereby stumbling across the carved graffiti in a window pane.) Commenting now many years later from his memory, "The mark dominus cuts two ways . . . entailing what transcends, what ascends and descends, what is exalted and what is abased."[34] This is a close cousin to what he alludes to in a footnote, what Levinas calls the trace of the other, referenced in Isaiah's question, "'What do you mean by crushing my people and grinding the faces of the poor?' declares the Lord, the LORD Almighty" (Isa 3:15). The faces of the expendable, the discarded, are indispensable to a transcendental approach to collective memory, a space for a discourse on justice. Of all the windows and stained glass, of the saints and scenes of the Bible, in one of the most historic churches, a window that pictures the murder of Thomas Beckett, another window of Thomas More, the courtyard built by Cardinal Wolsey; so much to remark upon, and our Oklahoma boy, with the trail of tears mentioned, he remarks upon this graffiti and an eaten

---

33. Keen, *After Crucifixion*, 54.
34. Keen, *After Crucifixion*, 204.

pear noticed in the moment. It is later that he adds footnotes on Augustine's confessions, Beckett's martyrdom, and More's ethic of prayer.

What seems evident to me is that in this third space, the tone is one of advocacy for the stranger, eventually finding a universal resistance, an impassioned pleading to restore the face of the other. It is on the same window, he remembers, there is the core of an eaten pear, consumed and discarded. The discarded fruit represents a kind of transcendence he describes. I was thinking that he might have naturally commented on the motto of Oxford, *Dominus illuminatio mea*, "The Lord is my light" (Psalm 27). Instead the explanation is of a generative metaphor with the eaten pear, for him this becomes an iconic memory used over a lifetime, operative for a triune deferment unfolded in this particular context.

One recognizes the reinvigoration of the critical potential of prophetic religion, with an advocacy for the stranger, that redefines responsibility as thinking otherwise in the face of the other by way of performative discourse that invites all as a meaning-maker. Allowing no smuggled baggage to empower the gatekeepers. This reminds me of Levinas' review of Kierkegaard's work in 1937, where he writes, "internal signification of all of the events that constitute my existence has to be respected, before interpreting them as a function of the universal order as constructed by reason."[35] Likewise, all religious traditions are based on generative metaphors capable of involving diverse and unfinished interpretations that remain exposed to the reason of the other, the human capacity for discourse based on mutual respect, if not a commitment to nonviolence. It is here that the "we" of any community is precariously exposed to the "thou" of others in a way that begins and ends in shared precarity. Such work or mutual laboring is a body-effect, described by Levinas, "Life is a body, not only a lived body where its self-sufficiency emerges, but a crossroads of physical forces, a body-effect."[36] It is in these terms that ecclesial language is put to the test. This body-effect performs like the plurality of precarious prayers offered at the Auschwitz crematorium in 1988. Perhaps also a little like the situation of an urban garden in South Central Los Angeles that Keen describes as the "weird" introduction to his theological work.

In more than one way gardening is like prayer, the work of homo precarious. One knows how to cultivate the land by some form of inheritance, whether directions from a book or an early memory of our parents digging

---

35. Levinas, *On Escape*. The journey embarked upon by Levinas in the 1930s is a walk with loved ones, both dead and living, also a walk with the pre-theoretical of existentialism. This is also Keen's ongoing journey, or one may say a pilgrimage always disrupted, led forward only by the shadow of the promise.

36. Levinas, *Totality and Infinity*, 164.

in the earth and planting seeds. In addition to this "know-how," gardening is an act of faith. Rain can wash seedlings away or hot drought may shrivel and burn them away. Then because it is also an act of faith it can be an act of solidarity—an act of a promise unfulfilled but also a promise that will not be let go. Gardens require our work and will. Last year my garden was washed away by flood, the year before that drought. But this year we cultivate the soil again. With perseverance, patience, and faith this spring the planting begins again.

The trope of a garden is well-known. Most especially the biblical notion of the garden is both creation and disaster. It is here that language first takes place, where a space is given life and order unfolds, then also where language becomes a means to pursue the death of the other as Cain asks Abel, "Let us go into the fields."

Neither is it Keen's habit to define meaning directly, once again he would have the reading find the analogy and try it on for size. Nevertheless the garden of South Central Los Angeles is a repetition, a retelling of the fall. It is the story of sin as well as the grip of the system. The community garden is a space for the people to work to cultivate a space together in the city, in the middle of an inhospitable world. A cultivation of communal cooperation and family renewal turns a place of violence toward a more peaceable kingdom. However, the story doesn't end there with the metaphor incomplete. The powers that be in the city, in this case the amalgamation of capitalist business and governmental oversight, combine to tear down the flourishing garden. The creation that resulted from an economy of gift is bulldozed by the system of capital.

So once again Keen writes with an apocalyptic tone. For him the legacy of apocalyptic is to see the world radically different, the conviction that this world is not all there is, not the end. He tries to call us out from ontological and objectivist concerns or at least give the effect of ontological clarity, by a sense of the face of the other. In this way Keen does his best to hang in solidarity with the damned and the dead, beyond any one cultivation. As "There is no social body in the abstract." His constant question is, "how to speak of a people not with a timeless essence, but with place and time, a transient season, footsteps, perhaps left across a wilderness on the backside of a promise given but never had."[37] It is to speak less of an uneasy peace enforced by armies pressed against national boundaries, where everything is weaponized, including our own bodies. Rather to listen and speak in proximity to body-effects, sometimes abiding and laboring together, albeit precariously.

---

37. Keen, *After Crucifixion*, 131.

PART III
Holiness

8//

Before Eucharist

The Politics of Food in Plato and Paul

Theodore Jennings

The theological work of Craig Keen presents us with a tightly woven tapestry that exposes to view the radical consequences of taking seriously the cross of the messiah as the beginning and end of theology. With the skill and precision of the poet, Keen articulates what is both a vision and a system (all things hold together in Christ said the author of Ephesians).

    One way of getting at the import of what Keen is up to is to notice the interplay of kinds of bodies: the crucified body of the messiah, the Eucharistic participation in that body, the becoming body of the crucified of the people of that messiah, and the attending to the suffering body of those who seek succor from suffering. With respect to the ideas thus expressed I find myself in substantial agreement even if my own approach is rather more prosaic and exegetical (and sometimes philosophical). In this contribution I intend to elaborate on one of the threads of this theological fabric: that which concerns eating and drinking, the sharing of food and drink that characterizes the messianic society in continuity with the messianic mission of Jesus. In particular, I want to draw attention to the political stakes involved in commensality, in the adoption of ways of eating and drinking together.

It is seldom noticed that manners of eating and drinking together are a basic theme of ancient political discourse. Now I know that Craig has a somewhat jaundiced view of what he supposes to be a sort of totalizing ambition of these ancient philosophical texts. But I am interested here not in their presumed metaphysics but in their attention to the rather mundane feature of the sharing of food.

In Plato's *Laws*, which for better and for worse was fated to become one of the most influential texts in the Hellenistic world, many pages, of this longest and perhaps latest of Plato's texts, we are presented with a treatment of the common meals of the citizens. This may seem arcane, but it is important to recall the stakes of the conversation that Plato invents in this text. Three companions are on a journey, one from Athens, one from Crete, and one from Sparta. Their theme is one that Plato had treated before in earlier dramatic stagings of conversation: in *The Republic* and in *Statesman*, all sharing the theme of what may be characterized as a just society. This is clearly a question of utmost existential as well as theoretical significance for Plato.

To understand why this is so we only need to recall the central trauma of Plato's life: the sentencing to death of Socrates for the crime of philosophy. It was this verdict agreed to by the gathered citizens of Athens as recounted above all in the *Apology* and the *Phaedo*, as well as other dialogs, that may be regarded as at the heart and center of all Plato's work, and most especially of his concern for the constitution of a truly just polity. Indeed, he had undertaken to engage in precisely this sort of practical task when he left Athens for Syracuse to assist his friend in the attempt to write a new constitution. Thus, both practically and philosophically Plato's work may be seen as a sort of memorial to a teacher executed by an unjust society. (I note in this regard that Plato had himself been a poet, a writer of Greek plays, before he left off that career to seek to practice philosophical improvisations in honor of his martyred teacher.) Obviously, I am pointing to certain odd parallels between the work of Plato and that to be undertaken by the apostle Paul (and other New Testament writers) whose work is spurred by a sort of homage to an executed leader.

But now briefly back to the *Laws*. Here Plato is staging a conversation between three people, each representing different polities, who agree to talk about what justice might look life in a new social order. In each case there is the invocation of the work of the great law givers of the Greek speaking world, Minos of Cyprus (the original source of the Greek renaissance), Lycurgus of Sparta, and Solon of Athens. Their goal is to take the best of these polities and then improve upon them. It is precisely in this connection that they agree in Book VI to take up the question of eating and drinking together most meticulously formulated by Lycurgus' Spartan polity.

Writing closer to the time of Paul, Plutarch notes in his *Life of Lycurgus* that Lycurgus had drawn the idea for some of his laws from a visit to Crete. He resolved to bring to an end the inequality among citizens: "to the end therefore that he might expel from the state arrogance and envy, luxury and crime, and those yet more inveterate diseases of want and superfluity."[1] Thus aiming "that they should live all together on an equal footing."[2] This would entail an equal redistribution of all land and the introduction of iron coins to inhibit the accumulation of wealth. But the third and perhaps most effective measure he introduced was the common meal. Plutarch writes: "The third and most masterly stroke of this great lawgiver, by which he struck a yet more effectual blow against luxury and the desire of riches was the ordinance he made, that they should all eat in common, of the same bread and same meat" and remarks that "the rich, being obliged to go to the same table with the poor, could not make use of or enjoy their abundance nor so much as please their vanity by looking at or displaying it."[3] These were called love feasts (*phiditia, philitia*).

It is precisely this communalist ideal that was to be liturgically enacted every time the citizen-soldiers ate and drank. Every meal was therefore a sort of liturgy. Plato has his three interlocutors agree to this as an essential feature of any society aiming at justice and meticulously spell out the manner in which this is to be done.

While in the *Laws* Plato has his three friends agree to this proposal, it is modified in two ways. First in order to account for a significant distribution of territory and increase in population the society is divided into districts, each of which will have its common meal. Even more importantly, Plato insists that these common meals should include both men and women. In Book V of the *Republic* he had maintained this to be necessary for the guardians but here makes explicit that this should be true for all regardless of rank. (Of course slaves and foreigners would still be excluded.)

In his *Politics*, Aristotle agrees to this proposal but notices a further practical difficulty.[4] If these meals are to be provided in turn by all members of the polis then there will be some who find this task more burdensome than others because of differences in the ability to provide these meals. (Here it is clear that Aristotle understands the provision of meals as a liturgy

1. Plutarch, *Lives*, 73.
2. Plutarch, *Lives*, 73.
3. Plutarch, *Lives*, 75.
4. Aristotle, *Politics*, VII.10.

in the basic sense of the term, the provision of something for the common good.) Since the text is somewhat fragmentary at this point, we have to guess at Aristotle's solution to the problem he has noted but it is most likely that this is resolved by a sort of tax on the wealthier members of the society or by provision from the common treasury.

The prestige of these great political thinkers insured that their influence would be felt in the development of Roman thought and practice. But a very important change occurs as Rome transitions from city-state to empire, from republic to a hierarchical social order. It is the transition from the common meal to the patronage banquet. The patronage banquet, so far from eliminating social inequality, actually was meant to display it and enforce it. The patron was responsible for inviting his retainers and supporters to dine. In turn they would constitute a sort of retinue whose task was to praise him in the streets for his munificence. We have a very illuminating depiction of this patronage banquet in the Satire VI of Juvenal. Here it becomes clear that the invitees were obliged to participate in ways that exhibited and underscored class divisions among them. For the poorer among them this was a sort of ritual of humiliation.

These exercises in commensality have become occasions to display the wealth of the host and his associates while underscoring the poverty of the invitees. Thus, Juvenal offers a series of contrasts between what the rich at such feasts consume and what is offered to the poorer faithful members of the coterie: the splendid aged wine for the host, or wine "so rough sheep's-clippings wouldn't absorb it"[5] for the retainer; the same or similar difference between the water offered and the servants who offer it; the bread either moldy tough bread or that of the finest flour; the rarest and most luscious fruit or a rotten apple.[6] The depiction of these differences, while perhaps exaggerated for comic effect, make clear that the feast aims to underscore the class divisions to the benefit of the wealthy. "The whole idea is to reduce you to tears of rage" warns Juvenal.[7] And if you accept this treatment then you will willingly accept every humiliation at the hands of your "benefactor," an outcome perhaps designed from the start by the patron.

Patronage was thus the mainstay of the imperial order. The temples of the gods (including of course divinized emperors and especially the great "Roma") were themselves sites of patronage. The "food sacrificed to idols," of which we read in Paul, was actually food offered to the masses by the patronal deity in whose name the food was consecrated and distributed

5. Juvenal, *Satires*, 29.
6. Juvenal, *Satires*, V.
7. Juvenal, *Satires*, 30.

thereby constituting a web of obligation that it was believed would hold the vast empire together. With this in mind we are prepared to (re)read Paul.

I have argued elsewhere that Paul is to be read as a political thinker, as one concerned with the question of justice and of a just sociality. And I have attempted to show that this brings him into intellectual company not only with the great political thinkers of antiquity by also with many of the radical political thinkers of late modernity (Derrida, Badiou, Agamben, Žižek, and so on.) I have generally focused on Romans as a key text in this regard but here I want to also give a few indications related to First Corinthians (with a glance at Galatians.)

In Galatians Paul indicates that the question of eating and drinking together had been a significant preoccupation of his since the early days of his apostolate. He recalls there a defining moment with respect to the question of whether it would be possible to include gentiles in the new messianic polity. It is a story about Antioch. At first he and Peter had freely eaten together with the gentile messiah followers. But then, sensing pressure from other Judean messiah followers, Peter had withdrawn from table fellowship with gentile or pagan messianists. We are not told whether what was a stake was eating pork, anathema to Judeans, perhaps essential to pagans. Obviously, a primary marker of belonging to the commonwealth of Israel had to do with certain nutritional customs that set off those belonging to that polity from those who are or have been excluded.

Here Paul seems to put forward the claim that the outsider has priority in determining what we shall eat and drink in order to be in solidarity with her or him. And this is so because the messiah himself was made one with the outsiders by being rejected by the insiders or those who presumed to legislate for the insiders and to judge on their behalf. Here Paul employs a certain christological theme not for its own sake but to undergird his intuition that a new messianic sociality must be exhibited in the ways we eat and drink together.

Now we come to Corinth where Paul notes that he has heard that there are divisions, schisms threatening to the very existence of these cells of messiah followers. And we recall that it is in relation to this very practical exigency that Paul makes reference to the centrality of the cross of the messiah as his principle theme. ("I resolved to know nothing among you but Christ and him crucified" [1 Cor 2:2]). Thus, chapters 1–4 become the classical statement of Paul's theology of the cross; but as a response to a very practical and political issue: how are we to live together, which according to Aristotle is the basic driver of political thinking and practice? And we recall that dissension and fragmentation had been the motivating force behind

Lycurgus's innovations in Spartan polity. Nor do we have to wait long for Paul to bring all this back to the question of eating and drinking together.

The difficulty confronted by Paul is that the assemblies of the faithful are beginning to adapt to or mimic the eating customs of the empire. We should think of regular occasions, perhaps even daily, when members of the assembly gathered to share meals. All gatherings of the assembly are gatherings under the aegis of the messiah; they are to reflect the messianic reality instituted, we recall, by an executed messiah.

Instead of exhibiting the new social solidarity, the generosity and partnership instituted by the gospel, these occasions have degenerated into a display of social differences, of class disparities. Instead of sharing, there is display of excess and humiliation of those who have little. In order to make clear what is at stake in commensality Paul offers us perhaps the oldest tradition concerning the messiah's meal with his apprentices:

> For I received from the leader what I also handed on to you, that the leader Joshua on the night when he was betrayed/handed over took a loaf of bread, and when he had given thanks, he broke it and said, "This is my body that is for you. Do this in remembrance of me." In the same way he took the cup also, after supper, saying, "This cup is the new covenant in my blood. Do this, as often as you drink it, in remembrance of me." (1 Cor 11:23–25)

Paul immediately connects this tradition with what he has said at the beginning of the letter concerning the centrality of the crucifixion of the messiah:

> For as often as you eat this bread and drink the cup, you proclaim the leader's death until he comes. (1 Cor 11:26)

Thus, the sharing of meals both proclaims the leader's death (that which is salvation for us he had said earlier) and anticipates the fullness of the messianic reality (until he comes). He then brings home the urgency of this matter:

> Whoever, therefore, eats the bread or drinks the cup of the leader in an unworthy manner will be answerable for the body and blood of the leader. Examine yourselves, and only then eat of the bread and drink of the cup. For all who eat and drink without discerning the body, eat and drink judgment against themselves. (1 Cor 11:27–29)

How are we to understand what Paul is saying here? What does it mean to be answerable for the body and blood of the leader? Who is answerable for that blood, that body, that death? Clearly those Paul had earlier described as "the rulers of this age" and as those who are perishing. But that is to point precisely to the very Roman society that they are beginning to imitate. By their way of eating and drinking together they become partners in the sociopolitical reality that executed the messiah, they become those who are therefore answerable for, responsible for, the torture and execution of the one they claim to be their leader.

It is therefore also clear how Paul could say:

> For this reason many of you are weak and ill, and some have died. But if we judged ourselves, we would not be judged. But when we are judged by the leader, we are disciplined so that we may not be condemned along with the world. (1 Cor 11:30–32)

By thus reflecting the values of this "world" they come under the same judgment as this world, which Paul had said is passing away. That some are sick and have died has nothing to do with a sort of magic in the elements but has to do with the sharing in the structures, the divisions of the world and so sharing in its fate.

Thus, to discern the body is not simply to suppose that this is the body and blood of the messiah but to recognize that participation or sharing in the messianic is to constitute a new body (as he will shortly maintain) in which together the sociality constituted by him becomes his new body, his presence as corporeal and corporate in the world and thus a sign of the inbreaking of a radically new sociality.

> So then, my brothers and sisters, when you come together to eat, wait for one another. If you are hungry, eat at home, so that when you come together, it will not be for your condemnation. About the other things I will give instructions when I come. (1 Cor 11:33–34)

It is very important, therefore, to notice that when Paul is addressing the way in which these societies come together to eat and drink in honor of the messiah he is not addressing a sort of private cultic act but rather the public and political act of the assembly. (Note that this is the term, political to the core, that he uses here). Moreover, there must be a fundamental difference between the polity of this new sociality in contrast to that of the decaying imperial order within which he takes shape. Indeed, we may say that it is precisely this difference that demonstrates the decline and fall of the imperial order as the new comes into being within and against it. Moreover, it is a question of the sharing of food and drink that creates social solidarity across differences, differences of religion, of culture, of opinion, and so on.

We get a further indication of this question of social solidarity in the long discussion in Rom 14:1—15:14 in which Paul deals with the question of folk eating together who have very different views about what should be eaten as appropriate to the honoring of the messiah. While the "weak" have certain scruples in this regard and the strong (like Paul) do not, Paul insists that they work to find appropriate ways to welcome one another as the messiah has welcomed them. That is, the basic feature of hospitality is that the strong defer to the weak while the scrupulous should not use their dietary principles to judge or condemn those who do not share their opinion and practice.

I have only dealt with some of the passages in Paul that deal with eating and drinking together. Let me just indicate what I think these passages may suggest to us and perhaps amplify some of Craig Keen's concerns regarding what he terms Eucharistic liturgy. The most important thing I would want to say is that eating and drinking in honor of the executed messiah is not something that has primarily to do with a Sunday ritual. Rather it has to do with all the ways in which followers of the messiah eat and drink with one another or with others in ways that are governed by the recollection of the messiah's martyrdom. Actually, the community "potluck" may be more Eucharistic in character than the ritual meal to which the name of Eucharist has been more narrowly applied.

If we are to continue to apply the term Eucharist to the cultic meal of gathered messiah-followers, then this may perhaps only be justified insofar as that meal becomes a paradigm for all forms of eating and drinking together that appropriately honor the executed messiah.

9//

"Sometimes Nothin' Can Be a Real Cool Hand"

Bryan Stone

Cool Hand Luke (Rosenberg, 1967) is the story of the incarceration of Lucas Jackson after a night of drunkenly removing the heads off of downtown parking meters with a pipe cutter. Luke, played brilliantly by Paul Newman, is sent to a Florida road prison where he is to serve out a two-year sentence of hard labor on a chain gang, and the film narrates his nonconformity to a violent and oppressive system designed in every way to break him. Though Luke is treated unjustly, he embodies a persistent and magnetic freedom that wins over his fellow inmates but eventually gets him killed. For these and other reasons, his character has often been taken as a cinematic Christ-figure.

The storyline of *Cool Hand Luke* does indeed invite a cursory comparison with the story of Jesus because of its creative biblical allegories and allusions and because of the narrative or visual parallels between Luke and Christ (betrayal, arrest, beatings, disciples, execution, burial, resurrection, ascension). That his name is Luke may be taken as pointing to the gospel of Luke, and his prison number, 37, is claimed by some to be an allusion to Luke 1:37, "For nothing will be impossible with God" (NRSV). In several ways, Luke clearly represents the arrival of "possibility," especially in relation to the laws laid down by the warden and his guards as well as those imposed by the hierarchy of the prisoners themselves, especially the burly Dragline, played to perfection by George Kennedy. From every direction, the system works on Luke in an attempt to bring him into line. But Luke will not be broken. He twice escapes but is caught and punished severely each time. When it looks as though Luke has finally been defeated by his captors, he escapes one last time. Betrayed by Dragline, who is more a Peter figure than a Judas figure, Luke is found and then shot dead. The film concludes with the prisoners regaling Luke's legend and resurrecting him in their stories. The camera then achieves a cinematic ascension as it cuts to the chain gang working on a road and pans out and upwards over a cross-shaped intersection.

Though the gospel parallels in the film are sometimes imperfect as a rendering of the Christ story, they still work fairly well, and in any case the artistic accomplishments associated with the cinematic rendering of a Christ story are not the product of strictly reiterating every detail of that story's plot and character. But the theological and christological significance of Luke's story goes well beyond the more obvious parallels to the gospel accounts. As an antihero, Luke is in several respects a unique and unlikely Christ-figure in the history of film, despite the fact that there is now a cluster of prison films in which Christ-figures or messianic archetypes appear—for example, *One Flew Over the Cuckoo's Nest* (1975), *The Shawshank Redemption* (1994), *Twelve Monkeys* (1995), or *The Green Mile* (1999). Luke is an outsider who suffers unjustly at the hands of a domination system and those who preside over it, much like the character of Randall P. McMurphy in *One Flew Over the Cuckoo's Nest*. Like McMurphy, Luke's interactions with authority unmask the insidious power of the system while at the same time subverting it, and he inspires devotion from his fellow prisoners along the way. But the sacrificial theme of laying down one's life for others that typically underlies a Christ-figure is inflected differently in *Cool Hand Luke*, and so also is the transformation of others around him. There is no Chief Bromden here who is inspired to break free as in *One Flew Over the Cuckoo's Nest*, nor is there a Red who finds new hope that is as bright as the vast, blue Pacific Ocean in *The Shawshank Redemption*. *Cool Hand Luke* gives us a very different kind of savior. He is perhaps more akin to Babette in *Babette's Feast*, whose actions and very presence constitute an excessive, unexpected, and self-emptying grace that stands in contrast to the law.[1]

---

1. Babette is all the more interesting in this regard since, as a Catholic in the midst of a legalistic Lutheran community, she turns the Lutheran protest against itself.

LUKE AND "NOTHIN'"

The reference to "nothin'" in the title of my essay is central to Luke's story, and surfaces when Luke bluffs his way to victory in a game of poker shortly after his arrival. Earlier in the day, Dragline calls out the new arrival in a prison yard fight, but Luke refuses to go down, despite being punched repeatedly by his towering opponent. Sisyphus-like, Luke rises repeatedly from the ground, raises his fists, and staggers again and again toward Dragline until everyone watching comes to realize, Dragline included, that the only way to beat Luke is to kill him. The prisoners walk away from the scene disgusted by the beating he is taking, and eventually Dragline drops his hands to his side, looking almost defeated himself, and returns to the barracks. Later that night, when Luke bluffs his poker hand and wins the game, Dragline reaches for Luke's cards. Dragline has been watching and inciting the other players first to call Luke's raises but then inevitably to fold against Luke's relentless bets. Upon discovering the bluff, Dragline exclaims with admiration that Luke had beat the other players with "Nothin'!" and he recollects the way Luke kept coming at him with nothing in the earlier fight. Luke responds with words that earn him his nickname, "Yeah, well sometimes nothin' can be a real cool hand."

On the surface, these initial encounters between Luke and the other inmates might have the look of a contest, a jockeying for position. But Luke's nonconformity is not really an assertion of his will or a test of competing wills, nor does he stage a revolt, fight for a cause, or recruit and ennoble others around him. His freedom is not that of individualism, but is something else entirely. His freedom is an abandon that comes with the juxtaposition of "nothin'" to systems that are all about "everything." He is a presence that is at the same time an absence, one whose identity can be neither inscribed within the world he has entered nor appropriated by those around him. Luke does not at all fit the modern tendency to celebrate the assertion of the individual will as the underpinning of messianism, salvation, and liberation. And this is what I think makes the film such an interesting dialogue partner for reflecting on the theology of Craig Keen, who writes of Jesus as one who suffers alongside those who cannot be assimilated into grand systems of insider and outsider, security and defense, progress and well-being:

> Jesus is reduced to nothing by the ideologies that keep us apart, that make strangers, widows, orphans, and the poor, the ideologies that rise to heaven to keep "the good" safe by excluding "the evil." Jesus is reduced to nothing by the architects of a future that builds on a settled past, those who know, like the board of a world bank, how to turn a profit before mountains of debt, the

forgiveness of which would constitute a leap into the abyss of certain economic ruin. Jesus is reduced to nothing by the same death-dealers who break the backs of the inefficient, the insufficient, the unproficient, the deficient—the "least" whom the champions of progress recognize intuitively as the sisters and brothers of the Jesus whose body they break and throw into the ditch with theirs. When this Jesus is created anew, he emerges from the depths of the darkness into which they have plummeted—made the redeeming, justifying, reconciling, forgiving sacrifice by which God has entered into creative, life-giving solidarity with the children whose dead bodies cry out mutely from the grave.[2]

If Luke may be thought of as a Christ-figure, he is one who, rather than exhibiting the classic transcendentals, is instead what Keen might call an "open wound"[3] in the prison where he has been sent. Luke enacts and embodies a kenotic freedom that transgresses not only the structures of domination designed to control him, but the politics of salvation and liberation that arise from within the world as an achievement, as something to be established through human might. Luke's individualism, if it can be called that, is not the triumph of the will, but the refusal to be confined and defined by the whole system of competition and hierarchy in which individual wills are set over against each other. If he is to be considered a Christ-figure, he does not serve as the Messiah of our expectations or the solution to our problems. Luke's "nothin'" is a very different kind of "somethin.'"

A FAILURE TO COMMUNICATE

One of the most iconic lines in *Cool Hand Luke* is spoken by the warden after Luke is returned to the chain gang following his first escape. The inmates are compelled to line up and watch as the guards hammer leg irons into place around Luke's ankles (yet another attempt to "nail him down"). The captain tells Luke that he will get used to the chains but he will never stop hearing them clinking. They are for his own good and will serve as helpful reminders. Luke replies sarcastically that he wishes the captain would stop being so good to him. As the warden's thin veneer of calm gives way to an eruption of violent blows, Luke is sent sprawling down a hill and

2. Keen, *Transgression*, 118.

3. In response to Tillich's theology, Keen writes, "It is a delusion to maintain that an open relationship with God will bring health, completeness, wholeness. In fact, in light of the cross (which remains the cross even on Easter), it seems that an open relationship with God is just that: open, as in 'open wound'" (*Transgression*, 182n3).

into the dirt. The warden composes himself and says, "What we've got here is . . . failure to communicate." He then goes on to add words that are just as significant where the christological dimensions of Luke's character are concerned: "Some men you just can't reach."

Here again Luke's "nothin'" stands in stark contrast to the domination system's "all" and a violation of its multiple levels of control. The warden recognizes that his spoken intimidations and rationalizations of violence are in Luke's case insufficient to achieve the aims of conformity. Language in this instance perpetuates, while simultaneously functioning as a smoke-screen for, the violence endemic in the totalizing "all" of the domination system—a fact that might not have been lost on audiences in the sixties who were familiar with the perverse use of language by the establishment to justify violence, whether in Vietnam or at home against protestors. But Luke's responses demystify the warden's rhetoric and reveal that communication is not really the issue. He exposes the warden's words as little more than an accessory to the violence that hides beneath them and at the heart of what we might call, using the words of Mark C. Taylor, an "economy of domination."[4]

The economy of domination in *Cool Hand Luke* includes an array of power formations ranging from the warden's more sophisticated and passive-aggressive intimidations and rationalizations to institutional rules and regulations outlined by persons such as Carl "the floorwalker" on the inmates' arrival, to the ever-present threat of violence represented by the walking boss, Godfrey, the "man with no eyes," whose face throughout the film remains expressionless and hidden behind a pair of reflective sunglasses, with hints of Foucault's panopticon, in which power is both "visible and unverifiable."[5] But that economy also includes the internationalization of domination among the prisoners themselves, inscribed within their own universe of unwritten hierarchies and rules. It also includes the simple following of orders by "innocent" guards, like the one who puts Luke in the "box" used for punishment. He apologizes to Luke with the excuse that he is just doing his job. But Luke reminds him that just calling something one's job doesn't make it right. Again, Luke does not so much fight the powers as he subverts them by standing outside of them. This "outside" is often

---

4. Taylor, *Erring*, 25. On this point, see also William Haltom, who describes the way "influence," "authority," and "power" interact within an "economy of violence" by which "prudent decision-makers will want to employ nonviolent influence as often as it gets the job done; to rely on routine authority when influence would be inefficient or insufficient; and to brandish power as an ultimate resort." While Haltom relates this specifically to systems of punishment, institutions of all kinds (including not incidentally the church and its educational institutions) are adept at enacting this economy. Haltom, "Laws of God."

5. Boyce, "Spectacle of Punishment," 61–62.

achieved cinematically by showing Luke sitting apart from the group or looking the other way during conversations.

Rowan Williams, in his book *Christ on Trial*, highlights the silence of Jesus before the Sanhedrin and Pilate in the gospel of Mark—a silence that is a recurring motif throughout the gospel. As Williams put it,

> Jesus knows more than he can say; he is like a naturally gifted musician trying to explain to slow or even tone-deaf listeners how basic harmony works. And when the transforming power of his presence breaks through in healing, he hurries to forbid people to talk about it. It is as if he knows they will only find the wrong words, the wrong categories.[6]

What is striking about Jesus, says Williams, is the way he stands outside the structures and languages of power by which he is being judged and how little leverage he has in that world.

> The world Mark depicts is not a reasonable one; it is full of demons and suffering and abused power. How, in such a world, could there be a language in which it could truly be said who Jesus is? Whatever is said will take on the colouring of the world's insanity; it will be another bid for the world's power, another identification with the unaccountable tyrannies that decide how things shall be. Jesus, described in the words of this world, would be a competitor for space in it, part of its untruth.[7]

That Jesus is not "a competitor for space" in the world does not mean Jesus is not a threat to the world. Rather, as Williams puts it, he "threatens because he does not compete . . . and because it is that whole world of rivalry and defense which is in question."[8] We can also think of Christ's victory along these lines, as a victory that is traced and gestured through a vulnerability and a disruption of the prevailing spatial and temporal maps of salvation and expectation, which must now be redrawn. To stand outside the world in this way, as Williams notes, is actually a way of saying "yes" to the world "by refusing the world's own skewed and destructive account of itself" and declining to "settle for the options set before us by the world's managers as the only things possible."[9]

---

6. Williams, *Christ on Trial*, 2.
7. Williams, *Christ on Trial*, 6.
8. Williams, *Christ on Trial*, 69.
9. Williams, *Christ on Trial*, 88.

Quoting from Anita Mason's novel *The Illusionist*, Williams claims, "There is a kind of truth which, when it is said, becomes untrue."[10] But if that is so, then bearing faithful witness to Christ may mean that more often than not we are left with the challenge of how to communicate Christ's silence. Indeed, one of the Christian practices that could use a healthy dose of Luke's "nothin'" is the practice of evangelism, especially in a world (and in a church) where, as Keen says, "success is all about counting."[11] Whether in its Christendom modes of achieving the spread of a morally thin, nominal Christianity across the planet or in its more current evangelical modes of securing personal relationships with Jesus on a grand scale, the practice of evangelism is rarely practiced as an act of prayer and gratitude that contradicts the way of the world, receptive and with a posture "exposed and vulnerable."[12] Instead, evangelism—and the science of apologetics developed in its service—is too often an attempt to win, to grasp, and to close one's fingers around the truth. That Jesus has come to fit so fully into this orientation means that even when one proclaims the lordship of Jesus, Jesus has already been made the pinnacle of a competition. The desire to triumph is strong—to win others, to secure converts, to shore up the truth, to eliminate the refusability of the gospel. The gospel has to be shown to be "credible" or to "help," and so it is brokered from within a logic of consumption, utility, and exchange. To be a Christian is to be well adjusted, to fit in, to gain "integrity." But the tighter the grasp, the more truth slips through our fingers like grains of sand.

But what if the good news we have to share with others is not a possession to be meted out, but rather a disposition of spirit, a brokenness and openness, a rupture of certainty so that like Luke we stand empty? What if, as Keen says, "faith were seeing in the mode of being seen, knowing in the mode of being known? What if faith were the gift of life, of an opening out into a future not to be achieved, but coming—coming for the weak, the lowly, the poor, the sick, the sinner, the dying, the dead, the damned?"[13] What if the church were "supported by nothing more solidly weight-bearing than a parable, an icon, a prayer"?[14] What if the good news was less a matter of information or answers but a wound that, like the body of Christ, opens us to both God and to the world? As Barth famously said in his commentary on Romans,

10. Williams, *Christ on Trial*, 6. George Lindbeck makes a similar point when he observes that "the crusader's battle cry 'Christus est Dominus,' [Christ is Lord] is false when used to authorize cleaving the skull of the infidel (even though the same words in other contexts may be a true utterance)" (Lindbeck, *Nature of Doctrine*, 64).

11. Keen, *Transgression*, 3.

12. Keen, *Transgression*, 145.

13. Keen, *Transgression*, 99.

14. Keen, *After Crucifixion*, 5.

> The people of Christ, His community, know that no sacred word or work or thing exists in its own right: they know only those words and works and things which by their negation are signposts to the Holy One. [If otherwise,] content would be substituted for void, convex for concave, positive for negative, and the characteristic marks of Christianity would be possession and self-sufficiency rather than deprivation and hope.[15]

The character of Luke represents just that kind of christological reversal.

THE "END" OF THE ROAD

Jesus, as Keen says, "was a constant affront to the given order," and "far before the last week of his life he was on a collision course with the powers of his world."[16] But that is not because Jesus was simply a "rabble-rouser" who asserted his own will against authority and order. Rather, it is because he was transparent to the coming reign of a Wholly Other God who is "on the move, breaking into this closed world from beyond it."[17] In his person are revealed, says Keen, both the contradiction between God and the world and the way the two touch. That contradiction and touch reveal the kenotic and downward movement that is a "transgression of the integrity of God":

> Jesus is in those narratives nothing but a drawing near to God that goes precisely where God goes; but this Jesus, "though he is in the form of God, empties himself, taking the form of a slave; humbles himself and becomes obedient to the point of death—even death on a cross" (Phil 2:6–8; translation altered slightly). The movement is from God outward. It is from exaltation to debasement.[18]

From the very beginning of *Cool Hand Luke*, as the image of a bright red "VIOLATION" sign from a parking meter fills the screen, we know Luke is a living, breathing contradiction to the world around him and to its laws and closed system of order and compliance. But Luke's character functions as a Christ-figure not primarily because he is someone who refuses to color within the lines, defying social convention and hierarchies. Rather, it is because the freedom he embodies enacts the downward movement to

---

15. Barth, *Romans*, 36.
16. Keen, *Transgression*, 12.
17. Keen, *Transgression*, 11.
18. Keen, *Transgression*, 13.

which Keen is referring and because he contradicts the domination system's "all" from a position of "nothin.'"

In another of the key scenes from *Cool Hand Luke*, the chain gang is given the crushing task of tarring a country road on a sweltering hot day. As the tanker truck full of tar proceeds ahead of the prisoners, spraying its thick black substance along the full width of the road, the men come behind shoveling a second coating of sand while being prodded and hassled by the guards whenever they slow down or stop. As Luke barrels along quickly, Dragline shouts to slow down and pace himself. Luke, however, continues to shovel harder, laughing, yelling, and inciting the others to move ever faster. The film editing and music provide a dizzying sense of the intensity of the pace as the bosses struggle just to keep up. Dragline himself begins to enjoy the adventure, and to join in the laughter and exertion. As the men eventually catch up with the truck at the end of the road, they discover they have finished far ahead of schedule, and have the rest of the day to themselves. As the men stand around asking themselves what to do now with their time, Luke replies, simply, "Nothin.'"

That the "nothin'" with which Luke infects his fellow inmates is surprising and unexpected is a function of the fact that it "arrives." It breaks into their world and cannot be predicted, determined, assimilated, or controlled by others. The "end" of the road is not an end and their work is not an "end" that they calculate, complete, or finish. It is a gift that comes to them. It is in that sense an "apocalypse." As Keen says, "We have all been trained to think that ends are achieved; they don't come."[19] And though we are used to lives dominated by planning, calculation, and production, the church is called to live according to a different imagination, "as a kind of corporate metaphor for an eschatos that no immanent metabolic process can produce. 'Thy kingdom *come!*' (Matt 6:10)."[20] The church is not a community marked by moral perfection or achievement for that reason, but rather a community that each day discovers the freedom by which it is constituted and that yet arrives from outside itself. *Cool Hand Luke* similarly subverts the economics of domination and control by introducing an alternative—one in which a gracious, "eucharistic" excess creates new possibilities and a new community.

EATING AND EMPTYING

This excess dovetails with the sacramental role of food in *Cool Hand Luke*, which has long been noted by Christian reviewers, and is first established

19. Keen, *After Crucifixion*, 59.
20. Keen, *After Crucifixion*, 59.

by the famous egg-eating scene where Luke miraculously downs fifty eggs within the space of an hour. The event is precipitated by Dragline's boasting about how much Luke eats and the fact that he can eat literally anything. Luke retorts that he can eat fifty eggs, and Dragline is left in stunned disbelief. But Luke insists he can do it. Dragline instantly gets on board, proclaiming that if Luke says he can do it, he can do it. The next ten minutes of the film feature the betting that moves like a wave across the entire prison camp, the preparation of both Luke and the eggs, and finally the contest itself, in which, of course, Luke triumphs.

It is not difficult to see the sacramental dimensions of the whole episode, especially when the camera captures Luke at the conclusion of the contest, lying alone on the table in a crucifixion pose, abandoned by the inmates who have moved on after the excitement. Likewise, the number fifty is intentional in the film, for there are fifty prisoners in the camp. On one level, as many Christian reviewers have noted, Luke's egg-eating can be taken as redeeming each of the men's lives, as he symbolically takes into himself the sins of the world. And of course the egg is a symbol of rebirth and resurrection. Frank Pierson, who was assigned to rework Donn Pearce's script (Pearce had also written the original novel after spending two years on a Florida State Prison chain gang) made the religious symbolism more overt in the story and gave it more prominence.[21] But on another level, while the scene is focused on Luke literally filling himself, his eating is in a very real sense not about becoming full but about an emptying, as with each egg he gives himself away over and over. In this way, it can be said that Luke performs a eucharistic liturgy of kenosis, atonement, and resurrection.

This liturgy gets reversed when Luke is returned to the barracks from his second escape, beaten, bloody, and reduced to nothing. He can barely stand, talk, or eat. When the men relentlessly urge him to amuse them with stories of his escape and freedom, he shouts at them to get out there themselves, and to stop feeding off of him. This reversal of eucharistic discourse may be interpreted theologically as a rejection of Christ's appropriation from within any orientation that would venerate and idolize him or gather a community around him without following him. It may well be that Luke's egg-eating can be interpreted christologically as an act of self-emptying atonement for others, with each egg eaten a life redeemed. But if that is true, it is also true that the Christ of *Cool Hand Luke* refuses to serve as a surrogate for others' own freedom; we are instead led to adopt a kind of thinking that, as Keen says, "let[s] the outside in without assimilating it."[22]

21. Eagan, "Cool Hand Luke," 628.
22. Keen, *After Crucifixion*, 11.

The eucharistic theme is continued in the very next scene after the warden and guards continue to go to work on Luke, mistreating and overworking him, and isolating him from the other inmates at night by placing him in "the box." As the men line up for evening chow, one of the guards piles Luke's plate as high as he can, reminding him that if he does not clean his plate he will go back in the box. As Luke struggles to eat even one bite, each of the inmates walks by and takes a spoonful off of his plate, "feeding off of him" in a powerful scene of eucharistic solidarity.

WORLD SHAKING

Despite these moments of grace and solidarity, it is clear that the inmates do not always "get" Luke's message (if it can be called that), and indeed they are much like Jesus' own disciples in this regard. Luke is their hero as long as they can celebrate his victories and escapes. So, for example, a few days after the inmates help Luke with his food, he is tortured by the guards by being made to dig a hole, refill it, then dig it again for a day and a night until he begs for mercy, professing to do anything they say. He grovels at the warden's feet, proclaiming to have gotten his mind "right." When the powers have finally broken his spirit, he is allowed to return to the barracks. But as he stumbles to his bunk, the inmates, all of whom have been watching the scene, begin to move away from him, looking the other way, shunning, abandoning, and refusing him, with clear parallels to the account of Christ's disciples having deserted him after his arrest (Mark 14:50). Luke collapses by his bunk, and shouts to his fellow inmates (and perhaps to God), "Where are you? Where are you, now?!"

It might be argued that *Cool Hand Luke* is a cynical, hopeless, and nihilistic film, perhaps even an atheistic one. In a number of scenes, Luke rolls his eyes, makes noises under his breath, or offers a knowing grin or sneer when he hears bullshit, as when the warden tells the new prisoners upon their arrival that his discipline is for their own good or when Dragline later that evening starts laying down his own rules. When he receives news that his mother has died, he moves away from the group to his own bunk and sings a satirical song about a "plastic Jesus," shedding a tear but refusing to be comforted by any sort of pious devotion or religious consolation. God is conspicuously absent in the film, or at least Luke's prayers might be taken as suggesting that. In one instance, as clouds gather and the sky begins to rain and thunder, the prisoners are told to stop working and get in the truck. Luke shouts at God, but Dragline urges him to stop, points toward the heavens, and reminds Luke that God can't be talked to like that. He asks

Luke whether he isn't afraid of dying. Luke replies that God is welcome to take his life anytime he wants to. He just wants God to let him know if he's there. "Love me, hate me, kill me, anything, just let me know it. And then after a quiet pause, Luke utters, "Just standin' in the rain. Talkin' to myself."

In another instance, at the end of the film, Luke is holed up in a church after his third and final escape and offers up a Gethsemane-like prayer. He calls out to God, offers both confession and protest, and asks what he is to do. After kneeling and waiting, Luke concludes that—just as he thought—no answer from God will be coming. He will have to find his own way.

Because of these and other examples, it is not surprising to find interpreters of the film refer to Luke as an atheist. Adam Kotsko, for example, refers to the film as "an atheistic apocalypse." Says Kotsko, "It cuts away the entire transcendent element and leaves only the immanent side of apocalyptic: the utter claustrophobia, the lack of any hope of escape. In this perspective, the only 'hope' he can offer his fellow prisoners is sheer fantasy" (Kotsko is referring here to a photo of Luke with two women that he sends the inmates after his second escape, which is later claimed by Luke to be a fake).[23] Thus, for Kotsko,

> The whole thing eventually becomes meaningless. Hope becomes a coping mechanism, a way of convincing yourself that it's better to contemplate Luke's gloriously failed escape than to stage one's own, and the net effect of actual "subversion" is to make the situation worse. After all, what does Luke concretely achieve other than winning the other prisoner's money and getting his most loyal sidekick put in shackles?[24]

Perhaps hope does, in fact, function for Luke's fellow inmates largely as a coping mechanism—though we might well ask if they are much different from the disciples in this respect, or for that matter, the church that has come after them. Indeed, critiques of Luke's failure to achieve anyone's liberation or salvation could well apply to Jesus himself, who must surely also be deemed a failure when judged by triumphalist messianic expectations and classical conceptions of transcendence. It may be a deficiency of Luke's Christ-figure (as for many other cinematic Christ-figures) that he does not provide a robust or positive announcement of what the reign of God looks like, with the accent falling instead on the experience of suffering and contradiction. But there is more going on in the film than this, and another reading of transcendence, meaning, and hope is possible.

23. Kotsko, "Cool Hand Luke."
24. Kotsko, "Cool Hand Luke."

As Keen puts it, Jesus is the one who brings "the otherness" of God close to humankind.[25] God's imminence does not remove God's otherness, however, and the God who is revealed in Jesus remains Luther's *deus absconditus*, the hidden God. When Jesus prays in Gethsemane or when on the cross he protests "My God, my God, why have you forsaken me?," God remains silent, just as God does for Luke. Luke's prayers and his singing about a "plastic Jesus" at one of the most sorrowful moments in his life may certainly be read as a cynical atheism, but they may also be read as entirely consistent with the way the deep experience of "nothin'" subverts and utterly transgresses stock conceptions of the sacred offered up for easy consumption. One might even argue that it is the latter rather than Luke's more honest "nothin'" that are in fact truly nihilistic.

Luke may understandably be considered a prophet without a proclamation, and most of Luke's actions have no design or purpose (he confesses to having never planned anything in his life at one point). Again, Camus's Sisyphus comes to mind, and the question is whether Luke's actions, because they appear to have no point, are therefore meaningless. But while there is an existential absurdity to Luke's actions, we can also see in his "nothin'" the irruption of the impossible that dislocates expectation and opens up new possibilities. Yes, Luke is an unlikely Christ-figure, but just because classical markers of grace, transcendence, and liberation do not predominate the film's plot, narrative, or visual imagery does not mean that transcendence has been excluded. Rather, as Keen might insist, in Christ the integrity of God has been "transgressed," inverting customary patterns of comprehending, utilizing, or consuming transcendence, and so making room for God in surprising and creative ways.

Likewise, hope is constructed throughout the film in ways that transgress triumphalist interpretations of resurrection that would gleefully skip past crucifixion on the way to Easter. Resurrection is symbolized visually in a variety of ways throughout the film—most notably when the photo of Luke with the two women is shown again at the conclusion of the film taped back together and superimposed over a cross-shaped intersection (one of the convicts had torn it up in disillusionment after Luke had been broken by the guards). Here especially, as this final visual image affirms, resurrection is not something that simply happens after crucifixion and as somehow moving beyond it. As Keen notes,

> In the narratives of the Gospels Jesus' resurrection does not erase his crucifixion. The resurrection reaches farther than that. It is the unmaking of an order in which life and death stare at

---

25. Keen, *Transgression*, 11.

each other in binary opposition. The resurrection of Jesus is the unsettling of his and every crucifixion. It engulfs them, hallows them, and saturates them with a new life. When he is raised, it is the scarred, broken, mortally wounded Jesus who comes forth from the tomb. His story remains the story of loss even as that loss is swallowed up in victory.[26]

Naturally, we would all like life to be free of suffering, imprisonment, pain, and death, and there is indeed an "already" in the Christian life that gestures toward life after crucifixion as it bears witness to Christ's resurrection. But this "already" is also an openness to a future that has yet to arrive. Thus, Keen can say quite rightfully, "Hope is the joyful wound of the eschatos, not the meeting of the need for a telos."[27] The Christian life is one that joins Christ in his sufferings while refusing to allow death to have the final word. In this way, Christ's crucifixion and resurrection create people of memory *and* hope. As Keen puts it, we bear witness to the resurrection "not by explanation, not by extrapolation, not by giving it a place in a worldview, not by settling the matter, but by working and waiting, by turning new eyes to a new dawn, by turning new ears to the pounding hoof beats of an approaching new world, by walking out into what is not-yet with a hope that need not avert defeat in order to overcome."[28]

The ending of *Cool Hand Luke* is far from unambiguously victorious, and for some reviewers, such as D. Eric Williams, the film's message is one of hopelessness, rendering Luke an inadequate Christ-figure: "Rosenberg's point is that there is no beating the Establishment—no beating The Man—and that there really is no messiah who will lead us out of our enslavement to the status quo."[29] Williams's reading is not without ample support, though I should like to argue that the film is hardly defeatist or bereft of hope viewed through the lens of a kenotic Christology. In one of the final scenes of the film, Luke and Dragline have escaped, but Luke decides to lay low rather than join Dragline in pursuit of his big plans now that they are free. In words reminiscent of Christ's commission to his disciples, Luke says that he has done enough "world-shakin'" for now. He instructs the others that they are to do the rest of it. They can send him a postcard.

Luke walks away toward the church where he spends his final moments. Dragline reappears, however, having been captured by the police and promising Luke on their behalf that if he just "plays it cool" and gives up

---

26. Keen, *After Crucifixion*, 39n5.
27. Keen, *After Crucifixion*, 143.
28. Keen, *After Crucifixion*, 181.
29. Williams, "Gospel of Cool Hand Luke."

peacefully and quietly he won't even be beaten this time. Luke, of course, knows how the domination system works, and refuses to submit. When he walks over to the window, he is immediately shot by the bespectacled boss Godfrey, the "man with no eyes."

Dragline helps Luke out of the church, and as they stagger toward the police cars, Dragline lunges for Godfrey and begins to choke him. As the two struggle in the mud, the boss's mirrored glasses tumble to the ground. As Godfrey gropes around to find them, unsuccessfully, Luke is placed in the warden's car to be taken to the prison rather than to the emergency clinic closer by, and thus to his certain death. Dragline reassures him to hang on, "There's gonna be some world-shakin' Luke. We gonna send you a postcard." In one of the most powerful scenes from the film, Luke in the backseat of the car turns his face and a formidable smile to the window, and as the car's tires move forward, we see a close-up of the boss's sunglasses crushed and driven into the mud as Godfrey's face and eyes are now exposed along with the corruption of the domination system itself. As William Haltom puts it, "This end reveals anew the superficiality of seeing *Cool Hand Luke* merely as a tale about meaningless existence."[30]

Luke does not seek death and there is nothing redemptive or sacrificial about his death. But his death, like that of Jesus, is not defeatist, for neither the domination system nor the death it wreaks can ultimately conquer him. When asked later by the other inmates what had happened, Dragline affirms that the powers knew they could never beat him. He recalls that "Luke smile of his" that was on his face all the way down to the very end. Haltom notes an additional small but significant detail in the film's ending as the warden's car takes Luke back to the prison. Symbolizing Luke's death, the green light on a stoplight under which the car is passing changes directly to red, without an intermediate yellow. As Haltom notes, "The green is on top and the red on bottom! It may be a small triumph, but Luke has turned an authority on its head. He never quite settled his score with the parking meters, but his score with authority backed by power has been settled before Luke slips into death. Luke has made a difference."[31]

CONCLUSION

A film such as *Cool Hand Luke*, because it fits within the wider genre of rebellious antiheroes and the antiestablishment sentiment of the 1960s can be viewed as forcing a particular reading of the Christ story that is about the

30. Haltom, "Laws of God."
31. Haltom, "Laws of God."

individualistic assertion of one's will against the powers of oppression and domination. But Luke's nonconformity is more than that of a dissident, but is instead born out of an inexplicable and apocalyptic "nothin'" that opens up new possibilities for freedom and community and thus it has the power to reshape the way we think about salvation and hope. Luke loses to Dragline in the prison yard fight, and yet it is Dragline who ends up his sidekick and follower. Luke is beaten and broken by the warden and prison guards, but he consistently gets the best of them. He is killed by the system itself, but exposes it and subverts it at the same time.

I close with the very same quotation from John Wesley that Keen uses to end his own final essay in *The Transgression of the Integrity of God*:

> I come, [Sovereign], to restore to thee what thou hast given; and I freely relinquish it, to enter again into my own nothingness. For what is the most perfect creature in heaven or earth in thy presence, but a void capable of being filled with thee and by thee; as the air, which is void and dark, is capable of being filled with the light of the sun, who withdraws it every day to restore it the next, there being nothing in the air that either appropriates this light or resists it? O give me the same facility of receiving and restoring thy grace and good works! I say, thine; for I acknowledge the root from which they spring is in thee, and not in me.[32]

Sometimes nothin' can be a real cool hand.

---

32. Wesley, "Plain Account," 441.

10//

On Loving Spiders

STEPHEN JOHN WRIGHT

IT WAS NEAR THE end of August that the morning light illuminated a hundred shining droplets on a spider's web and enraptured the heart of a young theologian called Jonathan Edwards. This vision transformed Edwards' perception of the world. He marvelled at the way that the web of a spider could span any distance. Some, he said, were "at such a height that one would think that they were tacked to the vault of the heavens."[1] A breeze blew, and Edwards observed intricately crafted webs floating past into the sky, and their tiny arachnoid passengers carried heavenward, "doubtless with abundance of pleasure."[2] As great as the joy of the spiders must have been, he added, his joy at beholding them was greater. When recalling the event in a letter, he writes as a man filled with love. He resolved to learn more about them, finally declaring, "I have become very conversant with spiders."[3] In spiders, he saw revealed the Creator's purpose, the wisdom of God. For God had filled their "bottle tails" with that "wonderful liquor" that thins

---

1. Edwards, "Spider Letter," 2.
2. Edwards, "Spider Letter," 2.
3. Edwards, "Spider Letter," 2.

out to a fine web that could carry them to the heavens.[4] Their lightness on their ethereal webs was matched by the lightness of their existence. Edwards noted the frailty of the spider's life, but also its persistent promulgation of offspring. There must be something of God, Edwards mused, in the fact that we are neither overrun with spiders, nor without them. In conclusion, Edwards declares that these, "the most despicable of animals" are "wondrous."[5] "Despicable" is not usually a very useful theological description, but we might get the following from Edwards: the animal that is most deplored by humanity, is loved by God. As "the wisdom of the Creator" shines from their "glistening webs," the despicable is seen to be wondrous, the unloved is the object of love.[6]

The theology of Craig Keen invites the reader to love the otherwise unloved. For Keen, theology is not a discipline undertaken to tame the world by the accumulation of knowledge, but an act that turns the practitioner toward the objects of divine love; this is what it means to follow Christ. He describes Christ as the "Galilean who walks relentlessly into solidarity with the forsaken."[7] Christ is the one on the move to "the marginalised, the poor, the dying, the sinner."[8] Christ is with the poor. Keen is cautious to prevent the Christian from mistaking themselves for Christ. The Christian does not redeem the poor, but by aligning themselves in solidarity with the poor, they create opportunities for grace. In *After Crucifixion*, Keen writes that turning to the poor is not "to teach them to fish" or "to give them a hand up."[9] Instead, the Christian is called to be with and like the poor. Both rich and poor are to stand "in solidarity with" the poor, "without demanding that they cease to be poor."[10] In this undemanding solidarity, a space opens for grace to arrive. Keen describes the encounter with the poor as a means of grace. It is at moments like this that we see hints of Keen's Wesleyan theological formation. In Wesleyan theology, a means of grace is a way of enacting Christian patience—it is the way that we wait upon the activity of God. This is exactly the

---

4. Edwards, "Spider Letter," 5.
5. Edwards, "Spider Letter," 7.
6. The violence of holding slaves, however, appeared not to trouble Edwards overly much. Any invocation of his descriptions of love and beauty should note this disjunction in his life and teaching. Elaine Scarry notes that the opposite of beauty is not ugliness, but injury—literally, the absence of justice. It is in this precise sense, then, that one can say unequivocally that Edwards's life lacked the beauty it taught, offering deep and abiding injury. Scarry, *On Beauty*.
7. Keen, *After Crucifixion*, 42.
8. Keen, *Transgression*, 31.
9. Keen, *After Crucifixion*, 31.
10. Keen, *After Crucifixion*, 32.

way that Keen frames the Christian encounter with the poor. "Grace," Keen writes, "comes particularly where calculation has come to an end."[11] Among the poor, the Christian ceases to require either themselves or the poor to meet an established expectation, to conform to a sanctioned pattern of living or existence. The means of grace are a way of divesting ourselves of control over a situation. They are an undemanding way of relating to the world and to others. They are a patient waiting upon the freedom of God.

Keen describes the pattern of human life altered by grace as eccentric. An eccentric life forsakes the ancient desire for integrity in favor of the more dangerous life of living for and with the neighbor. Graced life is not self-contained, but it is a life that opens outwards.[12] To describe this, Keen uses an unpopular word, and he uses it in a distinctly Wesleyan way: to be open outwards is to be *holy*. Holiness connotes separation. But, in the Christian gospel, it is not a separation *from* something, but a separation *to* something. To be holy is to be set apart, not to be isolated and remote but to a pattern of open living. To be set apart for God is to be separated to God. To quote Keen: "To be separated to God, to be holy, is to be separated with God to those whom God loves, the unholy."[13] Or again: "To be separated to God is to be separated with God to one's neighbor."[14]

When speaking of neighbors, Keen's focus falls primarily on the poor: "We are to care for the poor in particular and above all."[15] So holiness is dwelling with the poor. It is a life of love poured out into the hands and bellies of the poorest among us. In this way of teaching, Keen has an ancient ally in Basil the Great. Basil knew wealth in his youth. His family were esteemed, and his father was a well-known landowner. In his later life, he would describe with great detail the trimmings of opulence as he preached and wrote against the misuse of money. "If you truly loved your neighbour," he would preach to the rich, "it would have occurred to you long ago to divest yourself of this wealth."[16] Basil mocked the pursuit of wealth and the accrual of savings. Why, after all, should anyone obsess so much over pebbles dug from the ground, set to adorn our fingers?[17] If you truly love,

---

11. Keen, *After Crucifixion*, 32.

12. It should be said that concern for the poor is not antithetical to a theology of "integrity." The early church fathers who first formulated the doctrine of the Trinity as one that upholds divine integrity were also those that were concerned with living for and with the poor. For example, see Basil, St. Anthony, Chrysostom, etc.

13. Keen, *Transgression*, 28.

14. Keen, *Transgression*, 31.

15. Keen, *After Crucifixion*, 31.

16. Basil, *On Social Justice*, 43.

17. Basil, *On Social Justice*, 53.

he asks, why accumulate wealth? "If you want storehouses, you have them in the bellies of the poor."[18]

However, there is a marked difference between Keen and Basil. Keen's writing focuses very narrowly on the human experience, but it never quite gets around to fleshing out this account with a world. Basil, for instance, will say that the "fields are arid . . . because love has dried up."[19] The treatment of the poor, Basil conjectures, has a direct impact on the world. When describing the repentance of Ninevah, Basil observes the way that even the animals of the city are drawn into the deep and concerted act of penitence.[20] Keen's attentive focus on human frailty, by contrast, comes at the cost of a world. There is a certain ambiguous duality in Keen's account of the poor. There are the poor and the rich, or there are the poor and "I."[21] But the account can sometimes produce a claustrophobic reaction in the reader—in his detailed account of graced solidarity with human weakness, all other details of life seem to fade and disappear until we are left with a set of human bodies waiting in the pressing darkness. I don't intend to critique Keen's chosen point of focus, but ask whether this exhausts the eccentricity of life filled with grace? What does the world look like beyond the rich and the poor, waiting on the arrival of God?

BEING CREATURES

The categories of rich and poor are clearly anthropological and not intended as an exhaustive categorization of creaturely existence. Within Christian theology, the first and most fundamental distinction is that between God and creatures. This is a distinction that Keen maintains. However, Keen finds God in describing humanity in particular. His most detailed exploration of "nature," "Whom Shall I Send?," rapidly sharpens the pencil of nature down to the point of Christ's humanity.[22] Christ simply is the "concurrence of God and the world."[23] The use of "nature" becomes more intensively playful as the essay progresses, but the game carries the concept from the world to the purely human. Elsewhere, Keen appears to situate human reality as the capacious envelope of all other created reality: "If one understands that

---

18. Basil, *On Social Justice*, 68.
19. Basil, *On Social Justice*, 76.
20. Basil, *On Social Justice*, 77.
21. With great honesty, Craig's "I" is not a construction. Keen, *After Crucifixion*, 31.
22. Keen, *Transgression*, 183–213.
23. Keen, *Transgression*, 209.

human reality embraces nonhuman reality, then in him [Christ] is gathered together everything."[24]

The danger in giving such devoted theological attention to the human is that it can begin to appear that the human is another class of being, as though humanity had its own integrity not bound up in the fates of frogs and lizards and quasars. Rowan Williams voices the common critique here: "Being a creature is in danger of becoming a lost art."[25] Such loss is felt in either one of two ways: 1) we allow our anthropology to blur the lines a little in the distinction between Creator and creatures; 2) we allow our anthropology to produce a three-tiered ontology of God, creatures, and humans. The first critique does not fit Keen's theology, which takes care to avoid the conflation of God and creation. Divine transcendence provides a central impetus for much of Keen's thinking about Christ. However, Keen gravitates toward the second, situating the human as the prototypical creature, the very locus of the definition of "nature," and giving humanity the sacerdotal role of gathering up all nonhuman being in relation to God.[26]

In 1966, the historian, Lynn White, observed these patterns within Christian thought, and concluded that the marriage of technology and science that gave birth to the modern ecological crisis was a direct result of Christian theology.[27] Modern technology, White argues, is the "realization of the Christian dogma of man's transcendence of, and rightful mastery over, nature."[28] Certain features of White's argument seem indisputable. It is not wrong that a certain theological anthropocentrism can inform destructive relations between humans and the rest of creation. Keen, too, is mindful of this danger in his essay on *creatio ex nihilo*, where he describes the "dark night of modern technology" and its dreams of "dominion."[29] The dream, however, turns out to be as destructive for humanity as it does for the rest of creation. As Wendell Berry puts it, "If people are as grass before God, they are as nothing before their machines."[30] Such a form of relating to other creatures, Keen observes, is called into question by the identification of the Creator with the God of Israel.

---

24. Keen, *Transgression*, 176n11.

25. Williams, "On Being Creatures," 77.

26. I do not mean that Keen intends any of this, but rather his focus on the human tends toward such extremes.

27. White, "Historical Roots," 40.

28. White, "Historical Roots," 40. If my students are to be believed, this essay is still required reading for science majors in Australian universities.

29. Keen, *Transgression*, 115–16.

30. Berry, *Art of the Commonplace*, 97.

However, not all theologians have seen this the same way. Some Christian thinkers have embraced the idea that the human has dominion over creation, but have attempted to put that dominion to positive use. Ronald J. Sider writes, "Created in the divine image, we alone have been placed in charge of the Earth. At the same time, our dominion must be the gentle care of a loving gardener, not the callous exploitation of a self-centred lordling."[31] Even in this perhaps less-than-fortunate use of the concept of dominion, there is a tinge of eccentricity: Sider holds that dominion is only rightly exercised when it is not that of a "self-centred lordling." This qualification redefines dominion to be the exercise of love—this is what those who think long on such things call a "stewardship" ecology. That is, it is not clear that theological anthropocentrism in itself necessitates ecological degradation.

It is interesting to note that White suggests that the solution to the ecological crisis might just lie within the Christian tradition. He holds up Franciscan spirituality as a model for thinking about the human's relation to the rest of the world. Within Francis' well-known "Canticle of Brother Sun," creatures are not the stage upon which the human drama plays out, but they are brothers and sisters—"Brother Fire" and "Sister Water"[32]—"Praising the Creator," White says, "in their own ways as Brother Man does in his."[33] There is, in Francis's writing, a sense of commonality on the creaturely side of existence. But Francis did not sentimentalize nature. Francis, writes G. K. Chesterton, "was not a lover of nature," for a lover of nature entails perceiving "the material universe as a vague environment," something to be loved as a "background."[34] But, for Francis, Chesterton observes, "nothing was ever in the background. . . . He saw everything as dramatic, distinct from its setting. . . . St. Francis was a man who did not want to see the wood for the trees."[35] Each and every tree was interesting in its own particular creatureliness—specifically, in its appearance before him as a fellow creature.

Keen describes Francis as an "unassuming revolutionary."[36] Francis's "rapt attention" unsettles former assumptions of medieval epistemology. First, this attention directed toward Christ found the world within its purview, participating in "the growing sense of the connection between the human microcosm and the macrocosm within which it resides. . . . [I]tem after natural item was understood in its direct particularity as a symbol of

---

31. Sider, "Biblical Foundations," 48.
32. Francis, "Canticle of Brother Sun," 38–39.
33. White, "Historical Roots," 41.
34. Chesterton, *Collected Works*, 2.81.
35. Chesterton, *Collected Works*, 2.81–82.
36. Keen, *Transgression*, 188.

the great meaning of the whole."[37] Second, Francis's gaze privileged the particular over the universal. Keen hones in on this second reorientation of knowledge, and proceeds with it to consider human as knowing subject.[38] Within the broader scope of his work, Keen emulates Francis's "rapt attention" with the poor as the objects of his love. But Keen's is a love not of the poor-as-such—as one might love a forest—but a love of each life: a kind of Franciscan existentialism.

In the work of David Clough the Creator/creature distinction establishes a basis for a theology of animals. Clough is critical of anthropocentrism in Christian thought, but allows that a certain theological anthropocentrism focused on grace, love, and sharing is preferable to old-fashioned "it's all about us" anthropocentrism.[39] What is important, Clough argues, is to avoid the mistake of what he calls "teleological anthropocentrism," which suggests that not only is the world created for humans, but that the "human view of things is also the viewpoint of God."[40] God, in Christian theology, is not the creator of humans only, but of all creatures. It is overly presumptuous, Clough argues, to suggest that human self-perception matches divine perception. This would be to draw God into the world and reshape divine being into a human image. One might also remember with Ronald Osbourne that in the book of Job "the Lord of creation radically humbles all human pretensions to mastery and control over nature by declaring that the crocodile, not the human, is king over all the beasts."[41]

Clough traces the eradication of a hierarchy of being in favor of the Creator/creature distinction to Basil, although Basil's view has its antecedents in earlier thinkers such as Irenaeus.[42] In fact, Basil even shakes the accepted anthropocentrism of his day by relativizing the notion of human dominion to conversion and individual transformation: "Nobody is condemned for not catching a lion," he writes, "but one who will not govern anger is ridiculous to everyone."[43] Who can relate well to other creatures, Basil opines, who has not themselves undergone a radical changing of the mind? "See the earth," Basil writes, "and take it to heart."[44]

37. Keen, *Transgression*, 188.
38. Throughout this essay, Keen follows the lead of Louis Dupré, *Passage to Modernity*.
39. Clough, *On Animals*, introduction.
40. Clough, *On Animals*, xx.
41. Osborne, *Death Before the Fall*, 154.
42. Clough, *On Animals*, 26–27. Irenaeus, of course, would want no credit for this insight, insisting instead that we turn to the apostles.
43. Basil, *On the Human Condition*, 48.
44. Basil, *On the Human Condition*, 59.

Keen's theology has its roots deep within the Wesleyan theological tradition. I would like to examine this aspect of Keen's history and theology a bit more closely—particularly in relation to the concept of holiness. Wesley's theology of holiness gathers numerous descriptions: entire sanctification, Christian perfection, Christian perfecting, and others.

The word "perfection" has always been the most controversial aspect of Wesley's doctrine; it was not, as is sometimes assumed, a theology of "sinless perfection"—that is, of perfect moral performance. Christian holiness is, for Wesley, undivided love for God and for neighbor. Wesley described the person who has received a full measure of sanctification as the one whose love is as uninterrupted as the beating of their heart.[45] To quote from one of Keen's favorite sermons of Wesley's, "True Christian zeal is no other than the flame of love."[46] The sanctified life—what Keen called the hallowed life—is the one which heeds the call of grace and attends to the "distress of our neighbour, whether in body or soul."[47]

Wesley never admitted to this level of love himself. He died without testifying to the experience of Christian perfection. However, in his imperfect and troubled life, we see expressions of this love. He displeased the Georgian trustees who had appointed him after becoming embroiled in controversy for visiting and advocating for those he deemed to have been imprisoned unfairly.[48] He involved himself in the campaign for the abolition of slavery. He sought the end of the production of "hard liquor" in response to the plight of those who were without food after the rich land owners began diverting their crops to the production of alcohol instead of grain for food. It is common among contemporary Wesleyan theologians to describe sanctification in terms of deification or union with Christ. However, as Tom Noble points out, "being united to Christ, comes only through *kenosis*, self-emptying."[49] This is certainly the kind of theology that we find in Keen.

However, my contention has been that Keen's focus as he thinks through the issues of love, self-emptying, solidarity is narrowly set on humans. I would like to see what we learn when we zoom out a little to see how hallowed humans relate to other creatures, to see if Keen's preferred register of "transgression" communicates well. Again, we can find our basis for this discussion in the Wesleyan tradition.

---

45. Wesley, "On Patience," 176.
46. Wesley, "On Zeal," 312.
47. Wesley, "On Zeal," 314.
48. On this aspect of Wesley's early ministry, see Hammond, *John Wesley in America*, 178–89.
49. Noble, *Holy Trinity*, 52.

ANIMALS

Wesley did not limit the impact of Christ's work of grace to human creatures, and he marvelled at the limits of human knowledge about animals. "Who knows what animal spirits are?," he would ask.[50] We know that they have intelligence, but who knows their thoughts? Wesley admired the report that he heard of an elephant in Delhi that had the good sense to spray the inhabitants of a shop with water from its trunk after someone pricked it with a needle.[51] Wesley abhorred the cruelty of humans shown towards animals. Lions, tigers, and sharks might harm other creatures out of the necessity to feed, but, he writes, "the human shark, without any such necessity, torments them of his free choice."[52] Wendell Berry seems to be channeling Wesley when he recollects an experience he once had while hunting: "the sense had come to me that hunting as I knew it—the eagerness to kill something I did not need to eat—was an artificial relation."[53]

Wesley has what we might call a relative theological anthropocentrism: he thinks of the human as the highest creature in God's material creation, but he also believes that other creatures exist for their own unique relations to God and not to serve human interests. He conjectures that at the resurrection, when humans are made "equal to angels" that animals might be made as we are now: one step up the ontological ladder, as it were.[54] Wesley avoids the error of teleological anthropocentrism against which Clough warns us. Wesley argues against an expected objection: what use is it to dwell on the state of animals? This pursuit is worthwhile, he responds, because it may "soften our hearts towards the meaner creatures, knowing that the Lord careth for them. It may enlarge our hearts towards those poor creatures, to reflect that . . . not one of them is forgotten in the sight of the Father which is in heaven."[55] More specifically, Wesley says that it is the "creatures that appear vile in our eyes" who are transfigured into objects of love. Like Edwards's spiders, we are drawn to love the unloved. In Wesleyan theology, then, the animal creation can be a site of self-giving love. The human is turned outwards, not only to God and other humans, but to our nonhuman neighbors.

---

50. Wesley, "Imperfection of Human Knowledge," 577.
51. Otto and Lodahl, "Mystery and Humility," 128.
52. Wesley, "General Deliverance," 445.
53. Berry, *Art of the Commonplace*, 21.
54. Wesley, "General Deliverance," 448.
55. Wesley, "General Deliverance," 449.

Testimonies to sanctification were common in the early holiness movement. One of the best-known accounts is of Salvation Army Commissioner and theologian, Samuel Logan Brengle:

> I walked out over Boston Common before breakfast, weeping for joy and praising God. Oh, how I loved! In that hour I knew Jesus, and I loved Him till it seemed my heart would break with love. I was filled with love for all His creatures. I heard the little sparrows chattering; I loved them. I saw a little worm wriggling across my path; I stepped over it; I didn't want to hurt any living thing. I loved the dogs, I loved the horses, I loved the little urchins on the street, I loved the strangers who hurried past me, I loved the heathen, I loved the whole world.[56]

The holy life—the hallowed life—is lived in solidarity with all other creatures, from the orphan to the worm wriggling across the path. According to the Christian gospel, love is the precise way of relating to others. And, in Keen, love is also the mode of theological activity.

TRANSGRESSION

I will now turn this broadened scope back toward Keen's concerns, and see how including consideration of animals might impact upon Keen's thought. There are numerous motifs at play in Keen's theology. The titular essay of Keen's book, *The Transgression of the Integrity of God*, challenges the history of the notion of integrity and whether it fits with the demands of the gospel. There is a double transgression: the love of God transgresses one's integrity "in a Godward direction" and it "transgresses it again as one's identity is surrendered in and to one's neighbor."[57] One gives up the quest for integrity in order to stand with one's neighbor in solidarity and wait on the gracious arrival of God.

This highlights the fact that the concept of transgression is used in at least two ways in Keen's theology. First, the transgression of outgoing love. This is the kind of transgression that Keen is addressing in "The Transgression of the Integrity of God." However, in *After Crucifixion*, the body is presented as being in a natural state of transgression. Here, the body is transgressed, not only through eccentricity, but through involuntary intrusion. Keen sees this form of transgression in both personal and corporate bodies. Bodies are transgressed in pregnancy and childbirth, social bodies

---

56. Brengle, *Helps to Holiness*.
57. Keen, *Transgression*, 31.

are transgressed by those who are "outside," the lungs inhale, the body expels waste and discards dead cells. Integrity was always an illusion.

Keen's presentation of bodies is often marked by this transgression of integrity. Bodies are putrefying, mortifying, weak, broken, naked, mutilated, etc. Keen is wary of describing bodies as "whole," since this designation is caught up in structures of power—"who is in charge of [the] determination [of wholeness], and to what end?"[58] When the paralytic is lowered from the hole in the roof, Keen observes, Jesus' most pressing concern is not the "wholeness" of his body, not even the restoration of the paralytic's spiritual being, but instead Jesus announces his forgiveness.[59] Bodily "wholeness" is an afterthought. The summary of Keen's account of the body: "Life is hard, even for those who go to pains to prove it otherwise."[60] Such transgressions, it seems, are simply part of the messiness of embodiment.

No doubt, Keen has not given us a full picture of bodily life. As Clough reminds us, the human viewpoint is not the divine viewpoint. Nor is it a complete picture of reality. The human perspective is not necessarily true for all animals. However, humans share commonality with their fellow animal creatures in their embodiment. What is said about the human body must to some degree be true for animals at large. Animal bodies regularly succumb to violence in the quest for food. However, nature is not just struggle for survival. If we consider the lion, we note the way that its periods of hunting are mere moments among extended stretches of play and leisure. The same is true for the animals whose bodies will become meat for the predators, they dedicate themselves to extended periods of play or leisure. Bodies are not just broken or mutilated, they are enjoyed. It is this pleasure of the body that is largely absent from Keen's account.

Is the deepest truth of such joyful embodiment found in transgression? Julian of Norwich draws us into contemplation of Christ's gruesome suffering. Christ's praiseworthiness derives from his death. "We pray to God for His holy flesh and for His pretious blode, His holy passion, His deareworthy death and wounds."[61] Julian records in detail the vision of death conveyed to her: "In ghostly sight I saw the bodyly sight lesting of the plentious bledeing of the hede. The grete dropis of blode fel downe from under the garland like pellots semand [seeming] as it had cum out of the veynis, and in the comeing out it were browne rede, for the blode was full thick, and in the spredeing abrode it were bright rede. . . . This shewing was quick and lively and

---

58. Keen, *After Crucifixion*, 138.
59. Keen, *After Crucifixion*, 146–47.
60. Keen, *After Crucifixion*, 140.
61. Julian of Norwich, *Shewings*, 44.

hidouse and dredfull, swete and lovely."[62] What Julian saw in this vision was the secureness [sekirnes] of her soul. The ravaging of Christ's body opens her "blissid kindenes" and "endles life." She receives Christ's "sweete moder love."[63] The great joys of life have their source in Christ's harrowing death.

The human body, as an animal body, also knows play and leisure. In looking at such realities, I suspect that "transgression" begins to skew what we are seeing. Is it really the right language to describe what happens between animals during these periods of play and leisure? There is a certain self-giving love, yes, but this is not a love that is necessarily synonymous with words such as "mortifying" or "mutilated."

Attention to the world opens up the question of fallenness. The doctrine of the fall does not set us on a quest for completeness or restored integrity, but it allows us to see the world as simultaneously good and fallen: "quick and lively and hidouse and dredfull, swete and lovely." The harshness of life does not negate the joy that may be derived from it. Bodies are broken, indeed, but that does not mean that there is no beauty in them. Social order is messy and almost always entails violence, no doubt, but that does not mean that society is bereft of truth.

Elizabeth Johnson might help us frame the point with her distinction between the ethical and the biological. Considering the Darwinian account of biological development, suffering and death—transgression—are the precise means of the expansive liveliness of our world. "Orcas chase a sea lion through the waves, flipping it playfully in the air before devouring it; a lioness snags a wildebeest, knocking it down and biting its throat to cause asphyxiation; a hawk plummets to hook a scampering rodent with its sharp talons. The prey endures pain and death, but these are the result of interrelated life processes, not of some malign force."[64]

Johnson contrasts such biological transgressions with the ethical question of human involvement in the world of animals eking out their lives. The concern arises from the work of Celia Deane-Drummond, who questions the wisdom of establishing suffering as the baseline of existence. To

---

62. Julian of Norwich, *Shewings*, 46.

63. Julian of Norwich, *Shewings*, 45. In the seventh revelation, Julian regards the nature of such love and security. The peace of God was repeatedly disrupted by "hevynes and werines of my life and irkenes of myselfe that onethis [scarcely] I coude have patience to leve [live]." Though hope and faith were weakened by such experiences, she derived from her turmoil the lesson that we ought not to "folow the felynge of peyne in sorrow and mornyng," but pass through sorrow to "endless likyng." (58–59). One could also look to Hildegaard of Bingen here, for whom the church's "womb is pierced like a net, with many openings." This mutilated womb-net ensnares souls for their blessed rescue. Hildegaard, *Scivias*, 171.

64. Johnson, *Ask the Beasts*, 185.

suggest, as some have, that nature itself is cruciform, composed out of a web of transgressive engagements, "seems to subtly endorse . . . suffering rather than giving the moral imperative to seek its amelioration."[65] While in sympathy with Deane-Drummond's point, Johnson nevertheless finds that she has conflated the ethical and the biological. An indicative account of biological suffering need not amount to an ethical fatalism.

Following Johnson's lead, it seems wise to draw a distinction here, between the imperatives often laid out in ethical study, and the indicative descriptions of life offered by Keen. Transgression, perhaps, works better in ontology than it does in ethics. Or, perhaps, we could say that Keen's vision of transgression provides an ontologically indicative account of the ethical imperative to love.

CONCLUSION

I have already suggested that animals are rightful objects of human love; the life of sanctification is living with and for all creatures. Keen has argued that we are called to undemanding solidarity with the poor. For Keen, it is not our job to restore integrities—it may not even be God's job. But does the same outlook apply when thinking of how humans relate to suffering animals? When we enter into the landscape of ecology, the word "transgression" takes on new meanings that Keen does not seem to intend.

Historically, humans have transgressed ecological integrities with disastrous results. Keen calls us into solidarity with the poor. This means giving up on a self-enclosed life, and living in radical openness to one's suffering neighbor. However, to apply this same eccentricity to the human relation to animals, we see a slightly different picture emerge. In many cases, solidarity with suffering animals will mean withdrawal.[66] Withdrawal is a loving act when it allows another creature to thrive within its own ecological integrity. If there are ecological integrities that are worth preserving, what does this mean for the concept of "integrity" in Keen's theology at large? Given the disastrous history of human-animal relations, are there not some integrities—even relative integrities—that are worth attempting to preserve or restore?

Keen's theology attempts to articulate a vision of Christian life that is eccentric, that gives of itself for the sake of others, that loves. Solidarity with

---

65. Deane-Drummond, *Christ and Evolution*, 172.

66. Michael Welker proposes that we understand "free self-withdrawal" to be a mark of union with the crucified Christ in the Spirit. While the God-world relation is not contrastive, the creature-creature relation is. Withdrawal is an act of self-renunciation that lovingly opens space for others to be. Welker, *God the Spirit*.

animals might mean nothing more than accepting that we sit with them on the creaturely side of being, awaiting the grace of God and the resurrection of the body. Within Wesley's doctrine of Christian perfection, the human is drawn outward in love toward all creation. For Wesley himself, he was drawn to marvel at the wonder of the animal world, even in its harshest aspects. As Clough reminds us, humans are situated firmly on the creaturely side of being. The wonder of the incarnation, Clough observes, was not so much that the eternal Son became a *human*, but that the eternal Son crossed the fundamental divide between God and creation to become a *creature*.[67]

The body of Christ was an animate body. So what might other animal bodies teach us about Christ's body? I think that this is a question worth pursuing. For Berry loving the animal in its embodiment meant putting down his rifle. For Brengle, it meant dancing over the sidewalk to avoid stepping on a passing worm. For Edwards, it meant observing the spider atop its dewy web, and—crucially—stepping back, leaving the web intact.

---

67. Clough, *On Animals*, 100–103.

11//

The Hallowing of the Flesh in Biblical and Patristic Christology

THOMAS A. NOBLE

HOLINESS AND FLESH DO not seem to go together. Insofar as "the holy" seems to be linked to the "spiritual" (as in the name "the Holy Spirit"), there appears to be some kind of opposition here. "Flesh" appears to be so physical, so material, indeed so sensual, that it must surely be the opposite of "the holy." But this apparent opposition may have more to do with our present cultural context in the modern, rational, individualistic West.[1] It is no doubt a mistake to assume that the words have the same meaning for everyone in our culture. But broadly, there still seems to be a cultural lag here in that, despite supposed secularization, the new interest in the "spiritual" seems to be (if anything) a reaction against consumerism, materialism, the carnal and fleshly, capitalism and greed.

Arguably that has deep roots in our Hellenistic heritage. It appears to be the same old dualism, rooted in Plato's dichotomy between the eternal and the temporal, the transcendent and the earthly, the universal and the particular, and strengthened by the Cartesian dualism between the *res*

---

1. Or is it "postmodern"? Perhaps we need to continue to take that with a pinch of salt and ask critically just how "post" postmodernism really is.

cogitans and the *res extensa*, and the Kantian dualism between the noumenal and the phenomenal. It issues in a world-denying notion of spirituality that is ascetic and otherworldly.

Have we left that behind? With our minds dominated by the notion of fashion or "mode," we all tend to think that our particular generation has spectacular new insights, "thinking thoughts that never occurred to Socrates." But actually, our Western Augustinian heritage, with its roots in Plato, is still shaping our use of words and therefore our thinking in ways we often fail to detect. Rebellious youth in every generation—whether short-haired punk or long-haired hippie—comes to maturity when they begin to realize that the world did not begin when they appeared on the scene, and that we can never fully escape from our past and create a new world *ex nihilo*.

Realistically then, our Western heritage shapes our thinking and particularly the way we interpret Holy Scripture. When Paul writes of the enmity between the flesh and the spirit in Gal 5, we read that passage through this lens. Flesh is evil; spirit is good. When he writes about "the desires of the flesh" (*epithumiai tēs sarkos*) in Rom 13:14; Gal 5:16, 24; and Eph 2:3, we understand this to mean that these "desires of the flesh" are inherently sinful. Indeed, "desire" as such may appear to be evil in the New Testament (Rom 1:24; 6:12; 7:7; Eph 4:22; 1 Tim 6:9; Titus 3:3; Jas 1:14f; 1 Pet 1:14; 2:11; 1 John 2:16).

AUGUSTINE AND CALVIN

All of this became grist for Augustine's mill as he developed further the patristic doctrine of sin and the fall and introduced the terminology of *originale peccatum*, "original sin."[2] His thinking developed during his years as a bishop combating the Pelagians. In order to insist that salvation was *totally* by grace, he needed a corresponding doctrine of *total* sin. If we were saved by God's grace alone, that implied that there was nothing worthy in us. While there may be moral pagans, nothing we or they could do could merit God's grace. If we were only saved by *gratia praeveniens*, then it followed that humanity without God had to be seen as totally within the sphere of sin. And given Augustine's struggle with his own sensual nature, that had to include for him a matter of delivery from "the desires of the flesh." That was the significance of the text from Paul, which the child's voice urged him to "take up and read" in the garden at Milan:

---

2. This term first appears in a discussion of Rom 7:7–25 in *de diversus quaestionibus ad Simplicianum* written in AD 397.

> Not in riots and drunken parties, not in eroticism and indecencies, not in strife and rivalry, but put on the Lord Jesus Christ and make no provision for the flesh in its lusts.[3]

Under his influence, a strongly negative understanding of "the flesh" and its desires, which appeared to arise from the New Testament, became deeply embedded in the Western theological tradition. But it was Calvin who took this to its extreme. Interpreting the Fathers, including Augustine and the scholastics, as regarding desire as merely an infirmity, the *fomes peccati*, the "tinder" or "fuel" for sin, he goes further:

> We again regard it as sin whenever man is influenced in any degree by any desire contrary to the law of God. . . . Accordingly we hold that there is always sin in the saints until they are free from their mortal frame, because depraved concupiscence resides in their flesh.[4]

When we reach that point, questions arise. Granted that some doctrine of *total* sin is required as a complement to *total* grace, and granted that we are not talking just about sinful actions or sinful inaction, but about a condition of sinfulness that envelopes the whole human race, are we then to say that sinfulness so affects our very physical constitution that our natural desires are *in themselves* sinful, and if so, where does that leave the doctrine of creation? Calvin was aware of that question. He went on to write:

> We by no means condemn those appetites which God so implanted in the mind of man at his first creation that they cannot be eradicated without destroying human nature itself, but only the violent lawless movements which war with the order of God.[5]

That seems to be something of a concession: our natural desires are God-given and therefore good. It is their misuse that is the problem. But he goes on to muddy the waters by continuing:

> But as in consequence of the corruption of nature, all our faculties are so vitiated and corrupted that a perpetual disorder and excess is apparent in all our actions, and as the appetites cannot be separated from this excess, we maintain therefore that they are vicious. . . . We hold that *all human desires are evil*, and we charge them with sin not in as far as they are natural, but because

---

3. Henry Chadwick's translation of Rom 13:13-14 as quoted in Augustine, *Confessions*, 8:29.

4. Calvin, *Institutes*, III, 3, 10. "Man" here, translating *l'homme*, is the standard usage of the day, meaning "humanity" without respect to the division of the sexes.

5. Calvin, *Institutes*, III, 3, 10.

they are inordinate, and inordinate because nothing pure and upright can proceed from a corrupt and polluted nature.[6]

He grants that natural desires were implanted in us by the Creator. But the waters are muddied in that he seems to take two contradictory positions here as to how their present sinfulness is to be understood. The first is that the natural desires are God-given and therefore good unless they get out of control; the second is that human nature is now so polluted that the desires are evil in themselves. Which is it? The key question is how we are to understand "desire" and particularly "the desires of the flesh."

Perhaps the nature of the problem that arises from Calvin's position can be elucidated by employing the terminology of contemporary experimental psychology which speaks not of "desires" but of "drives." A drive is identified where a purposive activity is observed to be initiated by an internal state and external stimulation. The most obvious are hunger, thirst, and the sexual drive, but others which have been suggested include curiosity, fear, and aggression. The question then is whether the hunger, thirst, and sex drives, or any of the others, are the natural and good creation of God, which only become lawless when wrongly directed or out of control, or whether they are "polluted" in such a way that they have become "evil" in themselves. The latter view may not be Gnosticism strictly speaking, in that these drives were good when created, but have become evil. But it is perilously close to Gnosticism. It takes the Hellenistic devaluation of the physical and particularly of the flesh to extremes. Granted that humanity as a whole, including our drives, are within the sphere of sin, are we to say that they are actually evil? And what exactly is meant when Calvin says that our nature is polluted? This is presumably a metaphor, but what does it mean? Is this saying that it is evil *per se* to be hungry, thirsty, or to feel sexual attraction? It is clear that these lead us into sin when they are out of control, but are they sinful—indeed "evil"—in themselves? That seems to be the implication of the statement that "all human desires are evil." That may not blame God for this evil, but is it not coming uncomfortably close to the dualism that regards the material, physical life of the body (as opposed to the spiritual part of us) as in some sense evil, so that true "hallowing" only comes when the body is discarded by the eternal soul?

But even if we succeed to some extent in laying aside that dualistic Hellenistic heritage, dividing soul from body and the spiritual from the physical, and even if we reject Calvin's particularly strong interpretation of "total depravity," there still seems to be something of a contrast between holiness and flesh. Craig Keen recognizes that when he gives to his essay, "The Transgression of the Integrity of God," the subtitle, "The Hallowing

---

6. Calvin, *Institutes*, III, 3, 12; emphasis added.

of the Flesh." That subtitle assumes that flesh needs to be hallowed, implying that in itself it has to be understood to be unholy. How then shall we understand this?

"FLESH" IN OLD TESTAMENT THOUGHT

As Keen indicates, the starting point for our thinking must be Christ, for "The Word became *flesh*." How should we think about "flesh" then in the light of Christ? Does this mean that in becoming "flesh," the Son or Word of God became subject to sinful desires—the natural "drives" that are part of being human but which are polluted so that they must be regarded as "evil"? *Me genoito!* (as Paul might have put it). That cannot be. That offensively denies the sinlessness of the Son of God. So then, shall we deny that our Lord had those natural human desires? No, that too is inadmissible, for it would deny that he was truly human. How then could we understand how he was "tempted on all points as we are" (Heb 4:15)? Could it be then that our human drives and desires are unaffected by our sinful condition? No, that would offend against an understanding of our "totally" sinful condition which, as Augustine saw and the whole Western tradition (including Wesley) affirmed, was a necessary corollary of *sola gratia*. So how shall we understand this? Exactly how sinful is this flesh that needs to be hallowed, and what light is thrown on this when we hear that the Word became *flesh*?

Beginning then with trying to understand what is meant by "flesh," particularly in John 1:14, what does it mean to say that the Word became *flesh*? Reading the Fourth Gospel against its Old Testament background, the answer to that must lie in the Hebrew understanding of flesh. Walter Brueggemann notes that "the notion of humanity in 'the image of God' plays no primary role in Old Testament articulation of humanity."[7] He focuses instead on the central concern that "the human person *is a person in relation to Yahweh*."[8] Nonetheless, he does pay attention to what he calls "the physiology of human personhood," which revolves around the categories of *spirit* (*ruach*), *flesh* (*basar*), *living being* (*nephesh*), and *heart* (*leb*).[9] He considers it unfortunate that *nephesh* has been translated "soul," since that has imported a Greek understanding of the soul in contrast to the body, a way of thinking which is "precluded in Israel's way of speaking."[10] It is important to emphasize that these are not separable parts, but aspects of the one psychosomatic unity.

---

7. Brueggemann, *Theology of the Old Testament*, 452.
8. Brueggemann, *Theology of the Old Testament*, 453; italics original.
9. Brueggemann, *Theology of the Old Testament*, 452.
10. Brueggemann, *Theology of the Old Testament*, 453.

Brueggemann lists as "still useful" the work of Hans Walter Wolff in which Wolff notes that *basar* is used in reference to animals and humans, that it may refer to parts of the body or the body as a whole, but that it is also used in the context of human relationships.[11] It may be added that these relationships are seen within the context of what we have to call "corporate solidarity," but, as Wolff notes, the overall implication is of weakness and frailty. "Flesh"(*basar*) is, in fact, the Old Testament way of referring to what we call "humanity" or "human nature" or "the whole human race." The classic passage we may quote here is Isa 40: "All *basar* is grass, and all its beauty is like the flower of the field" (40:6). As the Lord God formed the *adam* from the mud and breathed into him the *ruach* of life, it was only then that the *adam* became a *nephesh*—a living being (Gen 2:7). Life and animation come to *basar* by action of the *ruach* of God. So the human creature is totally dependent on God for life and being, and when the human pair, who are of one *basar*, disbelieve God's word and disobey him, natural death is the inevitable result for them and for all their offspring, united as the one human "flesh."

It is inadmissible, by the way, to say that they only died "spiritually." That really imports the Hellenistic dualism into our interpretation of Scripture. Rather we are to understand that in Old Testament thinking the death sentence, which is the outcome of breaking fellowship with the Life-giver, is death not for a separable body, but for the psychosomatic unity of the human being and for the corporate solidarity of the human race as such. By sin came death.

What the narrative of creation and fall does not have, however, is any clear statement of the sinful condition resulting from their disobedience and from the break in fellowship with the Lord God. Natural, physical death is the consequence, along with banishment from the nearer presence of God in the protected sphere of the garden. But nothing is said there about a "sinful nature." What is said however about their sinful condition comes a few chapters later. God observes that "every imagination (*yezer*) of the human heart (*leb*) was only evil continually" (Gen 6:3). Here is another of Wolff's key Hebrew terms, the *leb* or heart. The *basar* is not said to be evil: it is weak and frail and condemned to die. But the thoughts of the *leb* are evil continually. The heart or mind, the center of human thought and action—*that* is what is actively engaged continually in evil. It is not that the desires of the flesh, the natural human desires and drives that are part of the human creature, are now inherently evil. They remain the good creation of God so that it is not sinful for the pair to eat or drink to satisfy their hunger and thirst,

---

11. Wolff, *Anthropology of the Old Testament*, 26.

nor is it sinful for Adam to *know* his wife Eve. The problem lies in the *leb*, the heart or mind, which is now consumed with sinful imaginings.

It is not that the natural bodily desires are evil, but that they are now out of control. It is not that the natural desires have corrupted the heart, but that the heart has become consumed by self-gratification so that the natural desires too are affected and the whole human being is defiled. It is not that flesh is inherently evil and has infected the mind: it is rather that the mind or heart—the voluntary, thinking, choosing center of human motivation and action—is sullying and prostituting the flesh. The God-given desires are now part of a sinful creature: but it is not because the natural desires have taken over against the heart and mind and will. It is rather that, having chosen to disbelieve and disobey God and exalt themselves as gods, the human creatures have polluted their whole being, disordering their natural desires. And this affects not only the first pair, but their offspring, so that they all die, and they all suffer from hearts that are far from God, consumed with their own self-interest. As part of the solidarity of human *basar*, they are born (*natus*) with a "nature" that is deeply affected, and they each choose to follow the path of their parents, not because their *basar* is evil, but because it is disordered in such a way that they cannot restore the original fellowship with the Lord God by their own actions and choices. Instead they all repeat and confirm the choice of their first parents to live for their own glory—to be "as gods."

PAUL'S PERSPECTIVE AND HIS NEW TWIST

It is not, of course, that this can be read off the surface of the text of Genesis. This interpretation is rather dependent on that of Paul in Rom 1:18–32, and also in Rom 5:12–21 and Rom 7:4—8:17. And the key to those passages is that Paul understood the human condition *in the light of Christ*. It is in the light of the Gospel of Christ from which he begins his argument in Rom 1:1–17 that he analyzes the human condition in the following passages. And his interpretation of Adam in Rom 5 is an interpretation that also springs from his exposition of the Gospel of Christ. He is not trying to understand Christ in the light of Adam. On the contrary, he can only understand Adam in the light of Christ. It is only because of the Gospel of Christ that the apostle *to the gentiles* can analyze the *human* condition and assert that Jesus is not only Messiah for the Jews, but the universal savior of *all of Adam's sinful race*. And after he has dealt with the corporate justification of "all" through the cross (Rom 3:23–24), and written about our corporate transference from the sphere of Adam to the sphere of Christ in Rom 5 and 6, he comes to the personal aspect. The first person singular in Rom 7 tells us that he is now for the first time thinking about the *ego* and of "the sin that dwells within" (7:17–20). That means that we live "according to the flesh" (*kata sarka*, 8:5) because we are characterized by "the mind of the flesh" (*phronema sarkos*, 8:5–7), which we may understand as the "mind *set on* the flesh." It is the motivation centered on merely human goals and values.

It is vitally important then to understand that in these passages and elsewhere, Paul has added his own unique twist to the concept of "flesh." Flesh in the Old Testament, in John, and in the rest of the New Testament is not in itself evil: it is weak and subject to corruption (*phthora*) in the sense of physical decay. It is falling away into disease and deterioration and dementia and death. Paul, too, shares that basic Hebrew understanding (Rom 8:21; 1 Cor 15:42, 50). Death is at work in our members. As N. T. Wright emphasizes, Paul's anthropology is not that of Hellenistic dualism, but of psychosomatic unity.[12] Our flesh is mortal flesh, not evil flesh. Physical flesh cannot think evil or desire evil: only the mind or heart (*leb, kardia*) can be responsible for evil thoughts and actions. The seat of sin is in the heart or mind. And so Paul's new twist is to write about *the mind* of the flesh. The root of our problem then is not that we are in the flesh—that we are physical human creatures: but that our minds are "set on the flesh." That is the very helpful NRSV translation of *phronema sarkos*, which we used to translate as "the carnal mind." It is the mind set on human goals and values, and of course since the word is *phronēma*, not *nous*, we are thinking of a tendency or bent or inclination or characteristic intention or habitual way of thinking. We may therefore helpfully interpret the phrase further as "the *self-centered mind-set.*" Paul adds yet a further twist when in one passage (Gal 5) he writes of "the flesh" as a power in opposition to the Spirit. But it is not an alien power. It is power of our own self-centered mindset to which we are enslaved and from which we cannot be delivered except by the Spirit of God.

Paul is clear that the sanctifying work of the Spirit in us is the outworking of that definitive hallowing of our flesh, which took place in the incarnation and in the incarnate life and sacrificial death of the Son of God:

> For God has done what the law, weakened by the flesh, could not do: sending his own Son in the likeness of sinful flesh and for sin, he condemned sin in the flesh, in order that the just requirements of the law might be fulfilled in us who walk not according to the flesh, but according to the Spirit. (Rom 8:3–4)

The phrase "sinful flesh" here in Rom 8 is best understood as "sinful humanity." Paul is not saying that physical human flesh is evil, but that the

---

12. See Wright, "Mind, Spirit, Soul and Body."

human race is a sinful race. And it was by becoming one of this sinful race that the Son of God condemned sin in the flesh. Human physical existence is sinful not in the sense that the physical flesh is evil or that it is wrong to feel normal natural human desires, but in the sense that, having chosen our own way in corporate rebellion against God, a path that we each confirm in our own lives, our very physical flesh has become disordered as we use our "members" as "instruments of wickedness" (Rom 6:13). In his physical incarnation in our human flesh, the Son of God began the hallowing of our common physical flesh by the power of the Holy Spirit.

Subject to the same infirmities and pressures and temptations coming from our weak, mortal physical existence, his holy choices sanctified human living. Where our birth in the disordered physical flesh led to a "mind set on the flesh" developing through all the stages of child maturation, in him that was never so. Faced as a growing boy with the same pressures belonging to our physical existence, he freely chose in the power of the Spirit to obey the Father on every occasion. Where we grow twisted and distorted, selfishly indulging our own natural desires and shaped by the dysfunctional sinful relationships of fallen human society, he grew straight and true. His heart and mind were so focused by the Spirit on the will of the Father that he was never characterized at any point in his life by the *phronema sarkos*, the mind set on the flesh. To use the Augustinian terms, he sanctified our common human nature by the power of the Spirit within his own holy person so that he was never subject to "original sin." He developed the archetypal holy *character*.

But his work in hallowing our common human flesh through his birth and life did not come to its culmination until his death. Paul had already made it clear in chapter 6 that corporate sinful humanity died in Christ's death:

> We know that our old humanity (*anthrōpos*) was crucified with him that the body of sin (*sōma tēs hamartias*) might be destroyed.... The death he died he died to sin, once for all, but the life he lives he lives to God. (Rom 6:6, 10)[13]

Now in chapter 8, he draws out the consequences of that for the believer of that once-for-all death and resurrection through the work of the Spirit:

> If the Spirit of him who raised Jesus from the dead dwells in you, he who raised Christ Jesus from the dead will give life to your mortal bodies through his Spirit which dwells in you. (Rom 8:11)

---

13. The translation, "our old self was crucified with him" introduces a modern individualism that is not there in the corporate term *anthrōpos*. It was our corporate Adamic humanity that was crucified, and since we are all one in that corporate solidarity, his death (as the Wesleys emphasized) was "for all."

PATRISTIC DEVELOPMENT

It is this Pauline understanding of the "hallowing of the flesh" that is developed in the Christian fathers, particularly in Irenaeus, Athanasius, and Gregory of Nazianzus. Unlike Paul, of course, the Greek fathers were Hellenes. Although educated in the Graeco-Roman culture, Saul the Pharisee was not a Hellene of the Hellenes but a Hebrew of the Hebrews. He may have inherited Roman citizenship and been educated in Greek rhetoric, but the springs of his thinking were in the life and literature of Israel. That was not true of the Greek fathers. Their cultural roots were in the sophisticated philosophical culture of the Hellenes. But they were aware of that, and even those educated in the schools of Athens such as Basil the Great and his fellow student, Gregory Nazianzen, were critical of their Greek cultural heritage. Perhaps those among the major fathers who were least influenced by their Greek heritage were Irenaeus and Athanasius. The pervading Platonist dualism between the spiritual world of the intellect (*kosmos noetos*) and the world of matter and the senses (*kosmos aisthētos*) is missing from their writings. The thinking of both of these fathers was rather shaped by their reading of Holy Scripture as interpreted by the apostolic gospel of Christ.

For Irenaeus, the first major theologian of the Christian Church after the apostles, theology is about the interpretation of the Hebrew Scriptures according to the teaching of the apostles. Every interpretative scheme has a *hypothesis*, a technical term in Greek rhetoric that indicated the assumption of a first principle from which one developed an argument.[14] For the Gnostics, the *hypothesis* was the hierarchy of *aeons* in the divine *plērōma*, but for the church it was the apostolic Gospel of Christ. God's only-begotten Word,

> who is always present with the human race, united to and mingled with his own creation, according to the Father's pleasure, and who became flesh, is himself Jesus Christ our Lord, who did also suffer for us, and rose again on our behalf, and who will come again in the glory of his Father, to raise up all flesh, and for the manifestation of salvation, and to apply the rule of just judgment to all who were made by him.[15]

Christ took our mortal flesh to death and raised it immortal in his resurrection. That is the Gospel—the descent and ascent, the humiliation and the exaltation, centered in the cross and the resurrection. That is the story of the Gospel, the shape of Christology, which is the key to the Holy Scriptures. And it is the story of the hallowing of our flesh.

---

14. See Behr, *Irenaeus of Lyons*, 112–15.
15. Irenaeus, *Against Heresies*, III, xvi, 6.

He took our humanity in order to sanctify it in his birth, life, and death. He was the second Adam who *recapitulated* our human life:

> He therefore passed through every age, becoming an infant for infants, thus sanctifying infants, a child for children, thus sanctifying those who are of this age . . . a youth for youths, becoming an example to youths, and thus sanctifying them for the Lord. So he was likewise an old man for old men that he might be a perfect master for all, not merely in the setting forth of the truth but sanctifying the aged also. . . . Then at last he came on to death itself.[16]

It was vital therefore that, unlike the first Adam, his flesh was not formed *de novo* from the dust or mud, but from the flesh of Adam's sinful race:

> Why then did not God again take dust, but wrought so that the formation should be made of Mary? It was that there might not be another formation [handiwork] called into being, nor any other which should [require to] be saved, but that the very same formation should be summed up [recapitulated].[17]

It was necessary that he come "in the likeness of sinful flesh," that is to say, assuming the very stock and corporate solidarity of Adamic humanity, precisely because it was *that* humanity, *that* flesh, which had to be sanctified. The hallowing of our flesh therefore was accomplished in his birth, in his victorious and obedient life, and finally secured in his sacrificial death.[18]

Like Irenaeus, Athanasius operates within the Hellenistic culture of the Graeco-Roman world, but is essentially shaped by his study of the Christian Scriptures. He is one of the most biblical of the Fathers. His life-long task was the defence of the deity of Christ against the Arians, but he also continued the doctrine of Irenaeus on the sanctifying significance of the humanity of Christ. He is particularly clear and direct when he writes:

> Our Saviour humbled himself exceedingly when he took upon himself our frail unworthy nature. He assumed the form of a servant in making our flesh, which was enslaved to sin, a part of himself.[19]

---

16. Irenaeus, *Against Heresies*, II, xxxii, 4

17. Irenaeus, *Against Heresies*, III, xxi, 10; see also the following chapter, III, xxii.

18. See the fuller study of Irenaeus' doctrine in Van Kuiken, "Relationship of the Fall," 122–37.

19. Athanasius, *Discourses Against the Arians*, I, 43.

But this assuming of our common sinful flesh did not make him sinful. Quite the opposite! For the whole purpose was "that, by his dwelling in the flesh, sin might perfectly be expelled from the flesh, and we might have a new mind."[20] Athanasius explains:

> For though it was after us that he became human for us, still he is therefore called and is the "first-born" of us because, all humanity being lost according to the transgression of Adam, his flesh before all others was saved and liberated as being the Word's body, and henceforth we, becoming incorporate with it, are saved after its pattern.[21]

The hallowing of our common flesh begins in the body of the Incarnate Word. The Word took our mortal body in order to raise it immortal in his resurrection. He took our sinful flesh in order to cleanse it *in the very taking of it* and by continuous, unbroken sanctification throughout his life on earth.

> For, the Word being clothed with flesh, as has many times been explained, every bite of the serpent began to be utterly staunched from out of it: and wherever evil spring from the motions of the flesh, to be cut away, and with these death also abolished, the companion of sin.[22]

The properties of the flesh became his, such as hunger, thirst, suffering, weariness. He bore "the infirmities of the flesh as his own."

> And well has the prophet said "carried," and did not say "he remedied our infirmities," lest, as being external to the body, and only healing it as he has always done, he should leave humanity still subject to death. But he *carries* our infirmities and he *himself bears* our sins that it might be shown that he has become human for us, and that the body which in him bore them was his own body.[23]

It was this corruptible, mortal body with its infirmities that he took to the cross and offered as a sinless offering to God so that through his death and rising again, our common human flesh might share in his resurrection.[24]

---

20. Athanasius, *Discourses Against the Arians*, II, 56.
21. Athanasius, *Discourses Against the Arians*, II, 61, referring to Col 1:15.
22. Athanasius, *Discourses Against the Arians*, II, 69.
23. Athanasius, *Discourses Against the Arians*, III, 31, with reference to Isa 53:4.
24. See Van Kuiken, "Relationship of the Fall," 138–48.

The hallowing of our flesh is finally completed when the corruptible puts on incorruption and the mortal immortality.

It needs to be underlined that when Athanasius writes about "flesh," he is not just writing about the material, physical aspect of being human. He has been accused of being Apollinarian, believing in the true physical humanity of the body of Christ, but having no role for the soul or mind of Christ. That has been supported by the generalization that while the Antiochenes had a "Word-man" Christology, the Alexandrians, and particularly Athanasius, had a "Word-flesh" Christology, making them all cryptic Apollinarians. This perspective was adopted by an older generation of scholars including Aloys Grillmeier and J. N. D. Kelly.[25] But this is now seen to falsify the picture. Khaled Anatolios points out that Athanasius does not work with the Hellenistic dualism between body/flesh and mind/soul, but that he has a fully biblical, Hebrew understanding of "flesh" as a comprehensive term for human nature in both its physical and intellectual dimensions. For Athanasius, the hallowing of "the flesh" is the hallowing of human nature as a whole.[26]

The common mind of the Christian Fathers on the hallowing of our flesh in the birth, life, death, and resurrection of Christ is often summed up in Gregory Nazianzen's dictum, "The unassumed is the unhealed." Nazianzen was writing in retirement to combat the influence of Apollinaris, who had denied that the Son of God assumed a human mind. He assumed a human body, according to Apollinaris, but not a human mind since the human mind was sinful. For Nazianzen, that was precisely why the Son of God *had* assumed a human mind! Only "that which is united to his Godhead is also saved."

> If only half Adam fell, then that which Christ assumes and saves may be half also; but if the whole of his nature fell, it must be united to the whole nature of him that was begotten and so be saved as a whole.[27]

As he had explained in his Fourth Theological Oration, the Son of God became human,

> that by himself he might sanctify humanity and be as it were a leaven to the whole lump; and by uniting to himself that which was condemned, might release it from all condemnation becoming for all humanity all things that we are, except sin.[28]

---

25. Grillmeier, *Christ in Christian Tradition*. Kelly, *Early Christian Doctrines*.
26. See Anatolios, *Athanasius*, 67. Also Leithart, *Athanasius*, chapter 5.
27. Gregory of Nazianzus, "Letters," 218.
28. Gregory of Nazianzus, "Oration 30," 317. See Van Kuiken, "Relationship of the Fall," 148–54.

Assuming our sinful humanity emphatically did not mean that the human nature of Christ was sinful. On the contrary, what it meant was that the hallowing of our flesh, our common human nature, began from the very moment of conception in the virgin's womb, so that he was sinless and undefiled, but that it was carried on through his sinless life until it was finally secured when the old humanity was crucified in his body, bearing our sins upon the cross, and raised immortal and incorruptible in his resurrection.

CONCLUSION

We have seen enough to conclude that Irenaeus, Athanasius, and Gregory of Nazianzus have a common mind on "the hallowing of the flesh" in Christ. Evert J. Van Kuiken's research concludes from his study including two more of the Greek fathers, Gregory of Nyssa and Cyril of Alexandria, and five of the Latin fathers—Tertullian, Hilary, Ambrose, Augustine, and Leo the Great—that this is the common doctrine of the *consensus patrum*.[29] The Son of God did not assume an *already* sanctified humanity created *ex nihilo*. He assumed our sinful humanity precisely in order to sanctify our common nature in his own person through his conception, birth, and life of obedience "unto death, even death on a cross." What deeper, more solid foundation could there be for our sanctification, the hallowing of our flesh?

As Craig Keen reminds us, however, it is the resurrection of the Crucified One that completes the hallowing of our flesh. The resurrection body of Jesus still has its scars. He remains even in the glory of his exaltation the One who shares common flesh with "the poor and diseased and outcast and frail," "the lost and forgotten," "the dying and the dead and the damned." He has not left them behind in his exaltation to glory. On the contrary, he is "touched with the feeling of our infirmities" (Heb 4:15). And as Keen goes on to remind us in the rest of his essay, it is by the Spirit that Christ is in us and we are in Christ. What was achieved *for us* in Christ is to be worked out *in us* as he dwells in us by his Spirit. And all of this is the gracious will and provision of the Father. This is how we are to understand the doctrine of the Trinity, which the fathers formulated at Nicaea and Constantinople. The trinitarian life of the church is the fellowship of the Spirit in which we share in the sufferings of Christ in reaching out to the lost and excluded, so bringing glory to the Father.

---

29. Van Kuiken, *Christ's Humanity*.

Afterword

12//

Tending to Dogma a Long, Long, Long Way from Home

CRAIG KEEN

ONE

IN THE OVER-INVOKED, BUT still disconcertingly suggestive year—1984—Random House released in English an anthology of texts by Michel Foucault, whose bright light went out in Paris on June 25 of that year, when he was not quite fifty-eight years old, the casualty of a neurological disorder consequent to acquired immunodeficiency syndrome. Among the writings collected in this volume is the essay, "What is Enlightenment?"[1] a previously unpublished lecture he had delivered the year before in Berkeley, while he was visiting professor at the University of California there, and had personally offered to the editor for the volume.[2] It is an inquiry into an even more famous essay published exactly two hundred years earlier by Immanuel Kant: "*Beantwortung der Frage: Was ist Aufklärung?*" Both thinkers, however

---

1. Foucault, "What Is Enlightenment," 32–50.
2. Miller, *Passion of Michel Foucault*, 456n41.

"patient [their] labor," it seems fair to say, were nonetheless characterized by a certain devotion to Enlightenment's "impatience for liberty."[3] "*Sapere aude!*"[4] Kant shouts in the first paragraph of his manifesto, *daring* his reader to *know*, to throw off the fetters of childhood,[5] to stand tall on the firm, level, graded ground of maturity, to break through the walls of dogmatism.[6] Foucault's dare . . . is of a subtler but more transgressive kind.

Though Kant, too, understands Enlightenment to involve the crossing of certain customary boundaries,[7] he is certain that it would be reckless to disturb *proper* boundaries. The mature *know* the difference. They do not wait for an authority to decree what they are to know, do, or hope—though, of course, as mature, they would never conduct their affairs with anything resembling anarchic intemperance.[8] Certainly, if they are to be autonomous

    3. Foucault, "What Is Enlightenment," 50.

    4. Kant, "What Is Enlightenment?," 3.

    5. Kant, "What Is Enlightenment?," 4.

    6. Foucault, "What Is Enlightenment," 38: "Kant in fact describes Enlightenment as the moment when humanity is going to put its own reason to use, without subjecting itself to any authority; now it is precisely at this moment that the critique is necessary, since its role is that of defining the conditions under which the use of reason is legitimate in order to determine what can be known, what must be done, and what may be hoped. Illegitimate uses of reason are what give rise to dogmatism and heteronomy, along with illusion; on the other hand, it is when the legitimate use of reason has been clearly defined in its principles that its autonomy can be assured. The critique is, in a sense, the handbook of reason that has grown up in Enlightenment; and, conversely, the Enlightenment is the age of the critique." It should also be noted that Kant explicitly contrasts "mankind" (Menschen) and the "fair sex" (schöne Geschlecht), i.e., the former is not presumed by Kant to be a generic term (3).

    7. Kant, "What Is Enlightenment?," 4: "Whoever throws . . . off [the fetters of an everlasting immaturity] makes only an uncertain leap over the narrowest ditch because he is not accustomed to that kind of free motion." One thinks, of course, of Lessing and of Kierkegaard, even if their ditch is considerably more ugly and broad.

    8. Kant, "What Is Enlightenment?," 3: "It is so easy not to be of age. If I have a book which understands for me, a pastor who has a conscience for me, a physician who decides my diet, and so forth, I need not trouble myself. I need not think, if I can only pay—others will readily undertake the irksome work for me." Cf. Foucault, "What Is Enlightenment," 36–38: "Kant in fact describes Enlightenment as the moment when humanity is going to put its own reason to use, without subjecting itself to any authority; now it is precisely at this moment that the critique is necessary, since its role is that of defining the conditions under which the use of reason is legitimate in order to determine what can be known, what must be done, and what may be hoped. Illegitimate uses of reason are what give rise to dogmatism and heteronomy, along with illusion; on the other hand, it is when the legitimate use of reason has been clearly defined in its principles that its autonomy can be assured. The critique is, in a sense, the handbook of reason that has grown up in Enlightenment; and, conversely, the Enlightenment is the age of the critique." Kant, "What Is Enlightenment?" 9: "this is the age of enlightenment, or the century of [Friedrich II]."

in any authentic sense of the term, their circumspective *critiques* of judgments, assumptions, procedures, conventions, and dogmas are not to be restricted—i.e., so long as they assiduously maintain the duties of their stations in life, e.g., as soldiers or taxpayers or clergymen.[9] Just as a lieutenant must obey his orders, even if he later publicly critiques them,[10] a clergyman must submit to the *dogmas* of the church to which he has pledged service, even though he, as a scholar, remains free all the while to publish reasonable arguments against them or in favor of alternatives. If he becomes convinced that what his church teaches is "contradictory to *inner* religion," he is duty-bound to resign his post.[11] The duties of his particular station in life are "private," Kant says, and there he lacks liberty. However, as a thinker, he is also a citizen of the wider world. Here is his "public" life; here each man is free to *think* and to *publish* what he thinks, even though he is not free simply to *act* on it.[12]

Foucault finds the fascination of Kant's essay to lie not in its challenging, its daring, us to throw off our "self-incurred tutelage."[13] The Age is loud with recruitment officers for "reason."[14] What fascinates in this text, he maintains, is the *manner* by which it makes its call; in the *way* it approaches the *time* one is to shake off one's childhood. That time, Kant says, is "*today*."[15] Kant's *today* is not a box on a calendar or the representation of an era in a succession of eras. It is an "*attitude*," "a *mode* of *relating* to

---

9. Kant, "What Is Enlightenment?," 5–6: "Many affairs which are conducted in the interest of the community require a certain mechanism through which some members of the community must passively conduct themselves with an artificial unanimity, so that the government may direct them to public ends. Here argument is certainly not allowed—one must obey."

10. Kant, "What Is Enlightenment?," 5: "Thus it would be *ruinous* for an *officer in service* to debate about the suitability of a *command* given to him by his *superior*; he *must obey*. But the right to make *remarks* on errors in the military service and to lay them before the public for *judgment* cannot equitably be refused him as a *scholar*." Italics added.

11. Kant, "What Is Enlightenment?," 6.

12. Kant, "What Is Enlightenment?," 4–7, 10: "A greater degree of civil freedom appears advantageous to the freedom of mind of the people, and yet it places inescapable limitations upon it; a lower degree of civil freedom, on the contrary, provides the mind with room for each man to extend himself to his full capacity.... [This] gradually works back upon the character of the people, who thereby gradually become capable of managing freedom; finally, it affects the principles of government, which finds it to its advantage to treat men, who are now more than machines, in accordance with their dignity."

13. Kant, "What Is Enlightenment?," 3. The German phrase is "aus seiner selbst verschuldeten Unmündigkeit."

14. Typically to a monolithic "reason," not otherwise qualified.

15. Foucault, "What Is Enlightenment," 38; italics added.

contemporary reality ... [indeed] a *way* of thinking *and* feeling." It has force and specificity, i.e., it is "a voluntary *choice* . . . a way, too, of *acting* and *behaving*" "by *certain people*." And "at one and the same time [it, first] marks a relation of *belonging* and [second] presents itself as a *task*." It is thus from the first a *battle* against "attitudes of 'countermodernity,'" ones that would bar the gates to freedom.[16]

To clarify Kant's vision, Foucault draws attention to the work of the nineteenth-century poet, Charles Baudelaire. Baudelaire attends in a paradigmatically modern fashion to the *temporary*, the *passage* of time, the *transient* moment that appears and then *disappears*, that *passes*. However, he neither glories nor despairs in the ephemeral. Indeed, there is something in what passes that does not pass: for Baudelaire, "being modern . . . lies in . . . recapturing something eternal that is not beyond the present instant, nor behind it, but within it." Modernity is as such an agonistic *attitude*—of boldness, of strength, indeed of "heroism"—before "the fleeting present."[17] "We are each of us celebrating some funeral," Baudelaire writes, Foucault reminds us. Modernity is "the will to *'heroize'* the present" precisely in the face of *death*![18] The modern man wills not to close the devouring jaws of time, but rather to *seize* out of them a *substantial* now—not to settle for appearance—but to pierce the façade of the moment that trembles before his gaze, in order to lay hold of its soul. "Baudelairean modernity is an exercise in which extreme attention to what is real is confronted with the practice of a liberty that simultaneously respects this reality and violates it."[19] To grasp the truth that waits in the "today" of ephemeral time, the modern man cannot remain as he is and has been; he must break out of his suffocating cocoon, rising to his full stature, assert himself, not as he was and is, but as he *can* become—i.e., if only he let his native power to create himself erupt.[20] As for Kant, who shouts for the autonomy of the *scholar*, so also for Baudelaire, who shouts for the autonomy of the *artist*, such creativity does not set its sights on "the body politic," but on something nobler, on the man himself—the man who would be autonomous—in his "permanent critique of our historical era."[21]

16. Foucault, "What Is Enlightenment," 39; italics added.
17. Foucault, "What Is Enlightenment," 39; italics added.
18. Foucault, "What Is Enlightenment," 39–40; italics added.
19. Foucault, "What Is Enlightenment," 41.
20. Foucault, "What Is Enlightenment," 42: "Modern man, for Baudelaire, is not the man who goes off to discover himself, his secrets and his hidden truth; he is the man who tries to invent himself. This modernity does not 'liberate man in his own being'; it compels him to face the task of producing himself."
21. Foucault, "What Is Enlightenment," 42.

Foucault is here anything but nostalgic. He does not long for a return to the eighteenth or nineteenth century; he does not propose that we take up Enlightenment doctrines anew. That, too, would be a surrendering to *dogmatism*, "simplistic and authoritarian." Yet he does call for a "permanent critique of ourselves" in the manner of Enlightenment, of modernity; not one, however, that looks for an elusive "essential kernel," say, "of rationality," or, to use Descartes's metaphor, an immovably solid rock upon which to build. Rather our task—in *our* "today"—Foucault says, is to keep moving, to inquire *historically* into "what is not or is no longer indispensable for the constitution of ourselves as *autonomous subjects*," i.e., to follow "a principle of a critique and a permanent *creation of ourselves in our autonomy*."[22] Unlike Kant, who would not counsel citizens to tamper with the duties of their assigned stations, Foucault looks hard for possibilities for the "transgression" of any constraint that is "singular, contingent, and . . . arbitrary," looking indeed for "the possibility of no longer being, doing, or thinking what we are, do, and think." That is, Foucault "is seeking to give new impetus . . . to the undefined work of freedom"[23]—concretely, on the ground of the "contemporary reality" that we living human beings face, not some abstract, ethereal, and hitherto always mortally dangerous "global or radical" "project."[24] Certainly, this inquiry and experimentation in the transgression of historical limits will never be "complete and definitive," it will always be "limited and determined";[25] "we are always in a position of beginning again." But without an incisive, albeit tentative, historical critique of the ways we have been constituted as "subjects of . . . knowledge . . . [,] power relations . . . [, and] actions," we are left with the *intensification* of those patterns that man and supply the containment forces that would keep us locked down and cut off from any "possibility of going beyond them."[26]

TWO

At Max Yasgur's dairy farm, in White Lake, New York, on August 15, 1969, the first of what was advertised as "3 Days of Peace and Music," the

22. Foucault, "What Is Enlightenment," 43–44. Foucault is adamant that what he is pointing toward is not to be confused with humanism. Italics added.

23. Foucault, "What Is Enlightenment," 45–46.

24. Foucault, "What Is Enlightenment," 46, 47: "I shall thus characterize the philosophical ethos appropriate to the critical ontology of ourselves as a historico-practical test of the limits that we may go beyond, and thus as work carried out by ourselves upon ourselves as free beings."

25. Foucault, "What Is Enlightenment," 47.

26. Foucault, "What Is Enlightenment," 49.

Woodstock Music & Art Fair opened. The unexpected volume of traffic it generated utterly overwhelmed every route to its rural venue. Its first act, guitarist and singer Richie Havens, a descendant of Caribbean African slaves and of the Blackfoot people of the northern American Great Plains, was on site, on time.[27]

> As the festival's first performer, he held the crowd for nearly three hours. In part, Havens was told to continue playing, because many artists scheduled to perform after him were delayed in reaching the festival location with highways at a virtual standstill. He was called back for several encores. Having run out of tunes, he improvised a song based on the old spiritual "Motherless Child" that became "Freedom."[28]

Neither of these songs, neither the spiritual nor its impromptu memorial, was formally composed. They rather *happened*, the way contingent events under pressure happen, the second an echo of the first, the first a lament from the strangled throats of slaves in the antebellum American Southeast, slaves ripped from their mothers' breasts, from their lovers' arms, from their sisters' sides, from their homes—and sold.

> 1—O, sometimes I feel like a motherless child!
> Sometimes I feel like a motherless child!
> O, Lord!
> Sometimes I feel like a motherless child!
> Den I git down on my knees and pray, pray!
> Git down on my knees and pray!

The lament continues, calling out one deprivation after another:

> O, I wonder where my mother's done gone . . . [and]
> 2—O, sometimes I feel like I'd never been borned . . . [and]
> O, I wonder where my baby's done gone . . . [and]
> 3—O, sometimes I feel like I'm a long ways from home . . . [and]
> I wonder where my sister's done gone . . . [and]
> 4—Sometimes I feel like a home-e-less child . . . [and]
> I wonder where de preacher done gone . . . .

Each time voices call out, not to the God of the auction block and the whip, but to the God who heard and hears the cries of slaves, in the brickyards of Egypt, on the plantations of Atlanta, and—we might add—in the sweatshops and brothels of LA

---

27. Siegel, "Richie Havens."
28. "Richie Havens." The punctuation has been slightly altered.

Den I git down on my knees and pray, pray!
Git down on my knees and pray!²⁹

Richie Havens's improvisational "Freedom" draws from the first and third verses of this song. It does not explicitly recall kneeling or spell out the word "Lord," but it laments. It is perhaps the extravagant repetition of the word "freedom"—shouted eight and then ten times in a row—that carries it most dramatically into conversation with the allusions of "Motherless Child," especially to the opening chapters of Exodus. Its even more abundant repetition of the word—"yeah"—constitutes its heart pounding "Amen!" Even the poetically awkward, "I've got a telephone in my bosom / And I can call him up from my heart," yearns for the beloved who have been ripped away—"a long, long, long way."³⁰ In the footage of his performance featured in the documentary *Woodstock*³¹ the song is shown to end as Richie Havens, drenched in sweat, exhaustedly dances off the stage, all the while strumming his guitar with determined, rhythmic energy. The final lyrics, a call and often inaudible response, speak concretely to the ones toward whom *this* freedom yearns: "When I need my brother, brother / When I need my father, father / Hey, mother, mother / Hey, sister, yeah / When I need my brother, brother / Hey, mother, mother, mother / Hey, yeah, yeah, yeah, yeah, yeah-yeah-yeah-yeah-yeah."

This freedom, the freedom of these two impassioned cries—neither of which was planned or formally composed, neither of which is agonistic, heroic, self-conscious, or plausibly seditious—*this* freedom differs from the freedom of the enlightened modern man of European reason. It does indeed revolt against the world order as it stands, the world order that—on the way to the auction block—would assign an exchange value to children, children who are about to be torn, root and branch, from their mothers and fathers. But it is not the freedom of one who would extrapolate a future from a dissected and monetized past and present. It is not the freedom of an aloof observer, a free agent, an analyst, a social engineer, a hacker, or a mole deeply embedded within the official channels of approved *quid pro quo*. It is not the freedom of the well heeled,³² the freedom to leverage investment opportunities, to exploit weak links, kinks in armor, soft underbellies, cracks in walls, signs of encroaching obsolescence, of a weakening grip, of a warder's inattention, of an unlocked gate, of a sheltered path, of a new day for autonomy. It is the freedom, rather, that *sings* . . . apocalypses,

29. Barton, *Old Plantation Hymns*, 18.
30. Cf. Morrison, *Beloved*.
31. Wadleigh, dir., *Woodstock*.
32. Or well healed.

that sways to the music of apocalypses, that imagines this fractured world through apocalypses, that does the sacramental work of apocalypses (Heb 11:1; 12:1-2). It is the freedom that would—without getting even, without shedding blood, without demolition professionals, and without the lawyers of thermodynamics—bring down the walls that enforce border policy and quarantine the outsider.

THREE

The *Oxford English Dictionary* surprises no one, when it defines "dogma, *n*." as "An opinion, a belief; [specifically] a tenet or doctrine authoritatively laid down, [especially] by a church or sect. Also: an imperious or arrogant declaration of opinion."[33] And this, our contemporary usage, does not significantly deviate from the formal, public trajectory of the word since the time Caesars and high priests commanded the poor of Galilee to be taxed. In the ancient Hellenophone world, though *dogma* often signified what "seems right or reasonable, . . . [especially] of philosophical doctrines,"[34] "[u]sually the emphasis [in the extant texts from that time] lies on the fact of 'publishing a decree,' i.e., [an] 'official ordinance or edict': of the king, . . . of the emperor, . . . [or] of the senate. . . . [In Philo and Josephus] Torah becomes a system comparable with the *dogmata* of philosophy."[35]

Seated thus in a tradition of the great and powerful whose interdiction the small and weak know as threat and injury, "dogma" would not likely stand out favorably to one whose knee would bend only to a disclosing God, a God who breaks into an otherwise colonized, subjugated world, a God who sets captives free, who transgresses boundaries, who is pleased to dwell in the dis-integrated body of Jesus. It is, therefore, not unexpected that *dogma* fails to be seen in a favorable light in two Pauline epistles. Colossians 2:13-15: "And when you were dead in trespasses and the uncircumcision of your flesh, God made you alive together with [Christ], when he forgave us all our trespasses, erasing the record that stood against us with its legal demands [*dogmasin*]. He set this aside, nailing it to the cross. He disarmed the rulers and authorities and made a public example of them, triumphing over them in it." Ephesians 2:14-16: "For he is our peace; in his flesh he has made

---

33. *Oxford English Dictionary*, s.v. "dogma," https://doi.org/10.1093/OED/1068414712.

34. *Greek-English Lexicon*, Liddell et al. (Oxford: Clarendon, 1996), s.v. "dogma," 441.

35. Further: "In the writings of the post-apostolic fathers the word comes to be applied to the teachings and prescriptions of Jesus." *Theological Dictionary of the New Testament* vol. 2, edited by Gerhard Kittel, translated by Geoffrey Bromiley (Grand Rapids, Eerdmans, 1964), s.v. "dogma, dogmatizō," 230-31).

both groups into one and has broken down the dividing wall, that is, the hostility between us. He has abolished the law with its commandments and ordinances [*dogmasin*], that he might create in himself one new humanity in place of the two, thus making peace, and might reconcile both groups to God in one body through the cross, thus putting to death that hostility through it." In these two passages, then, dogmas are said to be "nailed to the cross" and "abolished . . . through the cross." These, to be more specific, are dogmas that condemn us, that divide us from and set us against one another. Yet do dogmas function otherwise? Is it not their only function to set up boundaries that we are not to transgress? What in any dogma might incline otherwise? Could a dogma do anything other than set up a "dividing wall"? Is it possible to imagine a dogma otherwise than as a conclusion?

Luke-Acts is the only other place in the New Testament where the term is used. Luke 2:1 and Acts 17:7 use it to speak of the *decrees* of Caesar. The latter sets the activity of the church—"people who have been turning the world upside down"—in direct opposition to the decrees [*dogmatōn*] of the emperor," viz., by their obeisance to Jesus rather than to him. Here, too, dogmas seize and crush us, though this time in Rome's fist, not Jerusalem's. However, Acts 16:4, the only other place in the New Testament the word is used, is perhaps more ambiguous: "As [Paul and Timothy] went from town to town, they delivered to them for observance the decisions [*dogmata*] that had been reached by the apostles and elders who were in Jerusalem." The question here is whether this usage of *dogmata* resonates or clashes with its *imperial* usage. Does Luke-Acts here imagine walls buttressed or breached? Inasmuch as the *dogmata* of the apostles and elders had everything to do with yielding to the extraordinary work of the Holy Spirit among gentiles—with releasing them from any requirement of circumcision or other adherence to "the law of Moses" (Acts 15:5), with drawing them, no longer as a threat and adversary, into the widening history of Israel—metaphors of control or exclusion or confinement hardly seem apt.[36] These apostolic *dogmata* seem rather hastily cut avenues for the free acknowledgement of the prodigious influx of the Spirit and, by the Spirit, of those, now intermingling, who otherwise would simply recoil from or lay into each other.

A dogma that would set out to regulate the Holy Spirit of Luke-Acts would be a kind of blasphemy (Luke 12:10–12), a kind of falsehood (Acts 5:1–10), a kind of malign, strategic buyout plan (Acts 8:17–19), in any case a vain evasion of the Spirit. One wonders how anyone, however swift, might

---

36. "For it has seemed good to the Holy Spirit and to us to impose on you no further burden than these essentials: abstain from what has been sacrificed to idols and from blood and from what is strangled and from fornication" (Acts 15:28–29). (Scholars debate whether *all* of these prohibitions refer to common practices of Hellenistic idolatry.)

go about evading the Spirit *without* vanity. You "may as well try and catch the wind."[37] But what about the word "dogma" would suggest an open—rather than a closed—hand? Is it even logically possible to think and speak of a *dogma* of the *Holy Spirit*—even of a dogma so seemingly unrestrained as that the Holy Spirit is to be "worshiped and glorified [*sumproskunoumenon kai sundoxazomenon*] together with the Father and the Son," as it is put in the creed of the First Council of Constantinople—the most overtly pneumatological of the ecumenical symbols?

FOUR

In 1963, in his seventieth year, two decades prior to Foucault's delivering "What is Enlightenment?" Georges Florovsky, while professor at Harvard Divinity School, far from his native Odessa, published an essay in the *Greek Orthodox Theological Review* that examined, among other things, the *manner* of emergence of the dogma of the deity of the Holy Spirit in the fourth century, i.e., on the way to the First Council of Constantinople (381), chiefly by adding a few lines to the Nicene supplementation, half a century earlier, of long-standing baptismal credos.[38] Florovsky draws attention to the way Basil of Caesarea, in his treatise, *On the Holy Spirit*, distinguishes between *kērygma* and *dogma*. The only significant difference between the terms, for Basil, is that *kērygma*, quite often translated into English as "proclamation," is "publicized," while *dogma* is "unwritten" and "silent." "This was a tradition that was handed down to neophytes in mystery and had to be kept in silence."[39] Dogmas, Basil maintains, are sacramental, liturgical, ecclesial, pneumatological; they are thus mysteries, by definition,[40] never captured

37. Donovan, "Catch the Wind."

38. Meyendorff, "Light from the East?," 348: "At the time of the Council of Chalcedon (451) the predominant Eastern opinion was that the common baptismal creed adopted at Nicea (325) and Constantinople (381) was sufficient guarantee against recurring heresies.... [Dogmas] aim... not to exhaust the truth or freeze the teachings of the church into verbal formulae or systems."

39. Florovsky, "Function of Tradition," 111. Basil, *On the Holy Spirit*, 46-47 [26]: "What makes us Christians? 'Our faith,' everyone would answer. How are we saved? Obviously through the regenerating grace of baptism. How else could we be? We are confirmed in our understanding that salvation comes through Father, Son, and Holy Spirit. This would surely be grounds for great sorrow; if we now reject what we accepted at baptism.... If baptism is the beginning of my life, and the day of my regeneration is the first of days, it is obvious that the words spoken when I received the grace of adoption are more honorable than any spoken since.... May I pass from this life to the Lord with this confession on my lips."

40. The Greek word translated into Latin as "*sacramentum*" and into English as "sacrament" is "*mysterion*."

in the *ipsissima verba*, say, of Scripture or of creed, i.e., in the abstract. No matter how honored by time, decree, saint, and martyr, words in themselves, on the page in a closed book or repeated by rote, do not carry with them the way of life in which they are to do their work. That is, dogmas are to be understood as they are lived.⁴¹

This is not new with Basil; already Irenaeus maintained that Scripture is alive only as it lives in a:

> "living tradition" entrusted as a new breath of life, just as breath was bestowed on the first man. . . . The use of tradition in the ancient church can be adequately understood only in the context of . . . actual use. . . . The Word was kept alive in the church. It was reflected in her life and structure. Faith and life were [understood to be] organically intertwined. . . . "Liturgy," in the wide and comprehensive sense of the word, was the first and initial layer in the tradition of the church, and the argument from the *lex orandi* (rule of worship) was persistently used in discussion already by the end of the second century.⁴²

What will have been said and written and memorized will not have captured the sacramental act of testimony, of *saying*. Thus to *testify*, as a *martyr* might—e.g., that the Holy Spirit is to be worshipped and glorified together with the Father and the Son—is by the breath of the Spirit in and with whom the liturgical utterance of the symbol of Constantinople *prays* the baptized will always be gifted—by God's good pleasure, as an act of life, in the anointing with oil.⁴³

---

41. Basil, *On the Holy Spirit*, 98–101 [66]: "Concerning the teachings of the Church, whether publicly proclaimed (*kerygma*) or reserved to members of the household of faith (*dogmata*), we have received some from written sources, while others have been given to us secretly, through apostolic tradition. Both sources have equal force in true religion. If we attacked unwritten customs . . . we would reduce the Gospel teachings to bare words. . . . [Our fathers] had learned their lesson well; reverence for the mysteries is best encouraged by silence. The uninitiated were not even allowed to be present at the mysteries; how could you expect these teachings to be paraded about in public documents. . . . Dogma is one thing, kerygma another; the first is observed in silence, while the latter is proclaimed to the world. . . . We all stand on the day of resurrection to remind ourselves of the graces we have been given: not only because we have been raised with Christ . . . , but also because Sunday seems to be an image of the age to come . . . to follow the present age: a day without sunset, nightfall, or successor, an age which does not grow old or come to an end. . . . During this time [of standing] . . . our minds are made to focus on the future instead of the present."

42. Florovsky, "Function of Tradition," 102–3, 107, 108.

43. Basil of Caesarea, *Epistolae* 189.3, cited by Florovsky, "Function of Tradition," 112: "For the judge of the words ought to start with the same preparation as the author. . . . And I see that in the utterance of the Spirit it is also impossible for everyone

Protestants, Enlightenment deists, rationalists, naturalists, and "new atheists" are not the only ones who shake their heads before the phrase, "secret tradition." It does not take a cynic to regard it as an ace up the sleeve of an authorized ecclesiastical enforcer, who is ready to slap it on the table when the stakes are high enough. And yet a secret that remains secret, a mystery that remains mystery, a breath that will not be held without asphyxia, a speaking that does not settle into a line item on the transcript of a private business meeting of a closed fraternal society, will never lie in wait up anyone's sleeve or win a bet. It will rather always slip through the grasping fingers of those with plans and schemes, as Ananias, Sapphira, the Lucan Pharisees, and Simon the Magician discovered.[44] This is not to say that the theologian must cease teaching, say, the symbols of the church. The theologian is not to cease gesturing toward them and with them: *telling, showing, pointing, pointing out*. It *is* to say that theologians are expected to know how to keep a secret—or not this, but rather to understand that there is a secret that they cannot keep . . . or tell. Their task in fact *is* to gesture, to tell, to show, as often and in as many ways as an ephemeral occasion opens up, that there is a secret that they cannot by any means keep or tell. From Paris, where he lived in exile, studied, and taught, Russian Orthodox theologian, Vladimir Lossky, at the chronological midpoint between his birth in 1903 and Foucault's Berkeley lecture, wrote of all theological discourse: "The dogma of the Trinity is a cross for human ways of thought. The apophatic ascent is a mounting of Calvary."[45]

FIVE

In 2010, six years after passing fruitfully through and beyond her PhD program at Atlanta's Candler School of Theology, Shelly Rambo, then assistant professor in the Cradle of Liberty at Boston University, published *Spirit and*

---

to undertake the scrutiny of His word; rather, it is possible only for them who have the Spirit that grants the discernment."

44. See Meyendorff, "Light from the East?" 347–48.

45. Lossky, *Mystical Theology*, 66. Lossky would say this about any dogma. Cf. 42: "All that we have said about apophaticism may be summed up in a few words. . . . It is not a branch of theology, a chapter, or an inevitable introduction on the incomprehensibility of God from which one passes unruffled to a doctrinal exposition in the usual terminology of human reason and philosophy in general. Apophaticism teaches us to see above all a negative meaning in the dogmas of the Church: it forbids us to follow natural ways of thought and to form concepts which would usurp the place of spiritual realities. For Christianity is not a philosophical school for speculating about abstract concepts, but is essentially a communion with the living God."

Trauma: A Theology of Remaining. It is, among other things, a pneumatology of Holy Saturday, that *temporally* twilit, restlessly silent, bracketed space between Good Friday and Easter Sunday, that day when the *promise* of a light not yet seen plays unheard on a pitch black needle's point singularity.[46] It is the day that halts the ordinarily relentless, linear progression from early Friday through late Sunday. It is the day that will not concede, when the living won't stay alive and the dead won't stay dead. It is the day of tarrying, abiding, the day of "remaining."[47] "On the one side, there is death in God-forsakenness; on the other, there is eternal life. To get from one side to the other, we need a means of crossing. But Holy Saturday declares the impossibility of bridging the two."[48] The gospel is above all the tale of the embrace of the Father and the Son, but Holy Saturday is "the point at which . . . the love between Father and Son . . . is most fragile."[49] Yet how—when the body of the Son, newly pried from the rough hewn cross, lies cold, limp, and dead—does their embrace not break, how is it not reduced to a Pietà with God the Father in the role of Mary? By what inarticulable miracle, by what defiance of the sweep of the second hand, could the Holy Spirit hover over the face of *these* chaotic waters—not *bridging* the wide chasm between them, but rather—without mechanics—*bearing witness*?[50]

However, there is no *direct, unambiguous* witness to what is said to have transpired in, with, and under this peasant body—crucified, dead, and buried. Even on Easter Sunday, according to John's resurrection narrative, Mary of Magdala struggled both to see and to understand, as she sat before the empty tomb in the hour just before dawn. She knew Jesus at once, not at first, but unquestionably after he called her name—though at no time did she reach out, as she could have, and touch him, she would testify (John

---

46. Cf. Sir 13:1. Rambo, *Spirit and Trauma*, 56 (quoting Balthasar): "What is this light glimmer that wavers and begins to take form in the endless void? It has neither content nor contour. A nameless thing, more solitary than God, it emerges out of pure emptiness. It is no one. It is anterior to everything. Is it the beginning? It is small and undefined as a drop. Perhaps it is water. But it does not flow. It is not water. It is thicker, more opaque, more viscous than water. It is also not blood, for blood is red, blood is alive, blood has a loud human speech. This is neither water nor blood. It is older than both, a chaotic drop."

47. This is the word she uses as she translates the Greek, *menein*, a word to which "remain" is connected etymologically. "Remain" is also the language of trauma and "survival." See Rambo, *Spirit and Trauma*, 102.

48. Rambo, *Spirit and Trauma*, 74. She is drawing here in particular from the work of Hans Urs von Balthasar and Adrienne von Speyr.

49. Rambo, *Spirit and Trauma*, 71.

50. Rambo, *Spirit and Trauma*, 79. For the inadequacy of the metaphor of a bridge, see Rambo, *Spirit and Trauma*, 76–77.

20:16–17). Distance, darkness, tears, disorientation, the failure of speech, ambiguities of many kinds, would call into question her reliability as a witness either for the prosecution or for the defense.[51] Her testimony would crumble under cross-examination. The events of these days don't become useful or persuasive discourse, convincing to a dispassionate mind. Indeed, they mark "life in ways that cannot be cognitively grasped."[52]

Jesus had earlier told his disciples, as he bid them farewell, that they were to remain in him, in his love. And he told them that, even with his departure, he would not leave them alone, but would send another *paraclete* to them, one who would come alongside them, one who would dwell in them, *remain* in them, witness to him, as *they* became witnesses. "As witnesses, [however, they] experience the dismantling of sight, sound, and touch in the wake of the passion; it is through, rather than despite, these obstructions that they witness to life where life is not recognizable as such."[53]

> In the biblical accounts . . . [Spirit] signals God's presence in and with creation. . . . Jesus gives up his spirit, his breath, on the cross. . . . But the . . . breath of death . . . becomes the breath of witness to what remains . . . as a testimony to the inextinguishable remainder of divine love. This breath powers a testimony to what is unknown, unaccounted for . . . unsaid, unspoken, and inaccessible through language . . . [a testimony] that the Pauline text describes through the word "prayer." . . . In the middle, love is reworked as a . . . love that remains, that persists, that survives . . . a death.[54]

Rambo writes always mindful of those who suffer trauma, the trauma of war, of torture, of rape, of earthquake and hurricane, the trauma that breaks the body and the cognitive processes by which memory and hope, inside and outside, you and I meet and interplay, the trauma that breaks time and language. Holy Saturday speaks in particular to the traumatized, she maintains, those who do not have to be told that there is a blow that severs the body from its people, who do not have to be told that there is a dark past that will not stay in the past, who do not have to be told that there are words that won't be spoken, who do not have to be told that there is a trust, bound in chains, that in stirring awakens headless giants who drag it by its bonds irresistibly back into the shadows.[55] "Trauma tells us that

51. Rambo, *Spirit and Trauma*, 90.
52. Rambo, *Spirit and Trauma*, 97.
53. Rambo, *Spirit and Trauma*, 109.
54. Rambo, *Spirit and Trauma*, 117, 118, 120, 137.
55. Rambo, *Spirit and Trauma*, 19–21.

death returns, haunting the life that follows. In trauma, 'death' persists in life."[56] She remembers the traumatized as she remembers the Spirit of Holy Saturday and those who by the Spirit, as witnesses, remain in the darkness.

> Spirit is the breath that cannot be cut off, that does not cease . . . that . . . is handed over into the depths, [where] there are middle-day witnesses who receive that breath. . . . The middle space is the descent into hell, the furthest reaches from all sources of life. . . . The trackless trek of the Son in hell was not active and victorious. The trickle of love . . . was an image of . . . love's persistence. . . . This transformation, this redemption . . . , is not about deliverance from the depths but, instead, about a way of being in the depths, a practice of witnessing that senses life arising amid what remains. . . . Perhaps the divine story is neither a tragic one nor a triumphant one but, in fact, . . . the story of love that survives.[57]

SIX

Long, long before any of us uttered the first semblance of a vowel or consonant or found rhythm in her belly and throat, on her tongue and lips, through her hands and feet, her shoulders and her hips, long before she named the shadow marks of the lightning bolts released by intracranial storms to dance fleetingly across one after another ugly broad synaptic ditch, language held her, held me, held you, warmed and carried us, startled and comforted us, initiated us into deep pre-articulate ancestral secrets, softly and solemnly promising us times and places yet to come. We have always dwelt in language. It is our abode, our extended household, our neighborhood, our village, our tribe, our world—it is our home. It is the cosmos out of chaos—and it surveils us, keeps us, and guards us; polices us. It would have us carry on in a straight line or make an abrupt change of course.

It does so, certainly, in manifold ways. It does not need to generate, e.g., a special vocabulary in order to keep us safe and in place or to convince us that we are moving boldly out into uncharted territory. Familiar, ordinary, discourse works just fine. The most unequivocally orthodox identity markers—such as the phrase, "I am orthodox," and the performances that are expected to accompany it—may work *upheaval*; the most unequivocally heretical ones—such as "I am heretical," and *its* expected performances—may

---

56. Rambo, *Spirit and Trauma*, 156.
57. Rambo, *Spirit and Trauma*, 171–72.

work *retrenchment*—the former shape-shifting into the improvised explosive devices of insurgency, the latter into the patented riot gear, rubber bullets, and tear gas of homeland security. The turn may occur subtly. It may be enough to narrow the eyes, to set the jaw, and to add a certain cadence and intonation, perhaps fashionably accessorizing frightened flesh with the cloak of world-weary irony and derision.

What we say and what we write are never simply as they seem. Indeed, there may not be an utterance, no matter how apparently blandly benign, that is not Janus-faced, that may not from time to time (and perhaps every time) signify up to 180 degrees of variance from its pocket dictionary angle of signification.

Still, words do not come and go arbitrarily; they tend, they lean; they move with mass, velocity, and spin, their momentum transposed to other words with which they collide in discursive play. What a word will have done in particular, as it moves toward and into other words, marking them, being marked by them, is not always easily ascertained in advance. "The right word" is sometimes hard to find and not uncommonly, with its forthcoming, is acknowledged to be *right* less by adjudication from a lonely distance than by *listening*, memorially, for echoes and sound signatures—up close, intently, perhaps among passionately thoughtful friends.[58]

Words configure variously, as they are used. There are complex patterns of family resemblance,[59] but there are also the traces of their near and more remote ancestry, however illegitimate. (Even bastard words have ancestry.) As we hear tales of the historic journeys of familiar words, there may be moments when we, as if in talk therapy, are granted insight into what has been subtly at work in them all along. Thus, despite its contradiction to the ideal of independence and autonomy, there is something right about the day of discovery that the word "free" and the word "friend" have a common forebear.[60] Of course, a word's etymology is by no means always significantly at play in its usage, any more than the patterns of the childhood of one's great grandmother, a slave, say, in antebellum Atlanta or the British West Indies, significantly shapes one's way of reacting to the derisive asides of a colleague during

---

58. Wittgenstein, *Philosophical Investigations*, 31–32 [66]: "Consider for example the proceedings that we call 'games.' . . . What is common to them all?—Don't say: 'There *must* be something common, or they would not be called "games"'—but *look and see* whether there is anything common to all.—For if you look at them you will not see something that is common to *all*, but similarities, relationships, and a whole series of them at that. To repeat: don't think, but look! . . . And the result of this examination is: we see a complicated network of similarities overlapping and criss-crossing: sometimes overall similarities, sometimes similarities of detail.").

59. Wittgenstein, *Philosophical Investigations*, 32 [67].

60. See *Oxford English Dictionary*, s.vv. "free, *adj.*, *n.*, and *adv.*" and "friend, *n.* and *adj.*"

a professional meeting. However, there are times—and times between the times—when the past will not stay in the past, times when what we would have sworn was dead and gone rises to walk among the living, not as a ghost or some other cold apparition, but as a warm, living word.

Storytelling and songwriting, composing textbooks and sonnets or free verse, but also smiling and gesturing with one's hand, and, of course, the keying of theological prose into an electronic memory are all at the mercy of discourse. Even the theologian who would dare to speak of what has no place in any system of signifiers does so at the mercy of discourse, even if on occasion and after the fact its merchants would swear that they had been swindled. Still, at the risk of the appearance of ingratitude, when without calculative forecast a theologian, the upper limits of whose world have been ruptured from an impossible apocalyptic outside, writes of what cannot be written, writes of an uncanny life that will not be contradicted by death, it is difficult to understand how she might without unfaithfulness turn around and take any "tenet or doctrine" as "authoritatively laid down," especially "by a church," as anything but "an imperious or arrogant declaration of opinion" that denies, after it betrays, one into whom, through a rent sky, the Holy Spirit has descended like a dove.[61] There would in fact be for her no mountain of dogma, of imperial or philosophical or ecclesiastical decree, that would not be cast into the sea—with Pharaoh's army and the mountain upon which stood the temple that barred its doors to strangers and eunuchs. Yet she would also work trusting that the sea is in the end to give up its dead. And she would perhaps also admit that *every* language at the mercy of which she conducts theological work is an often subtle, but no less insidious, system of tenets and doctrines authoritatively laid down by some tribe of signatories. What she might do with tenets and doctrines, with dogmas, whatever their kind, trending or not, would and could rest on no established authorization; for when what is to come *comes* intemperately to make everything new, everything is disestablished—on *that* day, but also *now* by the audacity of a hope at work even in these fragmentary in-between days. Dogmas are to rise, but with all that is dust and ashes, with all that is human and humble and humous, into a glory not their own, a glory that would shine in a pariah's city without sun or temple, without magistrate or jury or executioner, without threat or fear. Even now, so far from sanctuary, such a theologian might look upon the dogmas of her ecclesial household not as authorized decrees, but as hastily written baptismal letters of martyrs witnessing to a coming insurrection.

61. *Oxford English Dictionary*, s.v. "dogma."

If the emperor's old clothes, red or yellow, black or white, are there for all to see after the last scrap of imperious garb has been pealed away from dogma, what kind of nakedness remains? Perhaps something humble—and the origins of dogma are indeed humble, as may be glimpsed already in its primary ancient Greek denotation, "that which seems right or reasonable, opinion or belief." It is a descendant of an even more humble Greek word, *dokeō*, which Plato takes in the *Gorgias* as "merely to seem" and contrasts with *einai*, "to be."[62] From *dokeō* is also derived another and quite similarly ambiguous word *doxa* that, as "mere appearance," is contrasted in Plato, this time in the *Republic*, with *ousia*, a word that is in Aristotle to become *the* marker of "being."[63] Yet *doxa* is also the word used in the Septuagint and the New Testament for "glory," the radiant disclosure of the holiness of Yahweh, a holiness that by Yahweh's good pleasure the creature may enter and with which she or he or it may be gifted, but which none can or may ever claim, own, possess, appropriate. To say "holy," to say "glory," is to speak not of something generic, e.g., a universal divinity, but of the *insubordinate particularity* of *Yahweh*, the one who *chose* Israel, the one who *liberated* Israel, the one who *promised* Israel a future—when Israel was nobody at all. Yahweh's radiant *doxa* is the coming of *that one*, that one who will have always come—*truly* come—to Israel and Israel's legitimate and illegitimate children, as the graceful God they—*we!*—are not and never will be.

If dogma, as Basil maintains, is sacramental, a mystery that remains, a mystery that never settles into the all-purpose public discourse, say, of the marketplace, a mystery that signifies only as its offering is greeted and welcomed, that signifies only as it prays by the breath of the Spirit of holiness, that prays only as a gifted hallowing work, and then, as with all sacramental works, to glorify the Father, the Son, and the Holy Spirit, then it is to be performed in the Spirit through the Son to the Father of doxology. However, any doxological movement out into the Holy Trinity of Holy Saturday is as surely a movement out into this ravaged earth, as leaping into a swollen, raging river is a movement downstream. This glory is an abiding mystery, one that remains *unspeakably* with the lost and the lonely, the poor and the dying, the despoiled and the despised. It is dumb (as a sheep before her shearers); in part because where a body—hands and feet, face and back, belly and brain—is cast down, there is silence. Even though surely universal compassion always has the right thing to say, *here* where universality stands with blood up to its elbows, a *particular* lover would let all eloquence go,

---

62. *Greek-English Lexicon*, Liddell et al. (Oxford: Clarendon, 1996), s.vv. "dogma," 441; "*dokeō*," 441–42.

63. Plato contrasts it with *ousia* this time. *Greek-English Lexicon*, Liddell et al. (Oxford: Clarendon, 1996), s.v. "*doxa*," 444.

deferring to mutilated hearts and souls and minds and strength, to queer sisters and queer brothers who, blank-faced, on hard times, under the lash—in the space between willing and unwilling—have learned to *forget* how to speak. It is here that dogma is to shine, in this darkness. It is to pray, to kneel, to bow its head, blindly exposing its neck to a fatal blow. Dogma is for broken people, survivors whose survival remains uncertain. Dogma is a word unspoken (even when spoken), a word whose breath, released, trailing off, is given to be heard (if heard) as the "nevertheless" of Gethsemane.

As much anxiety as such talk must evoke in the enlightened, a dogma that will not leave the side of glory—a *para-doxa*—works with a kind of freedom that demands neither independence from nor mastery of others, that demands neither a law inscribed upon its own Kantian practical reason nor the satisfying inclusiveness of a Hegelian *an und für sich*, that demands neither construction on a Cartesian solid rock foundation nor deconstruction in a condominium crowded with unraveled yarn. It is a freedom that—without mediating the otherness of the Father, the Son, and the Holy Spirit—calls out, agape—never mediating, but reaching out to embrace one who without being assimilated would nonetheless be my brother, father, mother, or sister. "When I need my brother, brother / When I need my father, father / Hey, mother, mother / Hey, sister, yeah / When I need my brother, brother / Hey, mother, mother, mother / Hey, yeah, yeah, yeah, yeah, yeah-yeah-yeah-yeah-yeah."[64]

The freedom of this uncanny dogma would thus resound with the prayers at play in texts with which ancient Israel traditioned its children: "The Israelites groaned under their slavery, and cried out." The freedom of this dogma is the freedom of a particular hope that remembers that, "Out of slavery their cry for help rose up to God. God heard their groaning, and God remembered his covenant with Abraham, Isaac, and Jacob. God looked upon the Israelites, and God took notice of them" (Exod 2:23–25). It is the freedom that cries out in hope for the coming of a paraclete—the way a farmer during a drought, alone in a dusty field, might raise her face to shout at the sky for a wind bearing dark clouds heavy with rain. It is the freedom that stands up to the coming God before the powers that presume to make and unmake the future. It is the freedom that, standing up, declares, "Thus says the Lord, the God of Israel, 'Let my people go,'" understanding that these powers will not understand why those who remember that they are as insubstantial as dust would ever long to "celebrate a festival to [some deity so unlike any of us—and of all places] in the wilderness" (Exod 5:1; cf. 2).

64. Wadleigh, dir., *Woodstock*.

Bibliography

Abell, Frances, et al. "Do Triangles Play Tricks? Attribution of Mental States to Animated Shapes in Normal and Abnormal Development." *Cognitive Development* 15:1 (2000) 1–16.
Anatolios, Khaled. *Athanasius: The Coherence of Thought*. London: Routledge, 1998.
Aristotle. *Politics*. Translated by Ernest Barker. Oxford: Oxford University Press, 1995.
Athanasius. *Four Discourses Against the Arians*. In vol. 4 of *Nicene and Post-Nicene Fathers*, edited by Philip Schaff and Henry Wace, 303–447. Grand Rapids: Eerdmans, 1971.
Augustine of Hippo. *The Confessions*. Translated by Henry Chadwick. Oxford: Oxford University Press, 1991.
Bangert, Marc, et al. "Shared Networks for Auditory and Motor Processing in Professional Pianists: Evidence from fMRI Conjunction." NeuroImage 30:3 (2006) 917–26.
Barth, Karl. *The Epistle to the Romans*. Translated by Edwyn C. Hoskyns. London: Oxford University Press, 1933.
Barton, William E. *Old Plantation Hymns: A Collection of Hitherto Unpublished Melodies of the Slave and the Freedman, with Historical and Descriptive Notes*. New York: Lamson, Wolffe and Company, 1899.
Basil of Caesarea. *On the Holy Spirit*. Translated by David Anderson. Crestwood, NY: St. Vladimir's Seminary Press, 1980.
———. *On the Human Condition*. Translated by Nonna Verna Harrison. Yonkers, NY: St. Vladimir's Seminary Press, 2005.
———. *On Social Justice*. Translated by C. Paul Schroeder. Yonkers, NY: St. Vladimir's Seminary Press, 2009.
Behr, John. *Irenaeus of Lyons*. Oxford: Oxford University Press, 2013.
Berquist, Jon L. *Controlling Corporeality: The Body and the Household in Ancient Israel*. New Brunswick: Rutgers University Press, 2002.
Berry, Wendell. *The Art of the Commonplace: The Agrarian Essays of Wendell Berry*. Edited by Norman Wirzba. Berkeley: Counterpoint, 2002.
Boyce, Benjamin S. "The Spectacle of Punishment: Cinematic Representations of the Prison-Industrial Complex," MA Thesis, University of Colorado, 2013.
Brengle, Samuel Logan. *Helps to Holiness*. North Carolina: Salvation Army Supplies, 1978.
Brown, Warren S., and Brad D. Strawn. *The Physical Nature of Christian Life: Neuroscience, Psychology and the Church*. Cambridge: Cambridge University Press, 2012.

Brueggemann, Walter. *Theology of the Old Testament*. Minneapolis: Fortress, 1997.
Butler, Judith. "Bodies and Power Revisited." In *Feminism and the Final Foucault*, edited by Dianna Taylor and Karen Vintges, 183–94. Chicago: University of Illinois Press, 2004.
———. *Gender Trouble*. New York: Routledge, 1990.
Butler, Judith, and Athena Athanasiou. *Dispossession: The Performative in the Political*. Cambridge: Polity, 2013.
Calvin, John. *Institutes of the Christian Religion*. Translated by Henry Beveridge. Edinburgh: Calvin Translation Society, 1845.
Calvo-Merino, B., et al. "Action Observation and Acquired Motor Skills: An fMRI Study with Expert Dancers." *Cerebral Cortex* 15 (2005) 1243–49.
Caputo, John D. *The Folly of God: A Theology of the Unconditional*. Salem, OR: Polebridge, 2016.
———. *Hoping against Hope: Confessions of a Postmodern Pilgrim*. Minneapolis: Fortress, 2015.
———. *The Insistence of God: A Theology of Perhaps*. Bloomington: Indiana University Press, 2013.
———. "Undecidability and the Empty Tomb." In *More Radical Hermeneutics: On Not Knowing Who We Are*, 220–48. Bloomington: Indiana University Press, 2000.
———. "The Weakness of God: A Radical Theology of the Cross." In *The Wisdom and Foolishness of God: First Corinthians 1–2 in Theological Exploration*, edited by Christophe Chalamet and Hans-Christoph Askani, 25–79. Minneapolis: Fortress, 2015.
———. *The Weakness of God: A Theology of the Event*. Bloomington: Indiana University Press, 2007.
Castelli, Fulvia, et al. "Movement and Mind: A Functional Imaging Study of Perception and Interpretation of Complex Intentional Movement Patterns." *NeuroImage* 12:3 (2000) 314–25.
Chesterton, G. K. *Collected Works*. Vol. 2. San Francisco: Ignatius, 1987.
Chomsky, Noam. *Chomsky on Miseducation*. Edited by Donaldo Macedo. Lanham, MD: Rowman & Littlefield, 2000.
Clough, David. *On Animals: Systematic Theology*. Vol. 1. Edinburgh: T. & T. Clark, 2012.
Collins, John J. *The Apocalyptic Imagination: An Introduction to Jewish Apocalyptic Literature*. 2nd ed. Grand Rapids: Eerdmans, 1998.
Collins, Paul, and Barry A. Ensign-George, eds. *Denomination: Assessing an Ecclesiological Category*. New York: T. & T. Clark, 2013.
Deane-Drummond, Celia. *Christ and Evolution: Wonder and Wisdom*. Minneapolis: Fortress, 2009.
Dewey, John. *Democracy and Education*. New York: Dover, 2004.
———. *The Early Works, 1882–1898*. Vol. 3. Edited by Jo Ann Boydston. Carbondale: Southern Illinois University Press, 1969.
———. *Experience and Nature*. Chicago: Open Court, 1925.
———. *The Middle Works, 1899–1924*. Vol. 11. Edited by Jo Ann Boydston. Carbondale: Southern Illinois University Press, 1982.
Donovan. "Catch the Wind." Track 2 on *What's Bin Did And What's Bin Hid*. Pye/Hickory, 1965, LP.
Dupré, Louis. *Passage to Modernity: An Essay on the Hermeneutics of Nature and Culture*. New Haven: Yale University Press, 1995.

Eagan, Daniel. "Cool Hand Luke." In *America's Film Legacy: The Authoritative Guide to the Landmark Movies in the National Film Registry*, 627–29. New York: Continuum, 2009.

Edwards, Jonathan. "The Spider Letter." In *A Jonathan Edwards Reader*, edited by John E. Smith et al., 1–8. New Haven: Yale University Press, 1995.

Florovsky, Georges. "The Function of Tradition in the Ancient Church." In *Eastern Orthodox Theology: A Contemporary Reader*, edited by Daniel B. Clendenin, 97–114. Grand Rapids: Baker, 1995.

Francis of Assisi. "Canticle of Brother Sun." In *Francis and Claire: The Complete Works*, translated by Regis J. Armstrong and Ignatius C. Brady, 37–39. New York: Paulist, 1982.

Foucault, Michel. "Of Other Spaces." *Diacritics* 16:1 (1986) 22–27.

———. "Truth and Power: An Interview with Michel Foucault." *Critique of Anthropology* 4:13–14 (1979) 131–37.

———. "What Is Enlightenment." Translated by Catherine Porter. In *The Foucault Reader*, edited by Paul Rabinow, 32–50. New York: Vintage, 1984.

Gallese, Vittorio. "Embodied Simulation Theory: Imagination and Narrative." *Neuropsychoanalysis* 13:2 (2011) 196–200.

Gibbs, Raymond W. *Embodiment and Cognitive Science*. Cambridge: Cambridge University Press, 2005.

Gregory of Nazianzus. "Letters on the Apollinarian Controversy." In *Christology of the Later Fathers*, edited by Edward R. Hardy, 215–32. Philadelphia: Westminster, 1954.

———. "Oration 30". In vol. 7 of *Nicene and Post-Nicene Fathers*, edited by Philip Schaff, 309–17. Grand Rapids: Eerdmans, 1971.

Grillmeier, Aloys. *Christ in Christian Tradition*. London: Mowbrays, 1975.

Haltom, William. "The Laws of God, the Laws of Man: Power, Authority, and Influence in 'Cool Hand Luke.'" *The Legal Studies Forum* 22 (1998) 233–56.

Hammond, Geordan. *John Wesley in America: Restoring Primitive Christianity*. Oxford: OUP, 2014.

Hauerwas, Stanley. *In Good Company: The Church as Polis*. Notre Dame: University of Notre Dame Press, 1995.

———. *Sanctify Them in the Truth: Holiness Exemplified*. Edinburgh: T. & T. Clark, 2016.

Hildegaard of Bingen. *Scivias*. Translated by Mother Columba Hart and Jane Bishop. New York: Paulist, 1990.

Hume, David. *A Treatise on Human Nature*. Oxford: Oxford University Press, 1978.

Irenaeus of Lyons. *Against Heresies*. In vol. 1 of *Ante-Nicene Fathers*, edited by Alexander Roberts et al., 309–567. Peabody, MA: Hendrickson, 1995.

Johnson, Elizabeth. *Ask the Beasts: Darwin and the God of Love*. London: Bloomsbury, 2014.

Jordan, Mark. "The Modernity of Christian Theology or Writing Kierkegaard Again for the First Time." *Modern Theology* 27:3 (2011) 442–51.

Julian of Norwich. *Shewings*. Edited by Georgia Ronan Crampton. Kalamazoo, MI: Western Michigan University, 1994.

Juvenal. *The Sixteen Satires*. Translated by Peter Green. London: Penguin, 1998.

Kant, Immanuel. "What Is Enlightenment?" Translated by Lewis White Beck. In *On History*, edited by Lewis White Beck, 3–10. Indianapolis: Bobbs-Merrill Educational, 1963.

Keen, Craig. *After Crucifixion: The Promise of Theology*. Eugene, OR: Cascade, 2013.

———. "A Glorified Mutilated Body at (Intercessory) Prayer." Unpublished paper.

———. "Homo Precarius: Prayer in the Image and Likeness of God." *Wesleyan Theological Journal* 33:1 (Spring 1998) 128–50.

———. *The Transgression of the Integrity of God: Essays and Addresses*. Edited by Thomas P. Bridges and Nathan R. Kerr. Eugene, OR: Cascade, 2012.

Kelly, J. N. D. *Early Christian Doctrines*. 3rd ed. London: Adam & Charles Black, 1968.

Kenny, Mary. *Irish Independent*. August 23, 2015.

Keysers, Christian. *The Empathic Brain: How the Discovery of Mirror Neurons Changes Our Understanding of Human Nature*. Kentucky: Social Brain, 2011.

Keysers, Christian, and Valeria Gazzola. "Towards a Unifying Neural Theory of Social Cognition." In vol. 156 of *Progress in Brain Research*, edited by S. Anders et al., 379–401. Amsterdam: Elsevier, 2006.

Kierkegaard, Søren. *Concluding Unscientific Postscript to Philosophical Fragments*. Translated by Howard V. Hong and Edna H. Hong. Princeton: Princeton University Press, 2013.

———. *The Point of View for My Work as Author*. Translated by Howard V. Hong and Edna H. Hong. Princeton: Princeton University Press, 2009.

———. *Practice in Christianity*. Translated by Howard V. Hong and Edna H. Hong. Princeton: Princeton University Press, 1991.

Kittel, Gerhard, ed. *Theological Dictionary of the New Testament*, vol. 2. Translated by Geoffrey Bromiley. Grand Rapids: Eerdmans, 1964.

Klinkenborg, Verlyn. *Several Short Sentences about Writing*. New York: Vintage, 2012.

Kotsko, Adam. "Cool Hand Luke: An Atheistic Apocalypse." An und für sich (blog), April 22, 2010. https://itself.wordpress.com/2010/04/22/cool-hand-luke-an-atheist-apocalypse/.

Leithart, Peter J. *Athanasius*. Grand Rapids: Baker, 2011.

Levinas, Emmanuel. *On Escape / De l'évasion*. Translated by Bettina Bergo. Stanford: Stanford University Press, 2003.

———. "God and Philosophy." In *Of God Who Comes to Mind*, translated by Bettina Bergo, 55–78. Stanford: Stanford University Press, 1998.

———. "Manner of Speaking." In *Of God Who Comes to Mind*, translated by Bettina Bergo, 178–81. Stanford: Stanford University Press, 1998.

———. *Totality and Infinity*. Translated by Alfonso Lingis. Pittsburgh: Duquesne University Press, 1969.

Lewis, C. S. "Meditations on the Third Commandment." In *Christian Reunion and Other Essays*, edited by Walter Hooper, 62–68. London: Collins, 1990.

Liddell, Henry George, et al. *A Greek-English Lexicon*. Oxford: Clarendon, 1996.

Lindbeck, George. *Nature of Doctrine: Religion and Theology in a Postliberal Age*. Louisville: Westminster John Knox, 1984.

Lossky, Vladimir. *The Mystical Theology of the Eastern Church*. Translated by Fellowship of St. Alban and St. Serguis. London: James Clarke & Co., 1957.

Lyotard, Jean-Francois. *The Postmodern Condition: A Report on Knowledge*. Translated by Geoff Bennington and Brian Massumi. Minneapolis: University of Minnesota Press, 1984.

MacIntyre, Alasdair. *Dependent Rational Animals: Why Human Beings Need the Virtues*. Chicago: Open Court, 1999.

Martin, Dale B. *The Corinthian Body*. New Haven: Yale University Press, 1995.

McAfee Brown, Robert. "Can Memory Be Redeemed?" In *Memory Offended: The Auschwitz Convent Controversy*, edited by Carol Rittner and John K. Roth, 191–201. New York: Preager, 1991.

Metz, Johann Baptiste. *Faith in History and Society*. Translated by D. Smith. New York: Crossroads, 1980.

Meyendorff, John. "Light from the East? 'Doing Theology' in an Eastern Orthodox Perspective." In *Doing Theology in Today's World: Essays in Honor of Kenneth S. Kantzer*, edited by John D. Woodbridge and Thomas Edward McComiskey, 339–58. Grand Rapids: Zondervan, 1991.

Miller, James E. *The Passion of Michel Foucault*. Cambridge: Harvard University Press, 1993.

Morrison, Toni. *Beloved*. New York: Alfred Knopf, 1987.

Mountainside Perennial: Memory for the Sake of Hope. Monrovia, CA: Mountainside Communion, n.d.

Mulhall, Stephen. *The Great Riddle: Wittgenstein and Nonsense, Theology and Philosophy*. Oxford: Oxford University Press, 2015.

Nancy, Jean-Luc. *Corpus*. Translated by Richard A. Rand. New York: Fordham University Press, 2009.

———. *Noli Me Tangere: On the Raising of the Body*. Translated by Sarah Clift, Pascale-Anne Brault, and Michael Naas. New York: Fordham University Press, 2008.

Nelson, James B. *Body Theology*. Louisville: Westminster John Knox, 1992.

Nieman, Susan. *Evil in Modern Thought: An Alternative History of Philosophy*. Princeton: Princeton University Press, 2002.

Noble, T. A. *Holy Trinity: Holy People: The Theology of Christian Perfecting*. Eugene, OR: Cascade, 2013.

Osborne, Ronald E. *Death Before the Fall: Biblical Literalism and the Problem of Animal Suffering*. Downers Grove, IL: IVP, 2014.

Otto, Marc, and Michael Lodahl. "Mystery and Humility in John Wesley's Narrative Ecology." *Wesleyan Theological Journal* 44:1 (2009) 118–40.

Plutarch. *Lives of Illustrious Men*. Translated by John Dryden. New York: John B. Alden, 1883.

Rambo, Shelly. *Spirit and Trauma: A Theology of Remaining*. Louisville: Westminster John Knox, 2010.

Reilly, Robert R. *Making Gay Okay: How Rationalizing Homosexual Behavior Is Changing Everything*. San Francisco: Ignatius, 2014.

Renteria-Vazquez, Tiffany. "Topic Modeling: Social Inferences in Individuals with Agenesis of the Corpus Callosum." MA diss., Fuller Theological Seminary, 2014.

"Richie Havens." Wikipedia, http://en.wikipedia.org/wiki/Richie_Havens.

Rogers, Eugene. *Sexuality and the Body: Their Way Into the Triune God*. London: Wiley Blackwell, 1999.

Scarry, Elaine. *On Beauty and Being Just*. Princeton: Princeton University Press, 2001.

Schultz, John A. "John Dewey's Conundrum: Can Democratic Schools Empower?" *Teachers College Record* 103:2 (April 2001) 267–302.

Scott, Bernard Brandon. *The Real Paul: Rediscovering His Radical Challenge*. Salem, OR: Polebridge, 2015.

Segal, Alan F. *Life after Death: The History of the Afterlife in Western Religion*. New York: Doubleday, 2004.

Severson, Eric R., ed. *I More Than Others: Responses to Evil and Suffering.* Newcastle, UK: Cambridge Scholars, 2010.

Sider, Ronald J. "Biblical Foundations for Creation Care." In *The Care of Creation: Focusing Concern and Action*, edited by R. J. Berry, 43–49. Grand Rapids: IVP, 2000.

Siegel, Robert. "Richie Havens: Face to Face with His Face." *NPR*, September 26, 2006. https://www.npr.org/templates/story/story.php?storyId=6140503.

Sloat, Warren. "Playing it Cool in Jail." *Christian Century* (April 10, 1968) 457–58.

Stendahl, Krister. "The Apostle Paul and the Introspective Conscience of the West." *Harvard Theological Review* 56 (1963) 123–44.

Taylor, Charles. *The Language Animal: The Full Shape of the Human Linguistic Capacity.* Cambridge: Harvard University Press, 2016.

Taylor, Mark C. *Erring: A Postmodern A/theology.* Chicago: University of Chicago Press, 1981.

Teske, John A. "From Embodied to Extended Cognition." *Zygon* 48 (2013) 759–87.

Tillich, Paul. *Theology of Culture.* Chicago: University of Chicago Press, 1959.

Van Kuiken, Evert J. *Christ's Humanity in Current and Ancient Controversy, Fallen or Not?* London: Bloomsbury T. & T. Clark, 2017.

———. "The Relationship of the Fall to Christ's Humanity: Patristic Theology as an Arbiter of the Modern Debate." PhD diss., University of Manchester, 2013.

Voparil, Christopher, and Richard J. Bernstein, eds. *The Rorty Reader.* Malden, MA: Wiley-Blackwell, 2010.

Wadleigh, Michael, dir. *Woodstock.* Warner Home Video, 2009 [1970].

Welker, Michael. *God the Spirit.* Translated by John F. Hoffmeyer. Minneapolis: Fortress, 1994.

Wesley, John. "The General Deliverance." In *The Works of John Wesley: Sermons II 34–70*, edited by Albert C. Outler, 436–50. Nashville: Abingdon, 1985.

———. "The Imperfection of Human Knowledge." In *The Works of John Wesley: Sermons II 34–70*, edited by Albert C. Outler, 567–86. Nashville: Abingdon, 1985.

———. "On Patience." In *The Works of John Wesley: Sermons III 74–114*, edited by Albert C. Outler, 169–80. Nashville: Abingdon, 1986.

———. "A Plain Account of Christian Perfection." In vol. XI of *The Works of John Wesley*, edited by Thomas Jackson, 366–446. London: Wesleyan Conference Office, 1872.

———. *On Working Out Our Own Salvation: Sermons on Several Occasions.* London: Forgotten Books, 2022.

———. "On Zeal." In *The Works of John Wesley: Sermons III 74–114*, edited by Albert C. Outler, 308–21. Nashville: Abingdon, 1986.

Weston, J. Kael. "The Graves of the Men I Lost." *New York Times*, May 29, 2016. https://www.nytimes.com/2016/05/29/opinion/sunday/the-graves-of-the-marines-i-lost.html.

White, Lynn. "The Historical Roots of Our Ecological Crisis." In *The Care of Creation: Focusing Concern and Action*, edited by R. J. Berry, 31–42. Downers Grove, IL: IVP, 2000.

Williams, D. Eric. "The Gospel of Cool Hand Luke." July 5, 2006. https://web.archive.org/web/20160815180831/http://dewms.com/article/cool.php.

Williams, Rowan. "On Being Creatures." In *On Christian Theology*, 63–78. Oxford: Blackwell, 2000.

———. *Christ on Trial: How the Gospel Unsettles Our Judgement.* Grand Rapids: Eerdmans, 2000.
———. *The Edge of Words: God and the Habits of Language.* London: Bloomsbury, 2014.
Wittgenstein, Ludwig. *Philosophical Investigations.* Translated by G. E. M. Ansombe. New York: Macmillan, 1953.
Wolff, Hans Walter. *Anthropology of the Old Testament.* London: SCM, 1973.
Wright N. T. "Mind, Spirit, Soul and Body: All for One and One for All—Reflections on Paul's Anthropology in His Complex Contexts (2011)." In *Pauline Perspectives: Essays on Paul, 1978–2013,* 455–73. Minneapolis: Fortress, 2013.
Yakovlev, Alexander. *A Century of Violence in Soviet Russia.* New Haven: Yale University Press, 2002.
Zarr, Noah, Ryan Ferguson, and Arthur M. Glenberg. "Language Comprehension Warps the Mirror Neurons System." *Frontiers in Human Neuroscience* 7 (2013) 1–5.

www.ingramcontent.com/pod-product-compliance
Lightning Source LLC
Chambersburg PA
CBHW031433150426
43191CB00006B/498